W9-AJU-468

Praise for
China Hans

"I just finished reading your excellent book. This I do not say because you mentioned me in it, but because it is truly fantastic and impressive. It is convicting, heart-searching, motivating, and inspiring. *China Hans,* no doubt, is one of the best mission books I have ever read. You are honest and vulnerable about yourself but also sensitive and forgiving to others. This is a must-read for every Christian, especially the young who are aspiring to a God-honoring life."
—**Dr. Werner Bürklin,** Founder, China Partner

"Some stories have to be written because they are so important to the biographer. Others have to be written because the story needs to be told. Hans Wilhelm wrote his story initially for his family, but it is one that deserves a much wider readership. This reviewer was immediately drawn into the epic, which is told with refreshing simplicity, honesty, and humility. *China Hans* deserves to rank among the best-sellers!"
—**Dr. Edmund Gibbs,** Senior professor of church growth, Fuller Theological Seminary

"From the trenches of wartime Europe to the bustling streets of modern Shanghai, Hans Wilhelm's journey spans continents and generations. His story is a testimony to God's unfailing protection and provision, and to the enduring power of the gospel in one whose life has been committed to His purposes. Hans' colorful and fond recollections of the mentors who shaped his life bring to mind a generation of leaders whose efforts furthered the spread of the gospel worldwide during the last century."
—**Dr. Brent Fulton,** President, ChinaSource

"It's too fantastic. Where in history can you find a member of the Hitler Youth who survived famine and an internment camp in China to go on to become a missionary statesman who served on all continents and is an avid marathon runner? Clearly, God's hand was on Hans Wilhelm and wrote this history for this generation. *China Hans* will bring laughter (how do you really smoke a cigarette?), sympathetic remorse, and a deeper sense and understanding that God's purposes are marvelous. In an age where putting together a resume is a learned skill, God shows how He puts together resumes for His servants."
—**Samuel E. Chiang**, International Orality Network

"*China Hans* is a must read for those seriously interested in finding the purpose of their life. An exciting record of the life of a man pursuing a destiny that takes him to five continents to minister in a variety of cultures. Throughout his journey he has had a contagious enthusiasm that has infected many of us. I have known Hans for over half a century. He is an authentic 'follower of Jesus Christ' who exudes zeal regardless of the mission he has or will be given."
—**Bob Vernon**, Assistant chief of police, Los Angeles Police Department (retired); founder, Pointman Leadership Institute

Hans is an excellent storyteller. I am sure his memoirs will be a most fascinating book to read in our time."
—**Dr. Aleck Lee**, General Director, Christian Missions Overseas

Few men could even begin to think of the life Hans Wilhelm has led, let alone live it. Born in China of German missionary parents, an ardent supporter of Hitler as a high schooler, then crushed by his defeat. All of this brought him to Christ and to a love for the once hated Americans who destroyed his youthful dreams. That's when the odyssey began.
From Taiwan to Brazil to America to Germany to South Africa and back to the United States, Hans has been used of God to

disciple leaders worldwide and create lasting ministries on virtually every continent on earth. And he's not finished yet. Today he serves Chinese churches in the US and has spoken to as many as 3,000 in China.

China Hans is a fascinating read from a dying breed — one of few men alive who has had worldwide influence, developed world class leaders, and continued to pioneer into the twenty-first century.

—**Dr. Bill Lawrence**, President of Leader Formation International, Senior Professor Emeritus, Dallas Theological Seminary

"Over the last forty-three years I have known Hans Wilhelm in many different roles. He has been my field leader, neighbor, fellow team member, colleague in leadership, confidant, and wise counselor. Through all these years and in these many roles Hans has been an example to all of us who have followed and walked with him. His steadfastness and discipline are legendary and nowhere are they better expressed than in his commitment to his friends. I am honored to be among them.

"It was a joy for me to go through the stories he included in his biography. There I found many of the people and situations that God used to form his character and mold his personality. A lot of the incidents related in *China Hans* I had heard Hans tell over the years, however, bringing them all together really fleshed out the evolving portrait of my friend, a man who has lived to honor our Lord and obey His Word."

—**Dr. Paul McKaughan**, Ambassador at large, The Mission Exchange (formerly EFMA)

God bless you!

1 Cor. 1:8

CHINA HANS

From Shanghai to Hitler to Christ

Hans M. Wilhelm

Hans Wilhelm

All Scripture quotations, unless otherwise indicated, are taken from the Holy Bible, New International Version®. NIV®. Copyright © 1973, 1978, 1984 by International Bible Society. Used by permission of Zondervan Publishing House. All rights reserved.

Other Scripture translations:
The Living Bible (TLB), © 1971. Used by permission of Tyndale House Publishers, Inc. All rights reserved.

The New Testament in Modern English, Revised Edition (PHILLIPS), © 1958, 1960, 1972 by J. B. Phillips.

Most Trafford titles are also available at major online book retailers.

© Copyright 2009, Hans Wilhelm.
All rights reserved. No part of this publication may be reproduced, stored in a retrieval system, or transmitted, in any form or by any means, electronic, mechanical, photocopying, recording, or otherwise, without the written prior permission of the author.

Note for Librarians: A cataloguing record for this book is available from Library and Archives Canada at www.collectionscanada.ca/amicus/index-e.html

Printed in Victoria, BC, Canada.

ISBN: 978-1-4269-2887 (sc)

ISBN: 978-1-4269-2894 (hb)

ISBN: 978-1-4269-2900 (e-bookl)

We at Trafford believe that it is the responsibility of us all, as both individuals and corporations, to make choices that are environmentally and socially sound. You, in turn, are supporting this responsible conduct each time you purchase a Trafford book, or make use of our publishing services. To find out how you are helping, please visit www.trafford.com/responsiblepublishing.html

Our mission is to efficiently provide the world's finest, most comprehensive book publishing service, enabling every author to experience success. To find out how to publish your book, your way, and have it available worldwide, visit us online at www.trafford.com

Trafford rev.7/27/2009

Trafford PUBLISHING® www.trafford.com

North America & international
toll-free: 1 888 232 4444 (USA & Canada)
phone: 250 383 6864 ♦ fax: 250 383 6804 ♦ email: info@trafford.com

The United Kingdom & Europe
phone: +44 (0)1865 487 395 ♦ local rate: 0845 230 9601
facsimile: +44 (0)1865 481 507 ♦ email: info.uk@trafford.com

DEDICATION

I do not remember how many times I have been asked over the years, "When are you going to write the story of your life?"

I knew that I had experienced much, but I always wondered whether anybody would truly be interested in reading about it—and whether it was worth the effort to put it all together.

Then the pressure started mounting from family, especially from my wife, Alice. One thing she said hit home: "When you are gone, your story will be gone too, unless you write it down." I had many times voiced my regret that I had not asked my parents more questions while they were still alive. There were so many things I did not know about them that I really wanted to know. I was about to make the same mistake by failing to record my story.

Then I came across this passage: "Remember the days of old, consider the generations long past. Ask your father and he will tell you" (Deuteronomy 32:7).

Years before, I'd been sitting in a hotel restaurant in Wuhan, China, having breakfast with the English-American pastor and teacher Dr. Stuart Briscoe, when he spoke these words: "Everyone has a story." I cannot remember the context of our conversation, but I have never forgotten his simple statement. Yes, indeed, every person has a story to tell, and in this book I am telling my story.

Obviously I had to be selective, because over the years I'd assembled a huge repertoire of events and experiences. But I wanted to present a picture of God's dealings in my life—the great moments as well as the defeats and struggles. My primary purpose was to leave a record of His faithfulness for my grandchildren, with the hope that they too will experience the same grace in their lives.

It is therefore to them that I dedicate this book:

Karl Martin, Heidi Marie, Kari Kay, and Mark Thomas Wilhelm

CONTENTS

ACKNOWLEDGMENTS

As I have shared parts of my story in public meetings, numerous people have urged me to tell my story in book form. Their faithful insistence finally paid off. I'm grateful to each of them.

My family, in particular, encouraged me to make time for this project and saw to it that once I started it was brought to conclusion. My wife, Alice, my children Marty and Lita, and my sisters Eva, Anita, and Peggy all joined forces to spur me on. Thank you!

In writing this story, I was blessed with some great resources: newsletters written over more than fifty years, other personal diaries and journals, and input from written accounts by my sisters and late brother which refreshed my memory. It would have been difficult to complete this project without them. I sincerely appreciate all of their help.

It was a great delight to work with Jim Lund in Bend, Oregon, who not only helped edit this book but also gave valuable and objective advice in making it more readable. Thanks Jim.

And finally, my special thanks to Lyndsey Barrett, who helped me design the book cover.

If there are any discrepancies and errors in this book, I, of course, assume full responsibility.

FOREWORD

In Hebrews 13:7 we read: "Remember those who led you, who spoke the word of God to you; and considering the result of their conduct, imitate their faith." To a significant degree, OC International is the mission it is today because of the faithful and sacrificial service of Hans Wilhelm. It is therefore a great honor for me, in my role as president of the mission and on behalf of our worldwide missionary family, to write the foreword to this book which traces the thrilling story of Hans' life and ministry.

Most missionaries have the privilege of serving in only one country of the world. In his extraordinary missionary career which now has spanned more than five decades, Hans Wilhelm had the incredible opportunity of serving as a missionary with OC International on five different continents! Beginning with his birth to missionary parents serving in China, this book relates the thrilling story of how God prepared and molded Hans into His servant through a unique series of life experiences, and then how God used him to have a worldwide ministry impact which began in Asia and progressed to Latin America, North America, Europe, and finally Africa.

The first time I met Hans was in the summer of 1974 when, as a young seminary student, my wife and I were beginning the process of preparation for cross-cultural missionary service. During the more than three decades which followed, Hans has been a faithful friend, a challenging model, and an invaluable mentor to me during my own missionary service and my progression through a variety of leadership responsibilities and roles. Just as the life and missionary service of Hans had been profoundly impacted by the godly men and women the Lord brought into his life, so my life and ministry were significantly impacted and shaped by his ministry to me over the years. What has been true of my life and ministry has been true as well for generations of men and women who have served with OC International in places of ministry around the world.

One of the verses, which the Lord has used powerfully in Hans' life, is Acts 13:36, which says: "For David, after he had served the purpose of God in his own generation, fell asleep." In this book you will read the thrilling story of a servant of the Lord who obediently and faithfully served the purposes of God in his generation, wherever those purposes took Him and whatever sacrifices they demanded of him. I wholeheartedly recommend this book to you, with the prayer that it will inspire and challenge you in your walk with and service for the Lord, even as the life and ministry of Hans have so significantly inspired and challenged me.

Dr. Greg Gripentrog
President, OC International

1

How It All Began

1931

Guizhou, China

It was during the first snowfall in the mountains of Guizhou province in southwest China, in January 1931, that I made my initial visit to this amazing country.

Seven years earlier, my dad—Papa—had embarked for China from Germany to keep a promise he had made during his soldier days in World War I. "Lord, if You bring me safely through this war, then I will serve You as a missionary," had been his pledge. God did protect him through the war years fighting on three battlefields in Russia, Hungary, and France.

Papa, like other soldiers, did not talk a lot about his war experiences. The trench warfare on the western front in France was anything but glamorous, and the deaths of comrades and enemies alike quickly turned a young soldier into a seasoned fighter.

Though my dad said little about his war escapades, one story is still vivid in my mind. It was during the time that he served in the Imperial German Army in France. His duties at that time involved carrying messages from the command post to troops on the front lines. He knew the terrain well and often dodged enemy bullets as he rushed with new instructions for the soldiers who were directly facing the enemy.

On one of these occasions, a dense fog fell on the battlefield, causing my dad to be disoriented. He thought he knew his way, yet the fog covered up all known landmarks. As he came upon a trench, he suddenly realized that he must have strayed across the lines, since all the soldiers were British. Instinctively, he reached for a hand grenade and was ready to release the firing pin, when all fifty troops in the trench raised their arms in surrender. Singlehandedly, my father marched these prisoners back to the German lines. For this he was decorated with the Iron Cross, First Class, the highest decoration awarded to a noncommissioned officer. My father wore it with pride!

While telling the story, Papa mentioned that before he went into the war, he had prayed that God would grant him the special privilege of fighting with distinction yet without taking an enemy's life. God mercifully granted both of these requests. To his knowledge, he never killed a single soldier during his war years.

It was during those World War I days that the German edition of the Christian magazine, *China's Millions,* carried the following announcement:

> A young man, who had committed himself to
> serve God through the Liebenzell Mission, has
> been killed in action on the eastern front. Who
> will become his substitute?

Within a week of reading this news, my father sent the following letter to Pastor Heinrich Coerper, founder and director of the Liebenzell Mission in southern Germany:

> With deep sorrow I have learned that once again,
> someone who was committed to serve in the holy

cause of world missions has become a casualty of this war. Because of that, I want to respond with an enthusiastic "Here" to your appeal for someone to fill the gap. If by God's grace I will return from the Great War, I will fulfill my vow which I gave Him as a youth to serve my Master as a faithful witness to spread His kingdom among the heathen.

Since my early youth, I have had a strong interest in missions, which has only increased as I grew older. But until that time comes, I will be a faithful servant of my Lord in where He has placed me at this time. Oh, may I clearly understand my responsibility and become a blessing to my fellow soldiers and comrades. May I request your intercession and prayers for me at this time? I am praying for you and the mission.

With warm greetings,

Max Wilhelm

As soon as the war was over, Papa signed up with the Liebenzeller Mission working in China as an affiliate of the China Inland Mission. After seminary training and practical internship, he left for China in December 1923, but not before he was engaged to a young deaconess working in an orphanage. They had met only a couple of times, but my dad had fallen in love with Anna Giessel, a petite, dark-haired gal with soft brown eyes who was devoting her life with a deep sense of love and commitment to helping young orphans. As the custom of the day demanded, my future parents had to secure permission from the mission director as well as the director of the orphanage for their engagement. Their commitment was to each other and to work together to take the gospel of Christ to China.

Mission policy at that time did not allow for married

missionary personnel to be deployed to the field, but insisted that only engaged couples be considered. This, of course, made for lengthy engagements. Added to this was the further stipulation that the future husband and wife both had to pass their first two language examinations and had to live in China for a period of at least two years before marriage could take place.

My mother-to-be departed for China a couple of years after my father. When she arrived at the language school in China, she was greeted by ominous news: her fiancé had been captured by Chinese bandits in an interior province and was being held for a high ransom. What a shock and test of faith for this young bride! God was preparing my parents, helping them realize that following Him was not going to be easy and would lead to many a sacrifice. Our Lord in His kindness did not reveal all of these things at once, but with each step of faith was able to teach them and later us children what it meant to follow Him.

My father's captivity was a horrifying experience. Other prisoners were executed daily. After each death, the executioners brandished bloody swords in my dad's face and said he would be next. Graciously, God intervened. My dad was set free without payment of the demanded ransom.

Two years later, after my parents successfully passed the required language examinations, a fellow missionary performed a simple wedding in Hong jiang, Hunan. The date was September 2, 1927. Two years after that, my sister Eva was born. I followed eighteen months later, on January 8, 1931.

Since this was in a small village in the mountain region of southwestern China, there was no hospital close by. Rosa Kocher, a missionary and nurse, assisted my mother with the delivery in our primitive home. Fortunately, all went well. Little did Rosa realize that the little guy she helped bring into the world would also be the one at her side when she was ushered out of this world! But more on that later…

My parents' first assignment was to assume pioneer missionary work in the province of Guizhou. It was the land of the Miao people, made up of over thirty different tribes, each speaking its own language. Although some of the men could understand Chinese, there was a mutual disdain between the Chinese and the Miao.

Strange stories circulated among the people about Germans and other foreigners. Once a boatman asked my dad if it was true that in Germany, the dead were not buried but laid to dry in the sun. Another story claimed that foreigners, or "foreign devils" as we were called, would steal Chinese children and cut out their hearts and eyes to make medicine.

One of the reasons for all this was that Guizhou's high mountain ranges made it one of the most inaccessible provinces in China. It certainly was and still is considered one of the poorest areas of the nation.

Travel was limited to walking or in some cases, boating. Yet the rivers were dangerous due to the many rapids, which easily swamped the boats and caused many people to drown. Walking along unpaved and often muddy footpaths barely two feet wide was the norm. When you arrived at night at a distant mountain village, a wooden bed with straw was the only lodging available. Everything was cooked over an open wood fire.

It was here that my dad began his missionary career. He would faithfully trudge up and down the mountain paths along with one or two Miao Christians, arrive at some remote village, and settle down for the night. The next morning, in the village square, he would use picture charts to present the Good News to the villagers. For all of them, this was their first contact with a foreigner and the first time that they heard the message of a God who loved them, a God who did not need to be feared, one who was stronger than all the demons in the world. Though not many were receptive to the gospel, some did come to believe.

One of the first converts was a teacher at the government school. During his baptism service he publicly confessed to persecuting Christians. This was a bold step for him, since in

5

those days it was not easy for a public servant to embrace a foreign religion. In later years he even became a preacher of the gospel.

Obviously, I do not recall any events of that first year in China. My parents told me that when I was just a few months old, I was stricken by tropical malaria and was close to death's door. My mother—I called her *Mutti*—showed her maternal feelings and voiced her concern with these words: "He is too good for this world. That is why God wants to take him to heaven." Once I found out what my mother had said, I did not allow my siblings to forget these words! But even at that early age, I experienced God's hand on my life. He had a purpose for me which He wanted me to fulfill. As Stuart Briscoe would often say, "We are immortal until we have accomplished God's purposes for our lives."

My sister Anita was born in early1932, and my parents prepared to return to Germany for a brief respite. My father had been in China for more than eight years, and my mother more than six. So with three little toddlers, the oldest being three, the long journey began. First it was down the river in small boats, then some overland travel by sedan chair, though my dad always shunned the ride, preferring to walk. From Changsha, the capital of Hunan province, it was on a small steamer that we made our way to Shanghai, the headquarters of the China Inland Mission.

The Saarbrücken, a German passenger liner, took us down the Pacific, around the subcontinent of India, and through the Suez Canal and the Mediterranean Sea to Italy. From there our journey took us through Switzerland to Germany.

We were finally home.

2

IN THE STEPS OF ABRAHAM

1932

Bad Liebenzell, Germany

Germany was going through major political and economic convulsions. It was still reeling from the Great Depression, and not just financially. As a country it had lost its moorings and was casting about for something new and fresh. There was a vacuum in the land.

Adolf Hitler, consummate politician that he was, recognized this vacuum and jumped into it full force. He appealed to the people to restore their self-esteem and climb out of their post–World War I doldrums. His charismatic personality attracted and convinced many, even Christian leaders, that he was a man who could be trusted, one who had the capacity to lead Germany.

My father's days were full. He traveled extensively throughout the country, reporting on what was happening in China and stimulating many congregations to redouble missionary vision and support. My mother was saddled with the responsibility of caring for her little children. During the next two years, two more additions were made to the family circle: my sister Esther was born in 1933 and my brother, Fred, arrived the following year. Little did my parents realize the impact these additional family members would bring. Dark valleys of testing and self-examination lay ahead. Yet deep within their hearts was the unshakable conviction that God had called them to China and that they needed to return, no matter what the obstacles might be.

The return trip to China originated from the mission headquarters at Bad Liebenzell, a quaint little resort town in the Black Forest. It was not an easy farewell. It meant saying good-bye to my sister Anita, three years old, who would be left behind in the care of my grandparents in eastern Germany.

How my parents came to this decision is still shrouded in mystery after all these years. From what I have been able to gather, there were two main factors that contributed to this momentous and life-changing choice.

First, an enormous amount of pressure was exerted on my dad by his family not to return to China. There was a general feeling that he had already fulfilled his missionary obligation to that land and that his future ministry could be exercised just as effectively in Germany. After all, had he not laid his life on the line when he was captured by bandits, never knowing from one day to the next if he would survive? He had kept his commitment made to the Lord in the trenches of World War I. Wasn't it just as important now to serve God here in his homeland? These were the questions constantly raised.

Besides, this was a time of considerable political unrest and instability in China. Nationalist forces under Chiang Kai-shek were locked in a bitter rivalry with the Communists led by Mao Zedong.

Two missionaries of the China Inland Mission with whom the Liebenzell Mission was affiliated, Alfred Bosshardt and Arnolis Hayman, were captured by Communist guerillas in Guizhou in

1934. This was the province where my parents had served during their first term in China.

In September 1934, these two missionaries and their wives were among a missionary party abducted by a section of the Communist armies and held hostage for a huge ransom (described as a fine for spying). The women were soon released, but Alfred Bosshardt and Hayman, a New Zealander, were taken by the Second Army on the epic Long March, the massive Communist army retreat to the north and west of China. Beatings and threats of execution heightened the sufferings of the hostages. Their fate attracted attention in the West and led to appeals for concerted prayer by the world Christian community. Hayman was released after 413 days, while Bosshardt was held for 560 days. He was released on Easter in 1936, after he had covered more than six thousand miles on foot. Bosshardt was desperately ill and needed a long convalescence.

Others were less fortunate. In December 1934, news reached Germany of the capture of John and Betty Stam, another young missionary couple affiliated with the China Inland Mission, by Communist forces. With them was their little baby. Their captors demanded more than $20,000 for their release, an incredible amount in those days. Reports graphically portrayed what happened next:

> The next morning the young couple was led through town without the baby. Their hands were tightly bound, and they were stripped of their outer garments as if they were common criminals. John walked barefoot. He had given his socks to Betty. The soldiers jeered and called the town's folk to come see the execution. The terrified people obeyed.
>
> On the way to the execution, a medicine-seller, considered a lukewarm Christian at best, stepped from the crowd and pleaded for the lives of the

two foreigners. The Reds angrily ordered him back. The man would not be stilled. His house was searched, a Bible and hymnbook found, and he, too, was dragged away to die as a hated Christian.

John pleaded for the man's life. The Red leader sharply ordered him to kneel. As John was speaking softly, the Red leader swung his sword through the missionary's throat so that his head was severed from his body. Betty did not scream. She quivered and fell bound beside her husband's body. As she knelt there, the same sword ended her life with a single blow.[1]

You can imagine the horror and fear this provoked in our extended family. You can understand their rationale for seeking to persuade my dad not to return to the mission field. My grandmother and my sister Anita had established strong bonds during the furlough years, which added to the family's resistance to giving her up to face the dangerous uncertainty China represented.

However, both of my parents stood firm in their conviction that God had called them to serve Him in China—no matter the cost. Had they not already experienced some of these trials of their faith in the past, especially when bandits had captured my dad?

But then came a second blow, and it came from the mission organization itself. When the time approached for my parents to return to China, a blunt mission directive instructed them to leave two of their five children behind. We were a family of seven, but the policy said only five could go!

In today's world, we can hardly imagine this sort of thing. But those were different days. Germany was in an economic crisis and the mission leaders did not believe they could support large families overseas. My dad protested this decision and in the process was nearly terminated by the mission leadership.

From mission archives, I discovered a letter my father wrote at that time to the mission leadership:

> We are very grateful that in this time of crisis in Germany you have expressed confidence in us by sending us again to the mission field. As much as lies in us, we will do our best with God's help to be worthy of this confidence. The path before us can only be taken by faith. And we are confident of this path before our Lord, even if the mission leadership can give us no other guarantees to accompany us except the unfailing promises of His Word. From a human perspective, our hearts may tremble and fail. Our faith is under constant tension, but the certainty of our "being sent" is our strength.
>
> Since extraordinary steps of faith mark our being sent to the field, we cannot comprehend that God could provide for three of our children, but not for four. Moreover, we firmly believe that our God who can command the raven to feed us five, can also order these birds to stuff the mouth of a sixth person. If we are willing to take this step of faith for three children, then we also will dare to take this step for a fourth child.

In the end, my dad's argument prevailed. But why didn't he ask for five children? Would that have been pushing the envelope? We don't know, and perhaps we will never find the answer. Four of us children set sail from Genoa, Italy, in the spring of 1935 when my parents returned to China for their second term of service. The close tie my sister Anita had with my grandparents determined that she would be the one to stay. We had no idea then how long our separation would turn out to be.

In a letter to friends dated February 22, 1935, just days before our departure, my father wrote the following. It reveals much of the man behind these lines, a man who left a legacy for those of us following in his steps.

> In view of the present crisis on the mission field of China, I have been asked numerous times in recent days how we could risk going with four little children into such an uncertain future. No one sees the difficulties ahead more clearly than we do. The most recent terrible reports from China have deeply affected us. I can assure you that we have examined our hearts before God and have wrestled in our souls to know His will, because we are committed to only do His will. We are sober-minded enough to realize that at this point the veneer of false missionary heroics has come to an end. At the same time, my heart did not find rest until I recommitted my heart to Him to serve Him among the heathen.
>
> Who am I, that I should spend my life in the service of the Master here in a comfortable and secure environment, since He called me from my youth to serve Him among the nations? He saved me from sin—called me into His service—saved me out of many dangers. Would I dare to hang on to my own life without defiling myself with disloyalty? The Great Commission has always been a service of faith and obedience.
>
> Returning on our second missionary expedition is especially a step of faith because we head into a perspective of a dark sea with stormy waves. Humanly speaking we feel like the disciples who cried out in fear, but He called to them, "It is I,

don't be afraid." So, we too are free to go with that assuring secret in our hearts: "I am certain that the Lord has called us to preach the gospel to them" (Acts 16:10).

We did not push our way to do this, but we heard the call of millions of unsaved, "Come over and help us." It was not an order from the mission leadership, but the conviction of our hearts: This is God's will! And this gives us joy to take this step... We have no financial guarantees as we set out, except the eternal, never-failing promises of God's Word!

Free from putting our hope in men, but firmly anchored on the foundation of His promises, we go forward with our little band of children following Abraham's way: "Go to the land I will show you..."

The difficulties were just beginning.

3

SLOW BOAT TO CHINA

1935

En route to China

The return trip to China took several weeks. The first leg was by train from Germany through Switzerland to Genoa, Italy. The train had to pass through the St. Gotthard tunnel, one of the longest alpine tunnels connecting northern and southern Switzerland, nine miles in length. When we finally saw daylight, my oldest sister Eva wondered whether we now had arrived in China!

Our hotel room in Genoa had a direct view of the Mediterranean harbor. I remember that evening when it was already dark and my dad showed us the German passenger liner *Trier*, which took us through the Mediterranean, the Suez Canal, the Indian Ocean, around Ceylon (now called Sri Lanka) through the Malacca Straits, past Sumatra, Penang, Singapore, Manila, and up the China coast to Shanghai.

We were fascinated at going through the Suez Canal, with Port Said being our first stop. We watched young boys dive for coins that passengers threw into the water. Soon they resurfaced, showing off the coins in their gleaming white teeth. We were terribly impressed by their skill.

I was four years old when we left Germany. I don't have too many memories of our six-week voyage. I do recall that Eva and I would explore the vessel and even find our way to the mess hall of the sailors. If they had left any beer in their mugs, we would pour the contents into one mug and drink it! Fortunately, our parents did not get wind of this.

My dad did hear of another caper I pulled when I went to the deck steward and ordered a lemonade drink. When he asked for payment, I simply replied, "My dad will pay for it." When he found out about this, the game was over!

From Shanghai we took a smaller ship that carried us up the Yangtze River through the Dung Ting Lake to Changsha, capital of Hunan province. From there we traveled to Liangtowtang, the little village that had been assigned to my parents as their new place of ministry. All in all, the journey took nearly two months. We were glad we'd finally made it.

Liangtowtang, literally "two-head lake," received its quaint name due to the fact that there was a lake on both ends of the little village. A street ran through the village connecting the lakes.

Our family was deployed here because of a missionary vacancy. We were the only foreigners in the village. Later, a Catholic priest, Pater Werner from Hungary, came to man the Catholic mission station. We did not see much of him, but I do remember him coming to our home for Christmas one year. He spoke German fluently, but what fascinated me was his violin. As we sang the familiar German Christmas carols, he accompanied us on his violin, which added to the festiveness of the celebration.

Apart from this, we were totally immersed in Chinese culture and life in a little village. I remember one day when I may have immersed myself a little too much. I showed a group of village boys a handful of coins. They immediately took me to a little store and pointed out that I could buy a whole string of firecrackers with the money I had. No sooner said then done. Followed by my band of newfound friends, I headed back to our home, attached them to a window sill, and lit the fuse. It did not take long for the sound of exploding fireworks to attract attention, including from my dad. He did not look too favorably on this and communicated it to me in no uncertain way.

On another occasion, I had my first experience with racial division. Due to our outward differences our family was often called *Yang guei tzu* or "foreign devils." In frustration, I hollered back that the villagers were *Zong guei tzu,* or "Chinese devils." Again, Papa did not take too kindly to this, explaining that we should never call anyone a devil.

Our home was a two-story brick house. Brick homes were not common, but this one had been built by a previous missionary who lived there and established the mission station. It was located in a compound containing a small chapel where Sunday services were held, quarters for employees, a stable, and a chicken roost. Surrounding all this was a brick wall with pieces of glass imbedded on top to prevent easy access by burglars.

We were also protected by two dogs, one of them a German shepherd. They were chained during the day but let loose at night to guard the property. Thanks to them, we never had a break-in during our time there. Whenever we went for a walk through the fields close to our village, they ran loose. When they encountered other dogs in these outings they would immediately give chase. However, one sharp whistle from my dad caused them to stop dead in their tracks and return meekly to my dad's side.

I've often been asked about the food we ate. We loved Chinese food, but it was not the kind you find in restaurants in the West. It was simple vegetable and meat dishes with rice as the main staple. In Hunan province we ate our food extremely hot, that is, spicy. Little red or green peppers were mixed in with everything. We got so used to it that even now, it is hard to eat Chinese food without these spices.

Otherwise, our meals were made up of typical German food,

including sauerkraut and sausage. A common change from eggs for breakfast was fried onions with liver or scrambled pig brains. It may sound bad, but actually was very tasty! My mom also excelled at baking, and at Christmastime especially we enjoyed a variety of Christmas cookies and breads.

We kept a stall of chickens to supply us with daily doses of eggs and meat. We also had a couple of cows for milk. Every now and then, my dad would butcher a calf. I still remember the smoked sausages strung across our attic.

On Sunday, of course, my dad conducted worship services in our little chapel for people from Liangtowtang and neighboring villages. Naturally, they were held in Chinese. He often accompanied the singing with his trumpet. We children always had mandatory seats in the front row. When the service became too long or too boring for us, we reverted to sibling warfare, pushing each other, elbowing, and showing other signs of restlessness. That's when Papa would interrupt the service and address us in German, telling us to behave.

A couple of older Christian women assisted in Bible studies for other women. The feet of these women were bound with bandages. Old customs held that small feet were beautiful. When these women were little girls, their feet were broken and bent underneath so that they literally walked on their folded-under toes.

One day, I had the occasion to watch the women as they unbound their feet, now no longer than four inches in length. Their feet were totally crippled and needed to be carefully washed each night, then re-bound with bandages. What a blessing that the government later outlawed this terrible practice.

My dad's study had a view of the whole courtyard in the compound where we lived. When he wasn't traveling, it was here that he spent much of his time studying. He also received visitors there; they were always served a steaming cup of hot tea. Papa's desk, pushed against a wall, was adorned with a series of photographs of the last German Emperor Wilhelm II, who had abdicated his throne at the end of World War I. Each year, my father received an autographed postcard with his picture, dated January 27, the emperor's birthday. It was with awe that I often stood and pondered these photographs. I am sure that events like these shaped my love for history, which became my major in college.

A large framed picture of Adolf Hitler, the German Führer, hung on the wall as you entered the office. There was a strong sense of German nationalism in the Wilhelm household, probably made more acute by our long and distant separation from the Fatherland. Limited news from Germany created in all of us a longing to identify with our homeland. Without a radio, the only news we received was from a Chinese newspaper, which Papa carefully studied for anything that might hint at what was taking place in our home country.

One day when I was about five, I had a sudden impulse to go fishing. Of course, there were no fishing rods available, so I decided to make one. I got a long piece of string and tied it to a staple from one of my notebooks. Then I got hold of a bamboo pole and connected it with the string. Now I had a fishing pole and was ready to go!

Proudly, I marched to my dad's office to show him what I had done. "I want to go fishing," I announced. Papa, taking a look at my fishing gear, wanted to know where I planned to go. We had a small water hole outside our compound wall. It was often used by farmers for their cattle and I was sure this was the perfect place. Unfortunately, my opinion did not coincide with my father's. He didn't think it would work. Then he expressly told me not to go there.

I had invested too much effort in this venture to be put off so quickly, however. When my dad's attention was diverted from the courtyard, I slipped over to the wall and gently opened the back door, which would allow me to leave the confines of our property. Right next to the wall was the water hole. I was ready to fish.

I dipped my pole into the water, convinced that a fish would soon swallow the staple hook and I could pull him out. But nothing happened. After several unsuccessful attempts, I determined that I needed to change positions. Perhaps the other side of the hole would bring better results. I tiptoed along the side of the water pond, not realizing that it was wet and covered with a green slimy surface.

Before I knew it, I had slipped and fallen into the water hole, which was too deep for me to stand in. As I splashed around and swallowed water, I didn't realize I was here alone, the gate to our compound firmly closed and out of sight of the caring eye of my dad. Humanly speaking, I had come to the end of the road!

But once again, God intervened. A man happened to be passing by and saw what was happening. He bounded down the hill, reached into the waterhole, and pulled out this little "foreign devil." He carried me to the compound and my dad rushed out to take possession of his soaked little boy. He tipped over a big water bucket, laid me on it stomach down, and rolled it back and forth until I vomited all the water I'd swallowed.

Later on, in a warm bed, he sat at my bedside and thanked God for saving my life. There was no rebuke for having disobeyed his word, only thankfulness for God's mercy.

I had violated my dad's command and this had led me to the brink of death. But God in His mercy had sent a savior.

Years later, on my tenth birthday, there was a special party. My folks hosted a Chinese feast and invited special guests to help celebrate. Seated at my side was Mr. Fan, the man who had saved my life. He was the guest of honor. After appropriate remarks were made, my father stood to publicly thank Mr. Fan for saving my life. Had he not walked by that day, there would have been no celebration!

Then, as was natural for a missionary, my dad talked about another rescue operation. Man was lost and alone in total darkness, drowning in his own sin. God saw it, and since He loved man, He sent someone to save them. It was His Son, His only Son. And even though His Son died to complete the rescue, this sacrifice was not too big to procure salvation.

God's purposes for my life were not complete, so He provided me with another opportunity for life. As I look back, I cannot help but thank Him for His great mercy and love.

4

LOOK OUT, THE COMMUNISTS AND JAPANESE ARE COMING!

November 1935–1941

Liangtowtang, China

One of my earliest memories of war dates to 1935. Ideological and political differences between the budding Communist party, led by Mao Zedong, and his former classmate Chiang Kai-shek, whose Nationalist party had assumed control of the government of China, soon led to armed conflict. Eventually it brought on the Long March and the Communist troop retreat into China's northwestern corner.

A few months after our return from Germany, my father wrote the following letter:

> "When I arrived home (Liangtowtang) on November 28, 1936, we received news that a Communist army was headed our way. This meant that we quickly had to grab basic necessities and pack for our flight. When we went to bed

around midnight, we realized that difficult days lay ahead. Around 2 A.M. a messenger arrived carrying a written order that we should flee right away, since the neighboring city, Paoking, had already been partially evacuated.

We will never forget that night. Outside it was pitch black. Icy rain beat against the windows— we shivered. Where should we flee with our children? When we yanked our little ones out of their warm beds an hour later and they stood shivering before us, our inward battle was over. We determined to go the longer route to Hengchow. Our verse for the day we read that morning was a comforting greeting from heaven above: You know the way, you know the end, guide us in our pilgrimage.

At dawn we left Liangtowtang with sadness in our hearts, leaving behind our congregation and practically all that we owned. My wife and the children traveled in sedan chairs. I walked the one hundred kilometers. The roads were bad. Twice the bearers of the sedan chair of my wife slipped and fell and it was only His grace that she was not injured.

On the evening of the third day we reached our destination. The troops of the central government in the meantime had intervened and had halted the advance of the Communist troops—we were safe for the time being. Eventually the Communists were driven out of the area and I was able to return to Liangtowtang, first alone, and then on January 11, I was able to bring the family back..."

This event is still vivid in my mind, even though I wasn't even five years old then. But it left an indelible imprint on me. Missionary life was not without its dangers, yet through them all, there was always God's gracious hand of protection.

But this was just the beginning of seeing the reality of war.

A few days after my sixth birthday, my sister Eva and I left home for boarding school in the city of Changsha, several hours' drive away. It was here at our German headquarters that a little mission school was located. Leaving home, and only coming home a couple times a year for school holidays, was traumatic. But having my sister Eva there gave me the assurance and security I needed. The whole school had only about twenty students, practically all of them missionary kids. There was basically one teacher, also a former missionary kid, who had come from Germany to assume this daunting task.

In May 1937, God blessed our family once more when my youngest sister, Peggy, was born. My mother was able to go to the mission hospital in Changsha where we attended school at the time and we soon heard the news of our latest family member.

Peggy arrived at a tumultuous time. Two months after her birth, the simmering conflict between China and Japan erupted into full-scale war. The outbreak of the Sino-Japanese war and the advance of Japanese troops called a sudden halt to the civil war between the Communists and Nationalist forces. Generalissimo Chiang Kai-shek had to turn his full attention to the new enemy, a much more formidable foe.

Soon Japanese troops had occupied most of the coastal territory of China and were beginning to push further west. The Nationalist army put up a valiant fight but was unable to resist the continuing advance of the enemy.

From that time on, practically on a daily basis, wounded soldiers appeared at our gate. There were no hospitals in our area, but they had heard that a foreigner was there who might be able to help them. Though my father was not a trained physician or a nurse, he had learned some medical skills in his early years in China when he assisted one of our mission doctors in his practice.

In Liangtowtang, Papa had established a small emergency clinic and dispensed medications, bandaged wounds, gave injections, pulled teeth, and tried whatever else might bring relief to these battle-weary soldiers. The war with the Japanese brought the fighting closer and closer to our area once again.

The Sino-Japanese war intensified. The mission leaders relocated our school to another town, feeling that we would be safer away from Changsha, the provincial capital.

I remember one night after we'd moved when, following a bombing raid on Changsha; we saw the sky turn red. The whole city was ablaze. We kids stood in our courtyard watching this spectacle unfold. The city had been set afire not by incendiary bombs, but by the Nationalist government, which feared a Japanese takeover. This "scorched earth" policy frightened us and eventually caused the mission to relocate our school once more, even further inland.

By this time the number of students had shrunk to hardly a dozen and we were under the care of another missionary family that acted as dorm parents. They were kind, yet strict, and did their best to be our guardians. We missed our parents, but they made every effort to take care of us. It was always an exciting day when Papa dropped by in connection with some of his itinerant preaching ministries. He would not stay long, but his visits made us appreciate home all the more.

One day he arrived with a huge basket of tangerines and told us we could eat all we wanted. Everyone thought he was Santa Claus that day! There was one rule, however, that we all had to follow: Every Sunday afternoon all of us had to sit around the large dining room table and write a letter home. It helped emphasize the importance of good communication.

Even in those early days, I had a sensitivity to spiritual things. Deep in my heart there was a searching after God. One Sunday morning I slipped away to a quiet room. I had acquired a little notebook and wanted to use it as a diary. I made my first and only entry. After entering the date, I wrote: "Today I have decided to become a Christian."

I walked out of the room with a sense of accomplishment and with a real desire to live and act as a "Christian," whatever that meant.

But, alas, my plan was short-lived. Nothing had really changed in my life and I was soon back to where I'd been before. I came to the conclusion that "this matter of being a Christian" really did not work, at least not for me. And this skepticism followed me all the way to my teenage years.

There was one other occasion when I was home from boarding school that a similar experience profoundly affected me. I was probably eight at the time. My father had invited a dynamic young Chinese evangelist to preach a series of meetings in his church. He was a member of the famous "Bethel Band" which traveled all across China. John Sung, a renowned Chinese evangelist, was one of the leaders of this group of traveling evangelists, though I am not sure if he was the one who preached in our church.

Whoever it was, I was enraptured by his powerful speaking. Each night I sat in the front row. One phrase he repeated over and over was "Shangdi-de-en-dian"—the grace of God. This was the most powerful sermon I had ever heard and it moved me deeply. But that is where it ended.

At school, our regular daily routine began each morning with a mandatory devotional time for everyone. We would sit in a large circle and listen to Bible stories, then kneel in front of our chairs for a time of prayer. I recall a rather unpleasant event during one of those meetings. It seemed that our time was dragging on interminably and to make it worse, I felt the urgent need to go to the bathroom. However, I dared not leave my place in the circle. The longer we prayed, the more urgent my need became—until nature took its course and I was soon kneeling in a puddle. When everyone got up to leave, it was my sister who saw my predicament and came to my aid. But you can imagine my embarrassment in front of all of my schoolmates.

It was also during those first few years of school, I think when I was about eight, that I was introduced to the game of chess. Since we could not buy a chess set in China, we made our own. We got a sheet of paper and drew the squares, white alternating with black, which we colored in with ink. Then we drew the chess figures on little pieces of white and dark cardboard. Simple, but it worked. I remember receiving my first chess set when I was eleven. What a thrill to have the real thing! I still have this same little chess set and have played on it with my dad, my son, and my grandsons.

We enjoyed ourselves during those years and took each day as it came. We never felt deprived of anything, since this was all we knew. But God was molding our lives in His unique way, preparing us for the future.

In early 1941, our family was transferred to the city of Shaoyang. The family that had been in charge of that mission station was readying to return to Germany for furlough and my dad was asked to take over their work. At the same time, my sister Eva was availing herself of the opportunity to return to Germany as well. She was not quite twelve years old, but the little mission school we attended was not equipped to educate students beyond the sixth grade. Now Eva could travel with this missionary family. They journeyed to the coast, made their way to northern China, and eventually boarded the Trans-Siberian Railway, which took them through the Soviet Union all the way back to Germany.

In God's providence, her train was one of the last to make it through the Soviet Union; in June, the German-Russian War broke out. Eva had passed through Moscow just a few weeks before! Now we had two members of our family in Germany: Eva and Anita. My younger sister had lived the past six years with her grandparents. Now she was able to see her big sister for the first time since she was three. When would we see them again? Only God knew.

Now air raids became more frequent. To protect us from direct bombing attacks, our family took refuge in mud bunkers that at least provided some cover from flying shrapnel. However, after digging only a few feet, we encountered ground water. Throughout our time there, the bunkers were generally half filled with water.

There were three siren signals that we learned very quickly. The first one was a warning of an impending air or bombing attack. The second siren announced its imminence and called everyone to take immediate cover. The last one sounded the all clear.

I recall the first bombing raid. We had taken shelter in a small storage room because it had been constructed of cement blocks. When we heard the roaring engines of approaching Japanese aircraft, we stuck our heads out and watched them descend lower and lower over the city. This struck panic into the hearts of our Chinese friends. "Be quiet! Don't talk!" they demanded. "The Japanese can hear everything you say."

"What are those eggs falling out of the planes?" I asked.

"Get back in there quickly," my father said. "Those are bombs." And already we heard the howling of the bombs and then the explosion on impact.

Later, when walking with my father through the ripped-apart streets, I saw dead people for the first time. The reality that life was over for them hit me. War was a terrible thing.

Because Germany was allied with Japan in the Axis agreement, we thought that we might gain some immunity from these attacks if we made known to the Japanese that we were Germans. So we obtained a huge rattan mat, perhaps twenty by thirty feet, and painted on it a German swastika flag. When the first siren sounded, we would unroll this mat on our front courtyard so that it would be plainly visible to the approaching aircraft. Whether they actually saw it or not, I do not know. But we never sustained any direct hits on our property.

War had arrived and was ever coming closer to home. We were just beginning to experience what this would mean for our family.

5

YOU MUST GO TO AN INTERNMENT CAMP

1941

Leiyang, Hunan, China

The Sino-Japanese war was moving into its fifth year. The Imperial Japanese Army was advancing further and further west. And with their advance, the frequency of air raids on Chinese cities increased. It seemed like the sound of air raid sirens was part of the daily routine.

Then came Pearl Harbor.

Not that we knew anything about the Japanese air attack on Hawaii. Since we did not have newspapers or radio, we did not find out about this event until much later. But the day before the fateful attack on December 7, 1941 we endured one of the worst bombing attacks on our city. Little did we realize that this was the overture to a sequence of events that would change our lives.

When we heard the news of the air strike against the Americans, we realized that as German citizens, we'd suddenly become enemies of the Chinese people. Germany, Italy, and Japan were committed Axis powers, which bound them to mutual defense. When President Roosevelt declared war on Japan, Germany was also drawn into conflict against the United States—and against China.

It did not take long before two armed soldiers appeared at our front door and took up posts to ensure that we did not leave our home without their knowledge. When my mother did her daily shopping at the open market, a soldier dutifully accompanied her and escorted her back home. The same applied to any other visits out of the house. The only exception was when there was an air raid. Then, everyone headed for the hills surrounding the city, including the armed guards. They dutifully returned to their posts once the all clear siren sounded.

The authorities soon issued orders for us to vacate our mission station in order to go to an internment camp along with other "enemy aliens." We did not know what this would mean.

However, our Chinese Christian friends and church members protested this decision. At the direction of the affable Dr. Yu, who spoke fluent German acquired during his studies of medicine in Germany and served as chairman of the church board, a two hundred–word telegram was dispatched to Zhongqing, the wartime capital of Free China. Generalissimo Chiang Kai-shek was implored to dispense with this regulation since my parents had never engaged in political activities but only served to bring the gospel of Jesus Christ to the Chinese people. After it was sent, my parents were encouraged and believed that God would answer their prayers by granting a positive response on the part of the Nationalist government.

But as the waiting for a reply continued, state authorities were losing patience. They finally established a deadline and told us in no uncertain terms that there was no further recourse. Everyone prayed.

The deadline came and to the great sorrow of our Chinese

Christian friends, we were picked up by armed escorts to be transported to our camp.

Only later did we learn that the central government had indeed responded favorably to the request of our church and had given permission for us to stay and continue with our work. However, the secretary to the governor of our state was very anti-Christian and refused to release the government's response. Only after we had left did he reveal the contents of the communication, but with a shrug of his shoulders said that it was too late for him to cancel our imprisonment orders.

Did God answer our prayers? Of course He did—even though the answer was quite different than what we expected.

When we were ordered to leave, all we could take with us was a small suitcase for each person. My parents packed up the rest of our belongings and left them behind with the hope that other missionaries might be able to save them for us and allow us to retrieve them at some future date. We never saw these things again. Other missionaries did pick them up, but they were attacked by bandits on the way and robbed of all possessions, including all our accumulated "treasures."

We realized afresh the importance of never clinging to earthly things, a principle that has been very important to us since those days. I have often said that it is important for us at some time in our lives to lose everything we have in order that we would put our trust not in things, but in God.

We boarded a military truck which would carry us 120 miles to Leiyang, a southern city in our province of Hunan. Obviously, we kids did not understand all that was happening. We considered this a real adventure. There was no hostility between the military and us or the police escorting us. It was the quiet confidence of my parents that provided us with a great sense of security.

Our destination was a Catholic convent run by Italian missionary nuns. It had been converted by the government authorities into an internment camp for Italian priests and nuns and German businesspeople and missionaries, all members of "enemy nations."

It was pouring rain when our truck stopped after passing through the main gate. Cold and wet, we sat there for a long time because of the confusion our arrival had created among the military guards. Apparently, the camp was full and there were no accommodations for us. After a couple of hours, they decided to hang a curtain dividing the room the guards were using and assign this newly created space for us. The space was small for a family of six. There was not a stick of furniture in the room, no lights, no stoves, no chairs, and no table. Dead tired, we just dropped and welcomed sleep as best as we could. We had family on one side of the curtain and guards on the other. Later, other facilities were found.

Slowly, we started to get acquainted with our new surroundings and other inmates. Most of them consisted of priests and nuns. There were some German businesspeople and one German missionary couple. Religious, language, and cultural barriers soon melted and we developed new friendships. I well remember some of the parties given by our Italian friends. It seemed that nothing could daunt their spirits. And how they could sing! I am sure some of them would have qualified for lead roles in many an opera, including jumping on a table and belting it out.

With little to do, a welcome change from school life, we had to find other activities. That is where I first discovered the "hidden" pleasures of smoking. As an eleven-year-old I had no access to tobacco. But I could improvise. I found out that the coarse Chinese toilet paper, rolled up as a cigarette, would do just fine. My brother and I climbed a tree that was a safe distance from where my folks were staying and started puffing away. To our youthful minds, this was an exciting adventure!

Shortly after arriving at this camp, Papa contacted the authorities and requested permission to leave China and thus relieve them of the burden to care of us. The authorities acted quickly upon receiving this request and took the initiative to "expel" us from their country. The prescribed route to the border would take us across our southern neighboring province of Guangxi to Guangzhou-wan. This was a small enclave in China's most southern province of Guangdong, which had been annexed by France in 1898 and was still under French sovereignty.

We traveled 450 miles by train and bus, and walked or rode in sedan chairs under military and police escort. At night we were quartered in simple Chinese inns where we also were served sparse meals. But this did not matter, since we were headed towards freedom.

One stopover stands out in my mind. We had arrived in Guilin, a major town where the Southern Baptist Mission had an active field of service. I am not sure how my dad arranged it, but he contacted the American missionaries and they immediately extended a hearty welcome to us. We were treated to a feast, which we had not experienced for a long time. The graciousness of our hosts and the loving way they embraced us was comforting and refreshing. It seemed like they had been lifelong friends.

Of course, this did not escape the attention of our military guards. It was incomprehensible to them that citizens of two countries engaged in a bitter war could reach out to one another in such a loving way. They asked my dad how this was possible. It was like another God-sent opportunity for him to share the Good News of the gospel. Through Jesus Christ we had all been made brothers and friends and this bond superseded everything else. Puzzled by all of this and still shaking their heads, our guards just shrugged their shoulders.

When after a couple of weeks of travel we finally reached the border, there was a formal ceremony where we were handed over to the French authorities after they duly had signed a receipt accounting for all adults, children, and pieces of baggage. We had now left China and were experiencing freedom on French territory. We were treading on new ground and were not sure what lay ahead. But my parents were assured that the God who had led us so far would also continue to lead us. They had experienced this many times during nearly fifteen years of service in China and their faith and confidence in God remained unshaken.

Quickly a plan developed to travel to Shanghai, which meant that we would reenter China. But this was the "other" China, which was now occupied by the Imperial Japanese Army. A huge chunk of eastern China was under Japanese rule, along with all the major cities on the eastern seaboard, including Shanghai. My parents knew that it had a large German community, including a school, and so felt this was the most logical place to sit out the rest of the war. Since Japan and Germany were allied, we looked forward to being in a place where we were no longer the enemy.

6

HAVEN'T YOU GOT
ANYTHING TO EAT?

March 1942

Macau, China

Our first major destination was the city of Canton, now known as Guangzhou. Our way there led us through the tiny Portuguese colony of Macau, where we had to make a brief stopover. This port city, though untouched by the war itself, was in the throes of a terrifying famine. Blocked off from the rest of China, it was not able to sustain itself without outside aid. Resident missionaries had departed long ago. The people were desperate, but there was nothing that could be done.

We arrived in the late afternoon after traveling all day. Someone had heard of our coming and was kind enough to provide us with shelter for the night. It was on a small houseboat which in former times had been used for evangelistic services for the boat and fishing people.

Happy to have found lodging for the family, my father asked

where we could obtain food. We hadn't eaten all day, so he was concerned about feeding these starving mouths. Fortunately, we were directed to a restaurant, where we children promptly gorged ourselves on sugar cubes until an unkind waiter removed them from our reach. We placed our order and waited.

The longer we had to wait, the hungrier we became. Why didn't our food come? But then our hunger pain was replaced by another pain, when the waiter announced that there was no more food in the restaurant. They had run out.

Slowly we trudged back to our quarters.

By this time night had fallen, and without electricity we didn't have much choice but to settle down for the night. We were all in one big room, the room used for meetings on the boat. We bedded down as best as we could on the benches but found it hard to sleep on empty stomachs.

Before Papa blew out the lantern, he led the family once more in prayer: "Lord, You have always provided for all of our needs. We have never had to go hungry. But today, we've had nothing to eat and we are hungry. For some reason, You have not seen fit to give us food. But we still love You and trust You."

With hunger still gnawing at our stomachs, we finally dropped off to sleep. It seemed only a few minutes when we were awakened by a loud knock at our door. A voice called out: "Pastor, open up."

After fumbling for the lantern, my dad finally opened the door. What we saw and heard was one of those incredible events which have been indelibly etched into our memories.

There stood a man with a bag in his hand, profusely apologizing for disturbing us. He said he had heard of the arrival of some missionaries that afternoon. Realizing that there was no food to be had anywhere, he had brought a little bag of cooked rice and vegetables for us. Again, he apologized for the meager meal he was offering.

For us, it was a veritable feast! Food never tasted better.

We devoured it and soon were asleep once more—this time fully satisfied.

This event taught us a lesson, one I have never forgotten: God not only is aware of our needs and hears our prayers, but He also is able to provide for all of our needs, no matter what the situation. This was His way of allowing us to experience this firsthand. He wanted us to remember this for the rest of our lives. As I look back, I realize that experience built a confidence into my life which has remained to the present day.

Our Lord cares about our needs. When our resurrected Lord saw His disciples struggling unsuccessfully to catch fish, He asked them directly: "Haven't you any fish?" When they said no, He promptly showed them where to catch them. But when they came to Him, He already had food prepared to feed them. Paul's experience echoed this as well when he told the Philippian believers, "My God will meet all your needs, according to his glorious riches in Christ Jesus" (Philippians 4:19).

For me, this is not just doctrinal truth; it is real-life experience. Just mention Macau and it comes flooding back into my mind!

7

EASTER MIRACLE
ON THE PEARL RIVER

Easter Sunday, April 5, 1942

Canton, China

We finally made our way from Macau to Canton, the big harbor city in southern China not far from Hong Kong. There we found refuge with German missionaries of the Berlin Mission who were able to carry on their ministry, since this part of China was now under Japanese occupation.

Our parents were anxious to get us children back into some sort of organized schooling. We were able to do this by attending a small missionary school located on the mission compound.

The famine we had experienced in Macau began to have its effect on us in Canton. I remember my mother returning from a trip to the open street market where she bought fruit, vegetables, and a loaf of bread. As she was riding back in her rickshaw with the bundles of groceries at her feet, a fellow come out of nowhere, raced beside the rickshaw, and grabbed the loaf of bread. He took a giant bite, and then ran off with it. My mother's comment to us was that he was probably hungrier than we were, and she let him have it.

On Easter Sunday, all Germans were invited to the German Consulate General for a special Easter celebration. The consulate was located on the other side of the mighty Pearl River running through the city. Having been separated from anything and everything German for so long, my parents eagerly accepted the invitation and rented a small *sampan,* or boat, to ferry our family across the river. It took us probably twenty minutes to cross. It was a gorgeous sunny day and we children participated eagerly in the festivities: games, an egg hunt, and more. This was a far cry from our internment camp experience of just a few weeks before. All too soon, it was time to make our return trip across the river.

Ominous clouds were gathering, and the two women who were to row the sampan across the river urged us to hurry. There were nine of us in the boat, including the two women rowing. Another missionary lady, rather heavyset, had decided to join our family at the last minute. Our little boat seemed overloaded. The sky turned darker and darker. I felt a terrible foreboding as the two women threw themselves into the oars to speed us across the river.

Then everything went dark. It seemed like someone had turned off the light switch. An eerie calm surrounded us. Fearfully, we all huddled a bit closer, not knowing what to expect.

Then the storm broke.

The wind picked up dramatically. The gentle ripples around us transformed into mighty swells up to fifteen feet high. They tossed our little sampan up and down at will. Heaven's windows seemed to open up cascading walls of rain on us. Horrific thunder and lightning took turns exploding around us. We were in the midst of a typhoon.

The two women, now in absolute panic, screeched for us to

sit still. I thought our last hour had come. There was nothing we could do. We were in a race not for time, but for survival.

It was then, and this is still indelibly etched in my mind, that I heard my dad pray out loud. It was probably one of the shortest prayers on record: "Lord, save us!" The answer was instantaneous.

From nowhere, a huge wooden wall suddenly loomed. It was the side of a Japanese salt ship which had anchored midstream to escape the typhoon. My dad whistled over the noise of the storm and attracted the attention of the ship's crew members, who tossed us a rope. After several tries, the two women were able to grab hold and pull alongside the ship. I wondered if the little sampan would crash against the side of the larger vessel.

One by one, we kids were pushed upward, where strong sailor hands pulled us aboard to safety. There was one more scary moment for us kids, when we saw Papa pushing up the heavyset woman who was traveling with us. As she left the sampan, she gave it a push. The women still on the boat were no longer able to hold on to the rope, and the sampan was tossed back into the waves. The lady was hanging down the side of the ship and only with extra effort was she finally pulled on board.

In time, the little boat reconnected again with the ship, and Papa, as the last one, climbed aboard. The two women, having securely fastened their little boat to the ship, decided to stay in their boat. I guess they were used to being tossed up and down by the waves.

We were soaked and cold. The captain invited us to his private quarters and made us feel as comfortable as possible by serving hot tea and candy. Of course, there was a language barrier since none of us could speak Japanese. Then I had an idea. I scribbled the swastika and German flag on a piece of paper and showed it to the captain. He immediately recognized it and said *doitzoo*, the Japanese word for German. Since our nations were allies, the captain was visibly overjoyed to learn he had saved the lives of German citizens.

Several hours later, after the force of the typhoon abated, we continued our return trip across the river to our destination. We later heard that no one had ever seen a boat anchor in the river before. It was God's providential answer to our prayers. Twelve other boats attempting to cross the river sank that afternoon. More than fifty people lost their lives.

What made this event so unforgettable was that it occurred on Easter Sunday. On that first resurrection day, God's power was demonstrated to the whole world when He raised Christ from the dead. We experienced this same power in our lives by His divine intervention. I have never been able to celebrate Easter without being reminded of this miracle on the Pearl River.

8

HITLER YOUTH IN SHANGHAI

1942

Shanghai, China

Two weeks later, we were on yet another ship—a Chinese freighter bound for Shanghai, China's largest city halfway up the eastern coast. The Japanese army had taken over the whole eastern seaboard and this made coastal waters all the more dangerous due to enemy activity. Quietly our convoy of ships snaked along the coast, hoping to avoid all possible contact with hostile forces, in particular, American submarines. At night we traveled under complete blackout. It was foggy for most of our voyage, and we often heard the ominous blast of the ship's foghorn.

As an eleven-year-old, I didn't fully realize the perilous situation we were in. That changed on the night we heard terrific explosions both in front of and behind us. The two other ships in our convoy had been torpedoed by American submarines. Both sank, leaving our ship as the only survivor. This was the second miracle at sea we'd experienced within the past month.

After a brief detour to northern Taiwan, we arrived in

Shanghai. Due to sickness on board, we had to lie in quarantine for three days in the Shanghai harbor. It was hot and humid, but we amused ourselves by marveling at the skyline of this huge metropolis from a distance.

Shanghai was something totally new. After growing up in a small village in rural China, I was overwhelmed by the hustle and bustle of a modern, industrialized city. Running water, electricity, streetcars, huge department stores, and many, many people—I'd never seen anything like it.

Initially we lived at the headquarters of the China Inland Mission, at that time the largest mission in China. The facilities were on a huge piece of property in Shanghai dominated by two five-story buildings. These housed the headquarters, administrative staff, mission offices, and a private hospital for missionaries, as well as accommodations for missionaries coming and going. After the war, my dad served as manager of the transportation department, which handled all travel for missionaries. He was the first person to meet them when they arrived and the last they saw before they left.

It was therefore a privilege to meet many of the China Inland Mission staff. One of them stands out in particular: Dixon Edward Hoste. He had been recruited by Hudson Taylor, founder of the mission and known as the Apostle to China, along with several other outstanding British university students known as the Cambridge Seven. Hoste's father was a general, and Hoste himself had been a commissioned lieutenant in the Royal Artillery. He had experienced conversion under the influence of the famed American evangelist Dwight L. Moody.

D. E. Hoste came to China in 1885 and in 1902 succeeded Hudson Taylor as general director of the China Inland Mission. He was already over eighty years of age when we met him, and we still have his signature in the old guestbook that my parents kept. During the war, the Japanese interned Mr. Hoste and other senior mission staff in special quarters. I accompanied my parents and some others who were allowed to visit this center.

43

When I was introduced to Mr. Hoste, he was not well and in bed. He had always been of slim build, but as he sat up his frailty was obvious. When he heard of my German background, however, he suddenly came to life.

"What do you know about King Frederick the Great of Prussia?" he asked me with a kind smile on his face and with his high-pitched, even squeaky voice. My knowledge and understanding of English was elementary, since I had only one year of English in our German school, but I got the drift of what he was saying. Then he began to fill me in on quite a bit of German history. I was surprised to hear this elderly gentleman and missionary leader talk so knowledgeably on this subject.

The Wilhelm kids enrolled in the well-known "Kaiser-Wilhelm-Schule," which provided education from kindergarten through grade twelve. It was a private German school, which had been founded in 1895 primarily to serve the German community. When we got there, it had a student body of over three hundred students, most of them Germans or from German-speaking countries, but also from about a dozen other nations including Holland, Scandinavia, and Russia. Then there were a number of Chinese, mostly from the diplomatic corps who had lived in Germany. Many of these men had married German wives and wanted their children to receive a German education.

This kind of school setting was a giant step from the little one-room school I'd been accustomed to. Even though this was China, I felt in a way that I was back with my "own" people. I had never seen so many Germans in one place in all of my life. To have a school with the name "Wilhelm" was icing on the cake! Later, when some of my American friends asked if I was related to the last German Kaiser, Wilhelm II, I would reply with a straight face that I was the seventeenth cousin of the German emperor! All classes began with the "Heil Hitler" greeting. This was the standard greeting for all official functions or meetings.

Besides the German school, we also had a German church

and a German community. This was the next best thing to being at home in our Fatherland.

I always had a fascination for uniforms, flags, bands, and march music. From an early age, I also had a strong interest in German history. One of the first books I ever read described the exploits of a German cruiser, the *Emden*, during World War I days. Of course, my father's involvement during that war was always a point of great interest. Sometimes he would pull out some of the medals he had garnered during those days, especially his two Iron Crosses.

One of the things that really fascinated me was a series of picture postcards Papa kept on his desk. All of them were portraits of Wilhelm II. Having served in the German army under his command, my father would send the emperor, living in exile in The Netherlands, a birthday greeting each year. In return he would receive a picture. I thought this was great, since I did not know of anyone else who had a dad who heard from the emperor!

Germany went through a terrible time of humiliation and depression following the end of World War I. When Adolf Hitler assumed leadership of what later was called the Third Reich, the number of unemployed had risen to over six million. But he understood how to appeal to the German psyche and was slowly rebuilding a sense of nationalism.

Even today, I vividly remember one of my first readers in first grade. In simple terms it described the needs of Germany after losing the war. Then it added these momentous lines, still inscribed into my mind: *"Und als die Not am größten war, sandte Gott einen Retter—und er hieß Adolf Hitler"* (And when the need was greatest, God sent a savior—and his name was Adolf Hitler).

Even here was an organized attempt to "educate" German youth. We all believed what we were told.

In Shanghai, the German community was so well organized that it had contingents of the German Nazi party and its subsidiaries. Of particular interest to me was the opportunity to become involved in the Hitler Youth movement. As a German youth, this was the most natural thing to do, and I entered into this new experience enthusiastically.

The Hitler Youth was a logical extension of Adolf Hitler's belief that the future of Nazi Germany rested in its children. The Hitler Youth was seen as equally important to children as their education in school. In the early years of the Nazi government, Hitler made it clear what he expected German children to be like:

> The weak must be chiseled away. I want young
> men and women who can suffer pain. A young
> German must be as swift as a greyhound, as tough
> as leather, and as hard as Krupp steel.

I was so fascinated and obsessed with that goal that I practiced becoming tough in my own way. Since scratching a wall with your fingernails would bring shivers down my back, I felt here was an opportunity to toughen myself. I would purposely practice this scratching and attempt to fight my weakness demonstrated by feelings of revulsion. I must confess that I never did quite succeed in mastering it.

Hitler wanted to occupy the minds of the young in Nazi Germany even more than this. Movements for youngsters were part of German culture and the Hitler Youth was created in the 1920s. By 1933 its membership stood at 100,000. After Hitler came to power, all other youth movements were abolished, and the Hitler Youth grew quickly. In 1936, membership had risen to four million. In 1936, it became all but compulsory to join the Hitler Youth. The Hitler Youth catered to ten-to-eighteen-year-olds. There were separate organizations for boys and girls. The task of the boys' section was to prepare the boys for military service. For girls, the organization was to prepare them for motherhood.

Boys at age ten joined the Deutsches Jungvolk (German Young People) until the age of thirteen, when they transferred to the Hitler Jugend (Hitler Youth) until the age of eighteen. Here boys were exposed to military discipline and Nazi history, which was nothing more than propaganda. Membership in the Hitler Youth was officially made compulsory in 1939 in Germany, but in China it was still voluntary. All of us felt, however, that joining it was part and parcel of our German heritage.

At the age of ten, girls joined the Jungmaedelbund (League of Young Girls) and at the age of fourteen they transferred to the Bund Deutscher Maedel (League of German Girls). Girls had to be able to run sixty meters in fourteen seconds, throw a ball twelve meters, complete a two-hour march, swim one hundred meters, and know how to make a bed. The requirements for boys were higher, and I well recall the day when I ran sixty meters in 8.8 seconds, besting all of my comrades.

We had weekly drills in which we acquired physical skills such as sports, marching, and shooting. Field exercises included crawling on our bellies between rice paddies, carrying messages from one command post to another.

We also were trained in political and military history. Nazi and patriotic songs provided us with an *esprit de corps*, which made us young people highly fanatical for the cause of our beloved Fatherland, even though Shanghai was thousands of miles away. Up to this day, some of these songs remain fresh in my mind. We found something to believe in, a cause to become involved in.

Often we lined up in formation and gathered around the flagpole, sang the German national hymn, and then listened to Hitler's speeches being broadcast through loudspeakers. We sensed a strong bond of loyalty that united us with Germans around the world.

Though the war with Russia raged thousands of miles away, I was eager to learn all I could about what was taking place on the frontlines. Every morning, I stood at the street corner and waited for the newspaper delivery. On the front page, I always looked for the latest report of the German High Command to learn what had transpired on the Russian front. We had a large map of

Europe in our living room, and I would pin small swastika flags on this map, charting the progress our German troops had made within the past twenty-four hours. Vicariously, I participated in the struggle of our nation against the forces of communism.

I shall never forget the day when I was inducted into the Hitler Youth proper. Other contingents of Nazi organizations were assembled, the flags were presented, and when at the drum roll our names were called out, we stepped forward to give our oath of allegiance. It was a threefold oath: To Hitler as our Führer, to our German Fatherland, and to our flag. By this oath we ultimately surrendered our lives to the cause of Germany—and we did so willingly and enthusiastically. This was not a Boy Scout oath to do our duty and be nice to old ladies. It was an oath which gave purpose to our life. At that moment I was willing to give up all I had for the cause of Germany.

There was but one regret. I was only fourteen and too young to bear arms and be shipped back to Germany to fight at the Russian front.

9

THE DEATH OF ADOLF HITLER

1945

Shanghai, China

As the war progressed in the Asian theatre, bombing raids on Shanghai by the Allies became more and more frequent. Where we once in the interior of China had been subjected to Japanese bombing attacks, we were now experiencing the fury of American B-29 bombers unloading their cargo over our city. Many an hour was spent in bomb shelters below our school building and air raid sirens became routine. If you found yourself on the streets during one of these air raids, the police roped off all traffic and no one could move. Pedestrians, cyclists, cars—everybody and everything was stopped, often for several hours. Only after the all-clear siren sounded were barriers lifted and the hundreds of people who had crammed the intersections allowed to proceed to their destinations.

Then D-Day came—the Allied invasion in June 1944 at Normandy. I was glued to our shortwave radio listening to live broadcasts covering the landing and initial battles on the beaches.

For the first time, a twinge of compassion arose in my heart for the American soldiers who were decimated as they hit the shores. How could anyone think they could overcome the German defenses?

But within months, it seemed that the progress of the Allies toward Germany was inevitable. While some entertained the thought that it would soon lead to a collapse of the Third Reich, nobody ever admitted this publicly. My own faith in Adolf Hitler remained unshaken. It never wavered. Had we not thanked God for saving his life in July 1944 when "treacherous" officers sought to assassinate him? What about the secret weapons he would launch against the enemy in the nick of time to once again restore German dominance?

I was convinced right up to the end that he would eventually lead us to victory.

There was that momentary flickering of the candle giving new light when the news broke that U.S. President Franklin D. Roosevelt had died. Some mentioned in this connection that one of the three archangels of Satan was now dead, and that the other two (Churchill and Stalin) would soon follow.

Not so. The end came for Germany instead. And it came very quickly.

April 1945 saw Allied and Russian troops advancing on the heartland of Germany. Many a day, all students of the Kaiser-Wilhelm-Schule had to assemble around the flagpole and listen to speeches given over the radio and loudspeakers. Whether it was Hitler who spoke or more often Joseph Goebbels, the Nazi propaganda minister, we all listened with rapt attention. Each assembly ended with the singing of the Nazi national anthem as well as *"Deutschland, Deutschland über alles"* (Germany above all).

Deep inside of me, there was always hope that in the end, our Führer would pull us through. After all, there were those miracle weapons that were on the verge of being unleashed against the enemy.

But as the days dragged by and more and more of Germany was occupied, even my spirit started to sag. Then the headlines in our German newspaper in Shanghai stared us in the face one morning: *DER FÜHRER GEFALLEN* (The Führer dead). The shock was instant and real. It was all over.

As I peddled home from school on my bicycle that fateful day on April 30, 1945, tears streamed down my face. A hopelessness never experienced before overwhelmed me. The one whom I had trusted in had failed. He was dead. What did I have left? There was no more cause, no more purpose in life—it was useless. Germany was destroyed and defeated. It was occupied by enemy troops and divided up among the victors.

My father, who had come to the school so he could ride home with me, peddled quietly alongside. He finally said, "Son, I know how you feel. This is the second time for me." Of course, he was referring to World War I and his return to a nation which had signed its surrender to the Allied Forces.

I have often been asked what I thought of all the concentration camps in which Hitler annihilated millions of Jews in what he called the Final Solution. How could I support something like this?

During the war, I never heard about the camps. I knew that many Jews had been forced to leave Germany. In fact, the Hongkew district of Shanghai was largely inhabited by about twenty thousand Jewish refugees from Germany, Austria, Poland, and Lithuania. The refugees were settled in the poorest and most crowded area of the city. Local Jewish families and American Jewish charities aided them with shelter, food, and clothing. Yes, there was a stigma attached to them, but as a family we did have some contact with them. Every week, for instance, a middle-aged Jewish man peddled to our home with a suitcase tied on the back of his bike. He would bring it to our home and unpack all types of German sausages and meats which we bought from him.

I took violin lessons and my teacher lived in that part of town. He was not a Jew, but his wife, an accomplished pianist, was. He was a little hunchback, but he could really play his instrument and gave me a deep appreciation for classical music. We knew that the Jews did not have an easy life there—an understatement—and so when my musician-teacher came to give me my lesson, my mother always made sure he was served a dinner. And enjoy it he did!

In the German Jewish community, there was also a small Christian group of believers. Since they did not have a pastor, the pastor of the German Lutheran church of Shanghai would go there on a monthly basis, particularly to administer Holy Communion. One day, however, the news broke that he had been fired. The German Nazi party authorities in Shanghai had given him warning and prohibited his ministry among the Jews. He had ignored this order, feeling that the party had no right to interfere with his ministerial duties.

Now that the church was without a pastor, my dad was asked to take over the leadership of the congregation, a position he held for about six years. Since he was a missionary and not under the jurisdiction of the Nazi party, he continued the regular visits to the Hongkew Jewish community. I accompanied him a couple of times and thought it strange there seemed to be a barrier between "us" as Germans and "them" as Germans. Weren't we all alike?

I well remember the first time I heard about the German concentration camps for the Jews. It happened a few months after the war ended, when I was 14, on a Sunday morning right on the doorsteps of our German church. As I waited for the service to begin, I encountered an old classmate from school. We had been friends, though I had heard—never from him directly—that he was half-Jewish. He began to tell me about the horrendous concentration camps in Germany in which millions of Jews were exterminated. I could hardly believe what I was hearing. And then he added, "Either Hitler will go down in history as the greatest pig that ever lived or as the greatest hero."

I was absolutely furious, struggling to contain myself since this happened in front of the church where Papa would shortly step to the pulpit and deliver his weekly sermon. I felt like slugging my old classmate. All I could say and think was now that Germany was down and out, anybody could say anything about a defeated foe and nobody could challenge the veracity of these statements. It was totally unthinkable, that my country would ever plunge to such depths of moral decay. No, this was not true—it never would be true.

It actually took several years before I would admit that this was not a myth, but fact. With it came a feeling of guilt that I sensed as a German, guilt over this horrendous crime committed against humanity. Though I was on the other side of the world, thousands of miles removed from my country when it happened, I nevertheless felt the burden of this atrocity. The years have passed, but I still remember the deep sense of shame.

The defeat of Germany marked the end of my dreams and hopes. My purpose for life was gone. I realized that if there was no purpose, then life wasn't worth living. Little did I realize the truth of this statement and how God would use this principle to open up a new world to me.

10

WHAT SHALL IT PROFIT A MAN...

October 27, 1945

Shanghai, China

The days following Germany's surrender on May 10, 1945, were a dark time in my life. Here I was at fourteen, living in a country which was not my own, with little choice as far as the future was concerned.

Staying in China was not something I desired or looked forward to. My parents had been called by God to the mission field, but I had not. After living here practically all my life, I was looking forward to the day when I could leave. But where to go?

To return to Germany at that time seemed out of the question. Germany had not only been defeated, it had also suffered tremendous destruction through the continuous bombing raids on its cities. Then it was occupied by four conquering armies representing the United States, Soviet Russia, Great Britain, and France, which divided the spoils by splitting it up into four different occupation zones.

Defeated, destroyed, occupied, and divided.

That was my Fatherland, my homeland, a place I did not even know yet so desperately craved.

We heard from our family of the pathetic circumstances they encountered on a daily basis just to survive. We scraped together whatever resources we had to send them regular food packages, CARE parcels they were called, to help them out.

So, China was out. Germany was out. Why not immigrate to America? Yet the U.S.A. had been our enemy these past several years—why would I even consider going there?

Why had God been so capricious with my life? Did He even care? Was this matter of faith a real thing? Or was it just a theory which might satisfy the philosophical bent of a certain few? I did not belong to this group and wondered a great deal about the real meaning and purpose of life.

I knew well enough not to voice these doubts and questions at home or publicly. Had I not been raised in a strong Christian home and taught the Scriptures from childhood days? Morning devotions with the family were followed rigorously. My father would read the Bible, talk about it briefly, and then pray, and we all would say a prayer in closing.

On Sundays, of course, we would go to church and listen to my dad preach in Chinese. At times, when we were getting restless on the front bench, he would switch into German and reprimand us.

Yes, it was great that Papa could preach to the Chinese. They needed it. They had never heard the story of God's love, which sent His Son to die on a cross. When my dad preached in surrounding villages, he would often take big picture posters with him which told of and depicted man's sin, God's righteousness, and heaven and hell. And people would respond, become Christian seekers, and were eventually baptized in our church.

At one time, there was even a tinge of jealousy in my soul, which wished that I could have been born in their setting. I would have then heard of this strange "foreign" man who had some Good News to share. I know that if I had heard it like they did, I would have quickly responded to this marvelous story.

But to me, this was old hat. I knew all there was to know about God, and yet He was not real to me. He existed in the Bible, He existed in the sermons I heard preached, but I could not get a hold of Him. As a teenager, I went to the German Lutheran Church where my father pastored during the war years. Sometimes I proudly wore my Hitler Youth uniform, since drills were often required on Sunday mornings. I remember sitting at the edge of my seat at church listening to what my Dad was saying, hoping that somehow I could catch the key that would unlock the secrets of knowing God.

But somehow all that I came away with was "Believe in God, trust Him." That was not the answer I wanted, the answer I was looking for.

I believed, yet I really didn't know what I believed. I believed there was a God, yet I did not know Him. And even if I believed in Him, what value was there in such a God?

That was my dilemma.

Thus, when my life was convulsed by the turmoil brought by the end of World War II, I'd become cynical and disinterested in God. He did not care. He did not love.

The way I was thinking gave proof to the fact that I indeed did not know God. God was far more interested in me than I was in Him. And He proved it by sending someone into my life.

Harold Binks was an Australian missionary kid who had spent the past few years in a Japanese internment camp near Shanghai. Quite a large group of China Inland Mission missionaries had been placed into these camps and survived the war. We had also supplied them with monthly food packages to supplement the poor diet rations they were given by their Japanese captors.

After the surrender of Japan, all the camp inhabitants were released. To the great joy of my mother, she met an old friend, Harold's mother. They'd attended language school together when they first arrived in China in 1925. Now, twenty years later, they renewed their friendship.

Harold and his brother naturally became acquainted with us. One thing that drew me to Harold was our common love of chess. We spent hours playing against each other. What I liked about this the most was that I did not have to speak English while we were playing. I needed to know only two words: *check* and *checkmate*.

One evening, Harold appeared at the front door of our apartment and invited me to go with him to a youth meeting held at the Free Christian Church. He explained that there was a special one-week conference for young people and he wanted me to accompany him.

In halting English, I replied that I did not have time, since I had to do homework for school. I was glad when he left, because I really was not interested in going anyway. In the first place, the meetings would be in English, which was out of my comfort zone with my limited German-school English. Then, it certainly would be about God and religious things. I just was not interested in pursing this subject.

However, my friend returned the next night, and again the following one, to invite me to go. He was tenacious. However, he had underestimated my own stubbornness. I steadfastly rebuffed his kind invitations, giving one reason or another.

Saturday night came, the last night of the conference. Again, Harold was at the door. I greeted him and he invited me to come on this the last day. I thought, *I have been consistent in not going, so I will remain consistent and say no a final time.* Harold turned and left as I closed the door.

I walked down the hallway and met my father coming out of the living room. He asked who had been at the door and why. I told him. He wanted to know whether I was going. I said no.

Then changing his voice ever so slightly, he said, "You *are* going, aren't you!"

I knew there was absolutely no other option. My dad had been raised in a generation where people did not know much about psychology or "lathering before you shave." In other words, I was not invited to sit down on the living room couch and discuss this matter with him. He was a man who knew what he wanted and was always firm in carrying out his intentions. It was this character trait, which, no doubt, had carried him through his World War I days as a soldier fighting in Russia, Hungary, and France.

I did not need to think of this when he told me to go. He told me to go and so I went. There was no other choice.

But I was fuming inside. I decided to take my time getting there.

When I reached the church, I was amazed at how full it was. They were all young people. I spotted a place behind a pillar in the auditorium and tried to be as inconspicuous as possible. But soon I was struck by a couple of things that were totally beyond my own experience in church. I had been used to the formality of a Lutheran service, with organ music and candles. But here was man in front leading the music. He wore a flashy tie and flailed his arms. After a while he shed his coat and rolled up his shirtsleeves. But he got the youth to sing—and sing with real gusto.

Then there were "testimonies," something else new to me. One thing impressed me deeply: each speaker had something in common. They all talked about God as if they knew Him personally, that He was real to them.

I am sure they had a sermon that evening as well, but I did not hear it. Rather, my attention became focused on the little song sheet we had been given. On the bottom of each page, a verse of Scripture had been printed. One of these captured my total attention:

> For what shall it profit a man if he gains the whole
> world but loses his own soul?

I translated the verse into German and recognized that it was familiar to me: Mark 8:36.

Then I experienced something amazing. What happened that night was what Scripture refers to as a *rhema*. It was a message from the Bible, directed by the Spirit of God for special application to my life. I heard God speaking to me through this verse of Scripture. It was not an audible voice heard by my ears, but one that spoke so powerfully to my heart that it drowned out all other voices around me.

> What is it that you really want? Is it success, fame, honor, reputation, education, money? Is that what you want? Tell me, what is it that you are after? Name it.

I had for all these months blamed God for ruining my life. He had allowed circumstances to wipe out any hope for success. I felt incapable of accomplishing anything. In fact, there was no more purpose to life.

Now I heard Him say, "Tell me what you want, and you can have it." With this kind of offer, how could I continue to blame God?

But then His Word came through with power:

> But what will it profit you, even if you gain everything you want in this world, but lose your soul?

And at that moment it was crystal clear in my mind: my soul was lost. If I were to die that night, I would not go to heaven. My mind recalled another passage of Scripture where Jesus mentioned a rich man who wanted to build bigger barns for storing all his goods so he could then take it easy for the rest of his life. God said to this man, "This night your soul shall be required from you, then whose shall all those things be which you have acquired?"

I thought, *What good is it if you gain everything in life, but lose your soul? What if your soul shall be required tonight?*

A terrific struggle took place in my heart as I sat in that meeting. I did not hear what was taking place around me. All I heard was the voice of God speaking and knocking at my heart's door.

I walked home alone—slowly. "What does it profit, if you lose your soul?" I could not shake this matter off.

When I got home, my mother told me that they had already eaten, but that dinner was ready for me.

"I am not hungry," I said. My mind was too occupied.

As I took my bath that evening, everything suddenly hit me full force. *This is as close as you possibly can come to making a decision*, I thought. *If you don't resolve this matter this night, then you probably never will.*

So, I simply turned to God and prayed, without even knowing that I was praying: "I have run from You long enough. I cannot run any longer. Please, take over the direction of my life. Come into my heart, be my Savior."

And then the miracle happened. No clap of thunder, no earthshaking event, but all of a sudden it seemed that the burdens I had carried with me all these years were gone. I was free at last! I felt like a new person, with a new sense of excitement for life.

Many people find the Lord in church, in a meeting, in private counseling with a friend. I found Him while sitting in the bathtub! Cleansed on the outside and on the inside, all at the same time.

The first people I sought out that evening were my parents. "I have asked Jesus to come into my heart!" I blurted out. I burst into tears. It was not that I was overcome with sudden emotion. It was something else. The moment I declared my faith in Christ, a sudden conviction of sin overwhelmed me. The Spirit of God brought an incident to my mind that went back quite a few years.

I had falsely implicated my younger brother for some mischief on my part and he had been punished for it. It had been a clear lie. The fact that now I was a new creation in Christ made me immediately aware of a new standard of right and wrong.

Turning to my dad, I cried, "Many years ago, I lied to you. I am so sorry. Will you forgive me?"

Of course, he did. Then my parents told me with tears in their eyes that they were filled with deep joy since they had been praying for this for many years.

Papa then gave me three important guides for my Christian life. They were *God's Word, prayer,* and *fellowship.* Make these a part of your daily life, he said, and you will grow spiritually.

I was awake bright and early the next morning—Sunday morning. I walked to the window and looked out into what seemed a brand new world. The grass looked greener, the air seemed purer, and the birds sang more sweetly. What teenager gets up in the morning and listens to birds sing? I was overwhelmed with an unspeakable joy and experienced firsthand the truth in 2 Corinthians 5:17:

> Therefore, if anyone is in Christ, he is a new creation; the old has gone, the new has come.

I looked over to where my younger brother still slept. A wild thought came to mind when I saw his shoes in front of his bed. I grabbed them, got some polish and shoe brushes, and started cleaning his shoes. I had never cleaned my brother's shoes before—but that morning it seemed to be the right thing to do.

My activities must have stirred him out of his sleep and he turned over resting on his elbow watching me for a while. Suddenly, it dawned on him what I was doing.

"Hey, those are my shoes," he said.

"I know," I replied

"Are you crazy?"

"No. I just wanted to do something for you."

A new life had begun and I sensed for the first time an inner excitement. I was embarking on a new experience. No longer was belief in God a theoretical matter. It had become a personal experience. I had started to know Him as a person, a friend, a Savior.

The night before, I had prayed for Him to take over the direction of my life. I was now sensing that He had taken the wheel. I felt safe trusting Him wherever He might lead me.

With this confidence came something else I had longed for. There seemed to be a new purpose for my life. Life was indeed worth living. And I knew that my soul was safe. I began to realize at that moment that the rest of my life was preparation for eternity. That was purpose enough.

I do not remember whether I had the chance to share this life-changing experience with Harold. He left with his parents to return to Australia shortly after this event. So, I am not sure whether Harold Binks ever learned about the big part he played in my life. But one day, in eternity, I will have the opportunity to tell him my story!

11

ANNA, FRANK, ARTHUR, ROY

1945

Shanghai, China

Now that I had committed myself to be a follower of Jesus Christ, I experienced a real hunger for the Word of God. You need the Word of God to grow, my father had said. I was eager to apply this truth.

I got up early each morning, climbed the two flights of stairs to the top of our apartment building, and made my way to the flat roof. There I opened my Bible and tried to make sense of what I was reading. Someone had once told me that the book of Romans contained the fundamental truths of our faith, so I tackled this book first. Alas, it did not make much sense to this young believer. What was I to do?

Again, I experienced God's supernatural intervention. He brought special people into my life who were a huge help in my Christian formation. I have been exceptionally blessed by the large number of people whose paths crossed mine over the years and left deep imprints on my life.

Anna Swarr, Frank Houghton, Arthur Glasser, and Roy Robertson were among this group. They helped me develop patterns that benefited my personal Christian growth and prepared me for ministry in days to come.

Anna was a secretary in the finance department of the China Inland Mission and hailed from Lancaster, Pennsylvania. She had followed God's call to come to China and had been assigned to administrative responsibilities in the mission office. She had a beautiful singing voice and radiated a deep love for God and for young people. Soon after her arrival, a number of young people started gathering around her to meet for Bible studies and youth meetings at the Shanghai Free Christian Church. It was here that basic foundations were laid for my life and this was where I attended the youth service that led to my salvation.

As a teenager, I had never prayed in public before. I was too scared. But Anna gently encouraged me to come to the prayer meetings and take part. Praying was hard enough as it was, but praying in English was even more intimidating. Anna encouraged me to write down a few sentences on a slip of paper and then read them during the prayer meeting. This was a practical challenge and it worked. The next time the sentences grew a bit longer, and in time I felt total freedom to pray along with the others.

Anna was always available to us young people. We spent many hours individually or in small groups, talking, learning, and praying together. She was a mentor to us in the truest sense of the word.

Anna never married and was more than ninety when she went home to be with the Lord. I saw her only once after I left China, but the fragrance of her life, her prayers and love for us, have remained with me forever.

Bishop Frank Houghton was the general director of the China Inland Mission, the third leader of the mission following Hudson Taylor. He had come from England and served as bishop in the Anglican diocese of the province of Sichuan before assuming responsibility for more than one thousand CIM missionaries.

Everyone referred to him in hushed tones as the GD (General Director) or the "Bish," but privately he insisted that I address him as "Frank." I was one of the few people ever privileged to do so.

How did this come about?

I first met the bishop when he came to Shanghai after the end of Word War II. The CIM had relocated its headquarters during the Sino-Japanese War to Chungking in western China and now was reclaiming its official headquarters in Shanghai. At his first visit, I mustered my courage and greeted him in my limited English. I had just found the Lord and must have conveyed that sense of newfound faith and love for the Savior to him.

When the mission leadership returned to Shanghai, the bishop and I developed a close personal friendship. He insisted that I spend at least half an hour with him in his apartment every day, during which time he would share principles from God's Word and life in general, as well as personal matters. How he as the director of the largest mission in China found time in his schedule to accommodate me is still a puzzle—but he did it. This went on for nearly five years. It is hard to enumerate all that I learned from this man.

Sometimes he would go through a whole folder of recent letters he had received from missionaries and mission business with me. Perhaps he needed to bounce some things off me, even though I was just a teenager! But he trusted me. I soon came to realize that missionaries were human and that they struggled like everyone else with their attitudes and relationships with others. It also taught me that leadership had more to do with servanthood than anything else. Administering a mission was no easy task.

I remember some funny situations where I overheard missionaries discussing one thing or another in terms of what the mission would do. I stood next to them, knowing all along what decision Frank had made, and I could only smile inwardly.

Whenever Frank traveled, he faithfully sent me handwritten notes, which I kept for years until a typhoon-caused flood in

Taiwan destroyed all of my files and treasured possessions. Even after he resigned from the mission in the aftermath of the Communist takeover in 1949, the letters kept coming. There was always a word of encouragement and challenge. I have often reflected on the example this man set for me in taking time to disciple others. I wish I had been as faithful as Frank was to me!

Arthur Glasser served with the First Marines as chaplain during World War II. He saw much combat and faithfully ministered to men before they entered battle, some never to return. His book *And Some Believed* vividly describes his years of ministry in the service. I found it in the CIM library and devoured it after I met him.

When the war was over, Art Glasser and his wife, Alice, sensed God's leading to apply to the China Inland Mission. That is where I first met them. Again, it was one of the unique experiences of my teenage years to rub shoulders with a man like Art Glasser, who later became a missionary statesman in his own right, a scholar (he succeeded Dr. Donald McGavran as dean of the School of World Mission at Fuller Theological Seminary), and mentor to many in the ministry today.

Art reminded me of a modern apostle Paul, in that he also wrote me letters once he relocated to southwestern China for his missionary assignment. These too were handwritten letters, often running six, seven, or eight pages, in which he shared with me basic biblical truths of the highest caliber. He introduced me to the depths of Romans 6–8 and other doctrinal truths, which I soaked up.

I remember that shortly after Art arrived in Shanghai, he was sent to the official language school to study Chinese. Our youth group was planning a conference and needed a speaker. Enthusiastically, I suggested Art, who readily agreed. There was only one hitch. He had to obtain permission to "cut" classes for a week and travel to Shanghai. The missionary leader serving as director of the language school declined to give permission. What were we to do?

A brilliant thought came to me: Why not appeal to the top? I marched to Frank's office and laid our case before him. Result: Frank contacted the language school director and requested he make an exception and allow Art Glasser to speak at our conference. And what a blessing it was. I still remember some of messages he gave at that time.

As a young believer, I had been encouraged to memorize a number of Bible verses, especially those dealing with the gospel. But it was Art who first introduced me to an organization called the Navigators, which had been founded by Dawson Trotman.

The Navigators had an effective ministry in World War II to American servicemen, principally within the Navy. Later that spread to the other branches of the armed forces as well. The motto of the "Navs," as they were to be called, was "To know Christ and to make Him known." Evangelism and spiritual growth through disciplined living was emphasized along with the challenge of training others in the same disciplines. The key verse was 2 Timothy 2:2: "And the things you have heard me say in the presence of many witnesses entrust to reliable men who will also be qualified to teach others."

One of these disciplines was Scripture memory. Before leaving, Art mentioned the Navigators to me. He added that Dawson Trotman would be coming to visit China, and that I should soak up all I could. Then he handed me a little booklet entitled "Initial Test," which gave a list of thirty-six key verses on a variety of topics of the Christian life. Art told me to start working on these. I jumped at the challenge.

I have stayed in touch with Art Glasser over these past fifty years, and he has been a faithful friend and supporter. I am humbled when I think of the privileges God gave to me through servants like this. I will be forever indebted to Art. Now in his nineties, he still serves as a living example to follow.

Roy Robertson was a naval officer and pilot who first made contact with the Navigators in Texas, his home state. Roy was a teacher, motivator, discipler, and evangelist. When Daws Trotman decided to send the first Navigator missionary overseas, it was Roy who went. Later, Roy often joked that his only missionary call was a telephone call from Daws asking him to go to China!

Roy arrived in Shanghai a few months before the Communists took possession of the country. We made an instant connection. Systematically—and everything Roy did was systematic—he introduced me to the skills of Scripture memory, Bible study, organizing prayer lists, and sharing my faith, as well as principles of spiritual maturity.

I remember Roy challenging me to memorize three new Bible verses each week. This did not seem to me to be enough, so I asked whether it was okay to memorize six verses. He smiled and said, "Go ahead, but be sure to daily review your old verses as well." I did, and after a year I had committed three hundred verses to memory. By the following year it was six hundred, and soon one thousand. More than anything, Scripture memory has assisted me in my spiritual growth and development and understanding of the Word. I will always be grateful to Roy for this.

Several others also had a tremendous impact on me when I was a teenager. I cannot say enough about the value of wise Christian mentors for anyone during their formative years. I thank God for those who went before me and faithfully shared the things they had learned in their spiritual pilgrimage.

12

AND HE CALLS HIMSELF
A CHRISTIAN!

1946

Shanghai, China

Things took a radical change in my life after the war ended, especially as far as school was concerned. Our days at the Kaiser-Wilhelm-Schule came to a conclusion. The school buildings were taken over by the authorities. Most of the teachers, along with the majority of the German community of Shanghai, were evacuated back to Germany.

A few teachers who remained behind organized private classes for those of us still in the city and were able to continue the regular curriculum on a reduced level. After the school year ended, so did this temporary educational arrangement.

What would happen next?

My two sisters and brother enrolled in the CIM school for missionary children, first in Shanghai and later in Kuling, a mountain resort in the interior. There were no classes available for my age group, so I had to find another solution.

I finally settled on enrolling at the Shanghai British School. The first school day was faced with great trepidation. Although I had studied English in the German school system and had contact with a number of English-speaking friends, I was not sure how it would be in the context of the school and classroom.

The whole approach was so different from what I was used to and it took a while to get in the swing of things. But before long, I began to learn the system and fit in.

We had the general subjects: mathematics, the sciences, English literature. I was fascinated with the study of history and the exceptional teacher we had contributed immensely to making this not only meaningful but inspiring. No wonder, later in college, this was the major I picked for my undergraduate studies.

In this school there was one more subject that was mandatory: Scripture. We actually were given instruction in Bible knowledge and here was one subject in which I excelled! In our grading system, teachers marked a grade of 75 percent as excellent. However, in my Scripture grades I would score over 90 percent, which astounded both teacher and students alike.

I wish I had been as good in all the other subjects. But, alas, this was not the case. Especially in French, I had great difficulties. Of course, when I arrived I was already two years behind the others. I never did catch up.

Besides my studies, there is something more from my years at the British school that left an indelible impression on me. We were writing a math exam, and to help me out in a real time of need, I resorted to a crib sheet, which I managed to hide between my knees, pressed against my desk. It had become a "very present help in the time of trouble" for me and I made it through the test just fine.

When I joined my classmates later, they were discussing the test and some of their creative ways of making it through the exam. As I approached them, one of them slapped me on the shoulder and yelled to his buddies, "You should have seen what he did, and he calls himself a Christian!" He began to describe in detail what he had observed me do during the exam. He told them that what they all did in cheating on their tests was nothing in comparison to what I had done.

In view of this lavish praise, I outwardly tried to smirk my way through this and enjoy the applause of my classmates. But inwardly, I was devastated. They certainly had every right to expect a higher standard from me, a Christian. Yet I had failed them in this. And even more so, I had failed the Lord. I had cheated my teachers as well, and I felt awful. Besides, I had brought shame to the name of Christ and had discredited my ability to witness to my classmates.

I knew that I needed to make things right.

When the grades were returned a couple days later and my grade was announced, I made my way to the teacher's desk and requested that I be given a zero. When the teacher wondered why, I simply said, "Because I cheated." To my great relief, the teacher obliged. He crossed out my grade and placed a big fat red zero across my paper. I walked back to my desk with a spring in my step—I no longer had to carry that burden!

I was learning the important lesson in life that failure is part of our existence. I was also learning that our failures can be stepping stones for success, and need not become burdens which cause us to live as prisoners of the past. Yes, just as Peter had failed our Lord, so I too could make things right and move on.

13

St. John's and the Fall of Shanghai

1949

Shanghai, China

I graduated from the Shanghai British School at the end of 1948 by passing my University of Cambridge certificate exams. With this certificate in hand, I registered for classes at St. John's University, the renowned institution in Shanghai. The faculty was mostly Chinese but there were a number of foreign lecturers as well. Classes were in English and Chinese. The student body of approximately fifteen hundred students, however, was totally Chinese, apart from the five of us who came from America, Germany, India, and Russia.

My classes were interesting, and I enjoyed the new atmosphere that was so different from what I had experienced in high school. I participated in interschool track meets and particularly enjoyed my debating classes.

Since St. John's had Episcopalian roots and been founded

by missionaries, we attended voluntary chapel meetings once a week. Once I was invited to take the place of a friend who could not keep his speaking appointment. I consented to do so and prepared a sermon. However, the closer the date came for me to speak, the more I began to dread and worry about it. In fact, I literally became sick, and had to stay home from classes that day.

I was not left off the hook on this one. A new date was set and I mustered all my courage to accept this opportunity. The morning came for me to speak, and I approached the podium with my sermon outline clearly in mind. I delivered it as best as I could, but found out that it had taken me all of three minutes! I took another stab at it and was able to consume another couple of minutes. My next approach was to lead out in prayer, but it seemed the clock was standing still. I believe that morning I set a new record for the shortest chapel service in the history of the school.

Shanghai, as well as the whole country, was going through the convulsions of civil war. The Chinese currency was being devaluated hourly. The exchange for one U.S. dollar rose to three million Yuan, the local currency. To make payroll for the Chinese office staff at the CIM headquarters, a truck was dispatched to the bank every three days. It retuned with bundles of local money packaged and sealed, but not opened. To go to the market required a suitcase filled with these packets of money.

Homeless people and refugees seemed to be everywhere. So were the beggars; their number increased daily. I remember peddling my bicycle to school one morning. It was bitterly cold and frost covered the ground. All of a sudden, a shocking sight made me forget about the freezing cold. I saw little bundles of newborn babies that had been thrown into garbage containers and left at the side of the road. Understanding supreme poverty was one thing, but seeing starving and desperate parents driven to such extremes left me shaken. This scene played over and over in my mind as I sat in classes—it was too hard to shake.

It would get worse.

When I returned in the late afternoon, I noticed dogs jumping in and out of those same garbage bins, feeding on these little bundles of human life. Was this possible? It turned my stomach. My heart ached for the people of China. Yes, it was a time of desperate need—and time for a change. Would Communism hold the answer for China and solve the misery of its people?

My college career came to a sudden halt. Chinese Communist troops under Mao Zedong were closing in on our city. Following the end of World War II, the longstanding conflict between President Chiang Kai-shek and his nemesis, Mao Zedong, had erupted once more. The war-weary Nationalist army under Chiang, after fighting the Japanese for eight years, was no match for the Communist troops. One city after another had fallen already to the "liberators." Now it was Shanghai's turn.

Chiang had pledged to fight for Shanghai to the very end, but when Mao's troops advanced, they met little or no resistance. We actually stood on the roof of our five-story mission building, watched the final bombing raids, and listened to rapid machinegun fire of advancing Communist troops entering the city. Before we realized it, the battle for Shanghai was over. The largest city in China was under Communist control. It was May 1949.

Of course, this meant that all schools were closed for the time being. When they reopened after a couple of months, St. John's resumed classes as well. But this time it was under new management. Instead of our regular classes, a new curriculum was introduced by Communist Party functionaries. "Political Orientation and Instruction" was the motto of the day. All students were brought together in the big university auditorium and schooled in the new system, which had been brought by the new People's Republic of China as proclaimed on October 1, 1949. There were endless lectures that we had to sit through.

For some of us foreign students this soon became a waste of time, since we generally sat in the back row of the auditorium and spent the sessions reading. After a few weeks, however, classes were suspended altogether. This was the end of my college experience in China.

Bishop Houghton was concerned that with the university closed, I would fritter away my time. He designed a course in English literature for me and held me to a strict program. I met with him on a daily basis.

Looking down the road, I and some of the new American missionaries who were studying Chinese often wondered what it would be like to attend a college in America. But as far as we were concerned, that was only a dream of the far distant future. Little did I realize that my days in China were drawing to a close.

14

STANLEY'S SONG

April 1950

Shanghai, China

The Communist takeover brought incredible changes in China. They were principally political, but in time economic and cultural as well. The people were weary of war and welcomed Mao Zedong. He had made huge promises, especially to the rural population. Optimism, often bordering on euphoria, greeted the new regime.

Soon, however, the foreign population felt pressure. Businesses were taken over by the government. Foreign personnel began to leave. Missionaries were also affected. Movement within the country was curtailed and for those living in Shanghai, this meant no travel beyond the city's borders. This began to restrict what they could do and how they could continue to minister. Local Chinese churches began to distance themselves from the mission organizations which had established them.

The China Inland Mission, the largest mission in China numbering approximately one thousand people, adopted a policy that would keep its missionary force in the country and reject any thought of withdrawal. This wait-and-see attitude was founded on the hope that given time, things would change and missionary work would return to normal. In retrospect, this was a mistake. It underestimated the real nature of China's new leadership.

The government took a page from missionary strategy when it began to promote the "Three Self Movement." Mission organizations had long recognized that their goal had to be the establishment of national churches which were self-governing, self-supporting, and self-propagating. Now that they had total control of China, the Communist government leadership felt it was time to implement their own principles nationwide. China did not need any more foreign missionaries! Churches could manage their own affairs without these capitalist agents from the West. Without much fanfare, over a century of missionary ministry in China came to an end.

As this truth began to dawn, missionaries began to withdraw, first in small contingents, then in increasing numbers.

My parents realized that this development would also impact our family. The question was, where were we to go? If Papa had his druthers, he would return to Germany at the drop of a hat. After all, we still had two sisters there and the whole family longed for a reunion with them. However, conditions in Germany were critical in the postwar years, particularly as far as the economy was concerned. My parents sent regular CARE packages to our extended family in Germany to help them in their struggle for survival. Would it be wise for the family to return to Germany under these circumstances?

There was another consideration: the future education of us four children. I had already made my shift from the German school system to the British. My two younger sisters, Esther and Peggy and my brother, Fred, had also transitioned when they enrolled in the CIM missionary school in Kuling, located in one of the interior provinces. To continue in the English educational system made sense. We all agreed that going to the United States was the best option.

We were granted our U.S. entry visa in early January 1950. That was a miracle in itself. Through the intermediacy of some good friends, my dad was invited to come to the States and assume the position of pastor of missions in a large church in Southern California. The pastor of the church expressed this invitation in a telegram to us. Armed with this sole document, my father went to the American Embassy in Shanghai and within forty-eight hours the officials granted the whole family a "non-quota" immigration visa for the U.S.A. Two consuls working at the embassy later confirmed to us that they had never before experienced such swift expediting of a visa with so little documentation!

This was a huge encouragement to all of us. We were convinced that God wanted us to make this move. One obstacle, however, remained. And the longer we waited for it to be resolved, the more formidable it became. We began to wonder if we had misread God's will for our lives.

In order to leave China, every person needed to apply for an exit visa from the Chinese authorities. Before granting it, all names of applicants were published in the local Chinese newspaper. This entitled any Chinese citizen to make a claim for compensation or voice his misgivings in his relationship with a foreigner applying to leave. Businesspeople often fell victim to charges made, some justifiable, others not.

Day after day, long lists of names appeared in the newspapers, including those of other missionary friends who were leaving China. However, our names were not among them. A couple of times, I accompanied Papa to the Chinese government office to inquire about the status of our exit visa. Finally, we were told in no uncertain terms not to come any more, that our visas were being handled efficiently and that we would be notified whenever they were ready.

So we waited.

Weeks and months passed. Still no word. Our daily perusal

of Chinese newspapers yielded nothing. In the meantime, our friends were leaving China, one by one. We just sat there and wondered what was taking place. A few months ago it had seemed so clear—now doubts started to assail us. Did we have it all wrong? Was God playing games with us? Had our future in America been a mere pipedream? Perhaps God never wanted us to go there in the first place. Maybe He wanted us to return to Germany after all.

So it seemed.

Then God sent a little visitor into our home.

His name was Stanley and he was less than four years old. His parents, Dave and Helen Morken, were good friends and fellow missionaries. Both of them were hospitalized along with their two sons. Helen was giving birth to "Shanghai John" while Dave was ill with asthma. On top of that, two of their boys were undergoing tonsillectomies! Their two older girls could take care of themselves. My parents offered to have this little towheaded youngster stay with us. We had no idea what a blessing he would prove to be to our whole family.

Before we even got up the next day, we heard that little crystal clear voice singing:

> Trust in the Lord, and don't despair, He is a friend
> so true.
> No matter what your troubles are, Jesus will see
> you through.
> Sing, when the day is bright, sing, in the darkest
> night.
> Every day, all the way, let us sing, sing, sing!

Stanley greeted us with it every morning. Before long we sang along with him: "Trust in the Lord, and don't despair..." It became our theme song.

But it was much more than that. It began ministering to our spirits that had succumbed to doubt and fear. This little fellow unknowingly began to turn our focus back on the Lord and away from circumstances. We had allowed ourselves to become absorbed by the hopelessness of our situation and now this little angel, a special messenger from God, reminded us to trust Him to see us through. And God is always pleased when faith and trust in Him supersede worry and anxiety.

The Wilhelm family will always remember Stanley Morken. He unknowingly restored and renewed our confidence in an all-loving, all-powerful God. From this point on, the burden was lifted, and we simply waited to see what God would do and how He would do it.

Many missionaries and friends prayed and reassured us that God was in control. Then the news came that an American ship would soon dock in Shanghai and transport the remnant of the American community still living in Shanghai. Also, all American embassy and consular personnel would be evacuated.

We received word from the American authorities that we should make every effort to get on this vessel, since this would be our last chance to make it to the States. But how could we? We had no exit visas, no permission to leave China.

More testing, more trials of our faith. But now we were singing:

> Trust in the Lord, and don't despair, He is a
> friend so true.
> No matter what your troubles are, Jesus will see
> you through.

Again God intervened. This time He used the Chinese government to block the ship from coming to Shanghai. It would not be given permission to enter Chinese territorial waters. Then the government officials changed their minds. At the last moment, however, they again blocked the ship from entering Shanghai harbor. This scenario was repeated several times.

Finally, in early April, an agreement was reached. The ship would stay in international waters just outside of Tianjing, a major city close to Beijing, about six hundred miles north of Shanghai.

There it would be available for boarding. The departure date was set for end of April. This meant that everyone in Shanghai would have to take a train trip north to board the vessel. One after another, our friends left Shanghai and boarded the train to Tianjing.

Except the Wilhelms. Things were coming down to the wire. We prayed and wondered. Others prayed and tried to encourage us. Would God come through, or did He have another plan for our lives? We just did not know, and so we waited from one day to the next to see what answer would come.

On Sunday, April 16—the week after Easter—I ran down the street and picked up a Chinese newspaper. Without opening the paper, I ran home and announced, "Our names are in the paper." It was wishful thinking at its best.

My hands trembled as I fumbled to open it. With everyone looking over my shoulder, we finally came to the page where a lengthy list of foreign names appeared. Quickly, my fingers ran down this list. There just had to be six Wilhelms, they just had to be there!

And then we saw them, beginning with K. Max Wilhelm, Anna Wilhelm, and all of us children.

You cannot imagine the gratitude and thanksgiving that welled up in our hearts and voices for the Lord who had answered our prayers and those of many others. He had done all things well. The happy news spread like wildfire through the missionary community, since all had been praying. Even in church that Sunday morning and evening, special mention was made of God's faithful provision for the Wilhelm family. God had answered prayer. He is never too late!

We obtained our Chinese exit visa and after a few frantic days of packing up our earthly belongings, we boarded a train to Tianjing. This journey took us three days, but we did not care. Our hearts were still overflowing with thankfulness for what we had experienced, as well as with excitement over what lay ahead.

After three more days in Tianjing, the day of our departure

from China finally came. We were ordered by the Communist authorities to report to the wharf at the harbor at 5 A.M. for customs inspection. We stood for hours as the sun rose and then began to beat down on us. Sweltering temperatures and humidity added to the discomfort, but what of it? We were leaving at last.

Finally, around noon, customs officials dressed in army uniforms arrived on the scene. There was more waiting. Eventually they approached their task to examine each individual gathered at the dock. They made us open every suitcase and trunk, and prowled through our belongings to ensure we were not taking anything "illegal" out of the country. Of special interest were paperwork, books, and letters. Then came full body searches. I saw the American ambassador a short distance from us. Both of his arms were raised high as a small young soldier conducted his search. No one was exempt.

It was evening when the first passengers were loaded on the large barge which would shuttle them twelve miles to the international boundary where the S.S. *General W. H. Gordon* was anchored. It was an American troop transporter from World War II days. Now it would carry over a thousand refugees and the remaining U.S. Embassy and consular staff out of China. This barge made several roundtrips before we were allowed to board. By this time it was past midnight.

A few more anxious moments arose when a sudden storm tossed us back and forth. Many got violently sick, but eventually we saw the bright lights of the *General Gordon*. It was about 3 or 4 A.M. when we clambered on board and were heartily welcomed by the crew. All of us were overwhelmed by a huge sense of relief and freedom. We had finally made it. We were free at last!

After stops in Hong Kong, Manila, and Yokohama, we were bound for Hawaii and San Francisco. Once again we were able to prove the truth of Proverbs 19:21:

> Many are the plans in a man's heart, but it is the
> LORD's purpose that prevails.

We had made the plans and had established deadlines which needed to be met. When these were not realized, we wondered why God did not intervene on our behalf. Yet ultimately it was the Lord's purpose which prevailed, and no power on earth could stop it. It was this demonstration of the power of our sovereign Lord which built and kept building our faith.

And this has never changed.

15

YOU ARE... YOU WILL BE...

May 1950

Pacific Ocean

We were on the *General Gordon* somewhere in the Pacific, making our way to San Francisco. It was a hot, steamy night down in the belly of this converted troop transport. We were sharing a huge dormitory with several hundred men stacked in triple-high bunk beds—all of us refugees from China bound for America.

Slowly I made my way to the top deck to get some air. I ended up spending most of the night up there. It was a beautiful night. The moon and stars were out, providing an even glow as the ship plowed through the sea. Apart from the churning of the ship's engines everything was quiet and serene. It was a night I would never forget, because in all that tranquility, I heard a voice. It spoke quietly at first then with an increasing force that will forever be etched in my mind and memory.

I was leaning over the railing pondering my future. What, I wondered, would it be like to live in the United States of America? There was a certain excitement, yet it was mixed with anxiety and apprehension. It would be a new experience for me and I was not sure how I would handle it.

As I stood there overlooking the mighty ocean, I began reflecting on my past, present, and future. Who was I?

I had spent seventeen years of my nineteen years in China. This had been my world, the only country I knew. Yet I was not Chinese and I could not imagine spending the rest of my life there, always being the "foreigner."

My heritage was German. My parents had left Germany in the 1920s in answer to God's call on their lives and had spent all these years in China with only one break of less than three years. I had attended German schools, had joined the Hitler Youth movement in China, and had always considered myself German to the core. Yet, I had to confess, I did not even know my own country.

Now I was on my way to America to begin a new life. I had a few problems with that. America had been our enemy during World War II. They all spoke English there, a language I had struggled to learn as a teen. Could I ever become a citizen of that nation?

These thoughts went rambling through my mind and I began to descend into self-pity. Who was I? Not a Chinese, not a German, and certainly not an American. Why had God allowed my life to get so mixed up? Why was I not born and raised in a home in my own country? I was a little bit of everything, but nothing completely. How could I ever make something out of my life?

I was in a fog.

It was then that I heard the voice. It was His voice and I recognized it. Not audibly, but ever so reassuringly:

> It does not matter who you are, what you are, or
> where you are going. The only thing that matters
> is what you will allow Me to make out of you.

Could I ignore my past and my present? This question was

quickly replaced by the assuring thought that God was bigger than all these concerns which had so weighed me down. Had He not tried to teach us that lesson when we were waiting to leave China? Yes, it did not matter who I was or where I was going, as long as God was going with me and I was willing to cooperate with Him in what He was doing in my life. A verse of Scripture leaped into my mind. I had recently memorized it and the Holy Spirit brought it to my attention.

> "My Presence will go with you, and I will give you rest." (Exodus 33:14)

A sense of peace settled on me. The burden was gone. The fog had lifted. I did not have to be a prisoner of the past anymore. I had a future, without limit—if I allowed God to mold my life and make me an instrument of His purpose.

And to that, I replied, "Yes, Lord. You hold the key of all unknown, and I am glad." The words of this well-known hymn had flashed into my mind. I was at peace and at the same time filled with a new sense of excitement and anticipation of what lay in front of me.

Had not Jesus assured Peter of the same truth when He called him to be His disciple? Jesus essentially said, "You are Simon… You will be Peter" (John 1:42). God was not limited by what I appeared to be at present, as long as there was the willingness on my part to allow the potter to continue to mold and form me according to His own purpose and will. As Max Lucado put it so aptly: "God loves you just the way you are, but He refuses to leave you that way. He wants you to be just like Jesus."[2]

As the first signs of dawn appeared on the horizon, a new day was dawning as well for this nineteen-year-old, China-born German on his way to America. A new and exciting life it would be. I knew it. And I grasped it with both hands. I was beginning to learn what F. B. Meyer meant when he said, "The main end of life is not to do, but to become!"[3]

That night on the water, a new desire awakened in my heart

to discover God's purpose for my life and to become all He wanted me to be.

16

ARRIVAL IN THE NEW WORLD

May 1950

San Francisco, California

The *General Gordon* sailed under the Golden Gate Bridge and entered San Francisco Harbor on May 23, 1950. I remember the date because it was my sister Peg's birthday. It was also the date marked on our travel documents, that our entry visa to the United States was expiring. Fortunately, we had already passed through immigration and customs formalities in Honolulu, the first U.S. port of entry. We were now "legal immigrants."

What were my thoughts as we set foot on American soil? I believe it would be accurate to say that I was overwhelmed. All of my life I had been surrounded by Chinese, and now I missed them. Everyone here spoke English, and all the street and store signs were in English as well. That took some time getting used to.

At the dock, what a wonderful surprise it was to see none other than Dawson Trotman of the Navigators welcoming us to the United States. I'd attended his talks in China in 1948 and was deeply impressed by his practical knowledge of Scripture. Daws greeted us warmly and invited us to visit his home as soon as we arrived in Los Angeles. It came as a real surprise when he asked me to join their office staff and later arranged for me to move into the home of Lorne and Lucille Sanny in Pasadena.

Lorne was vice president for the Navs and Dawson's right-hand man. He and Lucille became my second parents in the States. Lorne's transparency and humble unpretentiousness gave me hope that I would make it in my new home, and I will never forget the simple lessons Lucille taught me about learning to adjust to life in America. Their love and support was a continual encouragement and blessing.

In the Sanny home I shared quarters with six to eight other men working on the staff, and I received "orientation and training" both spiritually and in the mundane things of life, such as washing dishes after meals, cleaning floors, and sweeping driveways. Coming from China, where servants had done these menial tasks, this was a new experience.

I remember the first day of work in the Navigator office. The Navs were located in downtown Los Angeles, right next to the famed Church of the Open Door. Royally welcomed as the "new arrival from China," I was ushered into Dawson's office, where we chatted quite a while, and then I was invited out for lunch with him. I felt richly honored and privileged and enjoyed the company of this respected Christian leader. He personally guided me through the various offices and introduced me to the staff. We ended up in the shipping and supply department. That is where Daws turned me over to the staff there.

They introduced me quickly to my first responsibilities each morning: sweeping the long hallway as well as the supply offices, cleaning all the toilets and facilities, and emptying all the trash bins. I applied myself to these tasks. However, I must admit that after a couple of days, this began to grind on me. All this "servant labor" was new to me, and I thought I deserved better. I admired Daws, but I had not expected this.

It was then and there that I learned a major lesson in life and made a major decision. I began to realize that what I was involved in was not doing something for the sake of any man or even an organization. It was and had to be "unto the Lord." The minute I recognized that I was doing it for Him, the joy came back and I did not care how demeaning a job might be that I was asked to undertake. What an important lesson to learn!

Other responsibilities included preparing orders for shipment of literature supplies and handling the mail. One of the first things I learned about the American way, was doing it quickly. "Let me show you a faster way" was a slogan I encountered frequently during those early days.

That fall I enrolled in classes at Pasadena City College and shifted my work hours with the Navigators to afternoons and weekends. The conflict in Korea had begun a month after we arrived in the States, and it was the buzz on the college campus. To my utter amazement, I soon discovered that all the students talked about was how they could avoid the military draft. I was dumbfounded to hear them talk like this. I thought they would consider it an honor to serve their country. But I was mistaken.

Being over eighteen, I naturally had to register for the draft too, even though I was not a citizen. Not long after I was "invited" to present myself for a physical exam at the U.S. Army recruiting post to test my eligibility. I passed with flying colors.

I remember on a Sunday afternoon spending considerable time searching for direction for my life. Instead of being drafted into the Army, should I consider enlisting in the Navy or Air Force? I consulted with some of my friends and received mixed advice. I knew that my parents were not enthusiastic about this. So I waited. Eventually I received a student deferment, which would exempt me from the draft until I completed my college education.

There were, of course, also the fun remembrances of college life. Shortly after starting classes, I was invited to go with a group of students to the beach at Santa Monica. We left early and stopped at a coffee shop for breakfast. Ordering food was a new experience for me too. When someone ordered "shoe strings" with their hamburger, I wondered whether this was a new American cuisine. I didn't know they were fries.

That morning some of my friends ordered a stack of hotcakes. Not knowing exactly what they were, I joined in and asked for the same. I was very hungry and so ordered a double stack.

The order arrived and to everyone's amusement, my serving was absolutely enormous. I knew right then that it would be impossible for me to eat it all. What was I to do? Someone jokingly said, "Why don't you sell the extra order?" I thought that was an excellent idea. To the surprise of my friends, I picked up the plate of hotcakes and marched to a table where some new guests had just arrived. With my still pronounced German accent, I explained my dilemma to these people and asked whether they might want to buy this meal from me. They did! My friends had never experienced this kind of direct marketing before—they were impressed.

After my year at Pasadena City College, I transferred to the University of California at Los Angeles (UCLA) for my junior and senior years of college. Shortly after classes began at UCLA, Billy Graham held his first crusade at the Hollywood Bowl. I had first heard about Billy Graham when we were crossing the Pacific Ocean on our way to the States. My good friend David Morken had told me about Billy's big crusade in Los Angeles in 1949, which had propelled him to worldwide fame. Now I had the opportunity to experience one for myself—the first of many.

I enrolled in counselor training classes and attended every night of the Hollywood crusade. A special privilege for me was to assist in the counseling of those who wanted to make a commitment to follow Christ. I remember the first person I counseled and the joy I experienced when he prayed to receive Christ into his life.

Another important lesson I learned during those college years was to trust in God to meet all of my financial needs. My folks were not in a position to help me. In fact, when they arrived in the States, their mission organization cut them off from any further support and they were totally dependent on the Lord to provide for their needs. Papa ran from meeting to meeting and actually lived on the honoraria he received.

It was therefore a huge sacrifice for my folks to give me a one-time gift of $150, which paid for my out-of-state registration fee during my first semester at UCLA. After that I was completely on my own. Work provided for daily necessities, but not for any major expenses.

Then a visit to the dentist knocked the bottom out of my financial resources. My bill was $165. Since my work salary was ninety cents an hour, this was an incredible amount to come up with. I remember one weekend sharing the predicament with some of my roommates, none of whom were believers, and telling them of my confidence in God's ability to provide for this.

The Lord worked quickly. At church that weekend, someone slipped ten dollars into my pocket. Another person gave me thirty-five dollars. Then at the office, Daws Trotman handed me a personal gift of fifty dollars. And when I returned to my dorm, a letter awaited me with a check for seventy dollars. The total of these gifts was $165—the exact amount I needed to pay my dental bill. "Look what God has done for me!" I hollered to my stunned dorm mates. "I knew He would do it!"

Faith-building events such as these were priceless experiences in my early Christian life. God used them to build confidence into my life—confidence in His ability and grace to provide for every need I faced.

17

THE GREAT ESCAPE

Summer 1950

East Germany

As the Wilhelm family escaped the clutches of Communism in China and made a new start in America, something else took place on the other side of the globe which deeply affected our family. My two sisters, after spending the war years and the traumatic postwar era in Germany, were moving to end the years-long separation that had divided us.

While Anita was with our grandparents in the eastern part of Germany, Eva attended school and lived in a missionary kids boarding home in west Germany. After the Allied invasion in 1944, the fighting came closer and closer; Eva's town came under direct enemy fire. In the middle of one night, Eva and her aunt left in a blacked-out train. On their way to my grandparents' home they had to overnight in Erfurt, central Germany. That night there was another air raid; an incendiary bomb fell on the house where Eva and the rest had been sleeping. Fortunately, they'd taken refuge in an air raid shelter in the basement of the home. Their lives were spared.

The two sisters were together for the next four years. How relieved they were when American troops occupied their area. But then just as suddenly, the American troops left and the Russians moved in. As we learned later, this was all part of the Yalta agreement which had been made in February 1945. U.S. President Franklin D. Roosevelt, British Prime Minister Winston Churchill, and Soviet Premier Joseph Stalin agreed to demand Germany's unconditional surrender and planned to divide Germany into four zones of occupation.

Russian troops took over most of my grandparents' home and relegated the family to the top floor. In 1948, Eva, moved back to what was now officially West Germany to begin training as a nurse. Since she had previously lived in the west, she was permitted to return.

Anita, however, was another story. She had grown up in the home of my paternal grandparents. As soon as she heard that the rest of us had succeeded in leaving China, she yearned to be reunited with her family. As the days passed, this desire only increased. Yet all efforts to obtain permission from the Russian authorities to go to West Germany were fruitless. Every request was denied.

But Anita was determined. After a tearful farewell to family and friends, she made her way to Berlin with the hope of obtaining a visa to enter West Germany. Again, the results of all inquiries and applications were a firm "No." She decided to take the only other available step—enter West Germany illegally. As an eighteen-year-old, she knew this was risky and dangerous business, but the compulsion to be reunited with us made it worth the try.

Allow me to share her story in her own words, as recorded in .her book *Echoes of the Past* by Anita (Wilhelm) Osborn and with her permission:

I was hardly able to sleep the night before my departure from Berlin. I was so excited, but also a bit frightened to enter this new epoch of my life. The long and difficult journey had begun.

It was early in the morning on a cloudy and gray day in the summer of 1950 when I said goodbye and left for yet another train station. I bought a one-way ticket to a city nearest to the border between East and West Germany and traveled by train along the East German countryside until I reached the city of my destination...

When I arrived I inquired about a bus that would lead me to a village that was within walking distance to the border. I had to wait several hours for the bus to arrive and almost missed the opportunity for further travel. The bus driver informed me that his only passengers were employees of different companies who worked in the city but lived in the nearby village. I was crushed and asked him to please make an exception and take me along. With his right thumb he pointed in the direction toward the west and asked me if I intended to cross the border. I answered him with an emphatic "yes" and he let me enter his bus.

I was so happy to be on my way.

The bus we were traveling in was a very old-fashioned and dilapidated, rough-riding vehicle, but it did not matter to me, as it would take me to the road to freedom.

After we had traveled for some time, several Soviet Border Police who were controlling the area stopped the bus. The bus and its passengers were checked for valid passports. During these postwar years every citizen in East Germany was obligated to carry a current passport and/or identification papers with them at all times. Every person was registered at police headquarters and it was mandatory to report the departure of the town one was registered in and register again in the city or town that was to be visited overnight or longer. So it was not unusual that the bus I was on would have a "Razzia," a police raid.

Unfortunately, my identification was not valid in the area that I was traveling in and thus I experienced my first "close encounter."

The seats of the bus were open underneath and were placed facing each other. Several older men were sitting beside and across from me who turned out to be my guardian angels. When it became apparent that our bus was going to be stopped and inspected, I was quite frightened and my face must have given away my fear. One of the men said to me, "Hide under the seat and we will cover you up with our coats."

My heart was pounding as I crawled under the seat and awaited my fate. I heard the doors of the bus open up and the Russian Patrol guard entered to proceed with his inspection of passports. I trusted God who had brought me this far to protect me from the "enemy patrol."

As I hovered there, I watched the big boots, stopping at every seat to inspect the identification of the passengers and as he passed my seat I was sure that he would hear the pounding of my heart. But he passed my row of seats without noticing me hiding under one of them.

After several minutes the boots I had seen walking toward the back of the bus earlier were now walking past me in the opposite direction toward the front of the bus. Soon the guard exited and we were on our way. I slowly came out of my hiding place and sat back in my seat amidst my newly made friends and protectors. I was so grateful to these wonderful men!

The wheels of the old bus rolled on toward the border that divided Germany.

There was only one stop in the middle of the small village that was the destination of the bus trip. Everyone left the bus and in order not to look suspicious to anyone who might be watching me, I zeroed in on a house that was in my vision and walked toward it. Not knowing who and what I might find in that strange house, I knocked on the door.

A lady answered the door looking at me with a questioning expression, suspicion in her eyes, perhaps. I am sure that she saw a helpless creature in front of her asking and begging for help.

"Do you know of anyone who can show me the way across the border?" I asked her. What a chance I took in confessing what I had in mind doing. What if the lady was Communist, a spy, a sympathizer of the enemy or a German idealist? *Lord, help me,* I silently prayed.

"I have a grandson and a granddaughter who show people such as you where to cross the border and help them along the way," she said. "However, you will have to pay a good sum of money to compensate them for the risk they are taking."

"I will give them all of my East German money that I have," was my reply, and that was agreeable. The young teens were summoned and I was told that the time to start our venture would be immediately, for the time was right for the border guards to change their shifts. While they were busy exchanging their daily report, our chances of not being noticed easily were quite good.

So the venture to cross the border between East and West Germany, illegally, had begun!

The small convoy consisted of the teenage boy with his bicycle, his sister who was also a teen, and myself, who actually was a teenager as well. I carried a small bag, not much larger than a big handbag, that held my most needed possessions.

My young friend with the bicycle instructed us to follow his lead. He would ride along the road while we were to hide behind a bush, in a ditch bank, behind a tree or any other cover we could find. As soon as he got off his bike, we were to walk quickly until we saw him getting on his bike again. We followed that same procedure for quite some time.

At his last stop we caught up with him and he told me that this was as far as he and his sister would accompany me. He pointed to a farmhouse in the near distance and told me that once I reached that destination I had crossed the border. The two teens left me to return to their village as soon as I had given them all the East German money I possessed, as I had promised.

I can still remember how I felt when I stood at a crossroad in this German countryside, exhilarated and thrilled to have made it this far, but mostly I felt as free as a bird to have escaped the Russian government and the Communist regime that was so frightening and confining to me. I was one step further towards meeting my family in the U.S.A. Standing at this crossroad, which was actually an area that was called "No Man's Land," I was very uncertain which road to take to continue my journey.

I made a decision and as I started walking along this country road I encountered another obstacle. Two West German border policemen on horseback came riding toward me. They looked rather intimidating but I tried hard not to let it show.

"Well, young lady, where do you come from? And where do you think you are going?" the one officer said to me. I replied, "I come directly from Berlin and am on my way to the next town or city."

"Berlin," he said, "that is my hometown and I have not been back since the war ended. What does the city look like and what are the general conditions there?" he asked. Here was my chance to distract him and in a few minutes I told him everything I had ever heard or seen in Berlin.

He was very attentive, but soon interrupted me and informed me that it really was their duty as border police officers to send me back to where I came from. I pleaded with both of them to please let me continue my journey and told them my story of wanting to be reunited with my family in the U.S.

A miracle happened. They let me go! Not only did they let me go free, they directed me where to go next. The officer from Berlin wrote a little note instructing me to walk along the road we were on until I came to a Border Patrol station. On the note it said that he gave me permission to stay at the station until the daily postal truck arrived which would take me along to the next city. I could not believe my good fortune and again prayed a prayer of thanksgiving.

When I arrived at the little patrol station I was welcomed with something to drink. Fortunately, there was time for me to clean myself up a bit and to undo the lining of my coat to retrieve my West German money that I had hidden there. I was truly exhausted by that time and the ride in the postal truck, amidst bundles of letters and packages, was such a welcome relief.

It was late when we arrived at the city of Wolfburg, where my personal chauffeur of the postal truck took me directly to the train station. I immediately sent a telegram to my grandfather telling him that I was safe, and I am sure that he felt greatly relieved...

I had enough money to purchase a train ticket

for Bad Liebenzell, the mission headquarters of my parents. It was the Liebenzell Mission that financed my journey for which I was so grateful. The train was not due to arrive for another hour and it was the middle of the night by then. Few people were in sight and it was rather dark in the train station. To get to the platform where trains arrive and depart I had to walk down a flight of stairs, walk through a tunnel-like walkway and up the stairs to reach the platform where I would get on the train.

As I was walking along, I heard footsteps behind me and the faster I walked, the faster the footsteps became. I was terrified as my pursuer caught up with me, asking me, or rather telling me, to come with him to his place.

As I was arguing with him, trying to free myself of him, I saw a little control station on the platform near the stairs. I ran toward it and saw several men who controlled the train switches in the little glass control station. It displayed a sign saying, *"Eintritt verboten,"* which means entrance forbidden, but I ignored the sign and pounded on the glass door, which was locked, until someone opened it. I asked for help and was allowed to stay with the train officials until my train arrived.

I did not see the man who had pursued me again.

The train was nearly empty and as I sat on the hard bench on that dark train, it finally sank in what I had done, and in what grave danger I had placed myself.

I felt so alone…

It was then that I really became frightened and it was then that I knew that God Himself led me across the border and was with me every step of this dangerous journey. My tears were a combination of relief and gratitude.[4]

Soon after, Anita and Eva were reunited in West Germany. Now they both were free to pursue the next goal: to be reunited with the whole family in America.

18

SARAH WILL HAVE A SON

1952

Westwood, California

I started my senior year at UCLA with a major in history and a minor in German literature. How I made it through school, I still do not know. I started classes by 8 A.M. and tried to finish by noon each day. Part of that time I was in the library catching up on assignments. Then about noon, I hopped into my car and rushed off to work.

Work for me began at 12:30 each weekday. I ate my lunch as I drove. I'd started out in a steel factory, pretty dirty work, so I was delighted when a friend told me of an opening at a plastic factory where television parts were manufactured. Work there was clean, though often monotonous. After some time, I was given a new job in that company: driving deliveries all over the Los Angeles area. I think that I received this promotion mainly due to the fact that the wife of the owner was German too. Driving a new Chevrolet station wagon was a nice change and I enjoyed it. It made my thirty hours a week bearable, even if I was paid only $1.25 an hour.

I finished at 6:30 P.M. each day and headed "home." It was an off-campus house that I shared with about a dozen other guys. We usually were three to a room and so had little privacy.

To have my quiet time, I would slip downstairs and get into my car parked in the street. There was my opportunity to be alone. During my senior year, I was able to secure housing closer to campus which allowed me a private room. For that I was most thankful.

On top of this, I began enjoying excellent dinners a couple times a week. Two German ladies were employed in the household of a wealthy family in Westwood. One did all the cooking and the other attended the family during dinner. They would invite me come over and served me excellent meals in the kitchen before they even served their employers. I felt blessed and much preferred this to my usual fare of eggs and toast or cold cereal. Once, a school buddy introduced me to steak—horsemeat—and this also provided a bit of change.

With my heavy work schedule and weekends spent helping out at the Navigators office, my grades were only average (although excellent in German!). There was little room for any social life.

But there was something else missing in my life, and as I entered my final year at UCLA, this became more and more of a concern to me. I was beginning to sense God's call on my life and wondered just what I would do after college.

That summer I'd attended a Navigators staff conference at the Young Life Camp Star Ranch near Colorado Springs. This had been a welcome change from a busy study and work schedule. Listening and rubbing shoulders with committed men of God was a great privilege. I had been blessed.

As always, Daws Trotman's penetrating messages left a mark on many lives, including mine. I still remember them today. These were among his choice remarks:

Do you know why I often ask Christians, "What is the biggest thing you've asked God for this week?" I remind them that they are going to God, the Father, the maker of the universe. The one who holds the world in His hands. What did you ask for? Did you ask for peanuts, toys, trinkets, or did you ask for continents? I want to tell you, young people, it's tragic! The little itsy-bitsy things we ask of our almighty God. Sure, nothing is too small—but also nothing is too big. Let's learn to ask of our big God some of those big things He talks about in Jeremiah 33:3: "Call to me and I will answer you and tell you great and unsearchable things you do not know."

Daws was a man, a giant of a man, whom you could not help admire and follow—and love.

I vividly recall one night during this conference. After the meetings were over, I felt the need to be by myself and spend some time with God. It was a beautiful, clear, and starry night. Up at around eight thousand feet the air was clean and the stars seemed more brilliant. It was a good place and time to communicate with God.

That night, I heard His voice again. It was the same voice I had heard on several other occasions in my life. And each time I heard it, it marked a turning point in my life.

Are you willing to give your life to Me for missionary service?

The message was unmistakable. God wanted me to serve Him as a missionary. Was this part of God's unfolding of His purposes for my life? If so, I was not sure I was ready for it. Yes, I did want to serve Him, but would it have to be overseas? Couldn't it be here in a comfortable setting?

I recalled having talked earlier that week with a young missionary leaving for ministry in my home country, Germany.

He was excited about the opportunities he was facing and the responsiveness of German young people he had encountered on previous visits. Now he was looking forward to his move there. As we talked, I wondered how I would fit into a situation like that. There were a lot of advantages I had in being German, speaking German, and understanding the culture of my people.

But this call was not geographically oriented. It was far more a challenge to give my life to God for missionary service, wherever that might lead.

> Are you willing to give your life to Me for missionary service?

This was a call which required an answer. And I knew it.

I knew what missionary life was all about. Had I not spent most of my life growing up as a son of missionaries in China? The adventure, the romance, the excitement of living in another culture was not a motivating factor as far as I was concerned. I needed more than that.

> Are you willing to give your life to Me for missionary service?

The call kept coming. I knew what I needed to do. When God called, there was only one option, and that was to obey Him. It did not matter how I felt about this. But it did matter whether I listened and obeyed His voice.

So that night, high in the Colorado mountains, my answer was unequivocal: "Yes, Lord. If that is what you desire from me, I will give my life to you toward that end. And I will do so gladly."

Again, like at many other times when I had yielded to His will, there was instant relief in my spirit and a joy that flooded my soul.

Weeks later, when I began my final year of classes at UCLA, it was this experience that began to eat away at my soul. No, I did not have second thoughts about my response to His call. But a nagging question had not given me any rest. How could God use me overseas if I had not been fruitful in my service right here?

I wrestled with this question day after day. And I was afraid of the answer.

The climax came one day when I returned to my home. I dropped to my knees, laid my Bible on my bed, and cried to God to do something in my life. I felt what Jacob of old must have felt. I did not want to leave this place until He had blessed me.

God's answer came from a most unusual place—a passage in Genesis 18. I cannot recall what turned my attention to this portion of Scripture that day. But as I was kneeling in front of my bed, this passage came alive to me: "Is anything too hard for the Lord? I will return to you at the appointed time next year and Sarah will have a son" (v. 14).

It was these last five words that God quietly, not audibly, yet firmly, whispered into my ear:

> Sarah will have a son.

Though my name was not Sarah, I knew God was speaking to me. And what He said gave me a tremendous sense of hope. It was a promise of "spiritual offspring"! God was promising me that I would experience the privilege of having "spiritual children."

This was what I had been looking for and this was what God was telling me now. And then to confirm it, He added:

Is anything too hard for the Lord?

I got up from my knees with a huge burden lifted. God was going to do something special, as He had done for Sarah. I had heard His promise and I trusted Him to fulfill it.

It could only have been a few days later that I sat in the crowded cafeteria on the UCLA campus, grabbing a quick bite of lunch. A fellow student walked past the little table where I was sitting, then turned back and asked whether he could sit with me. "Of course," I said.

His name was Gene. Before long we entered into a conversation that turned to spiritual matters. As I saw Gene's openness, I sensed that here was a heart God had prepared. I began to share my own testimony with him and then presented the gospel and his need to come to Christ. Gene responded immediately, and left the table as a new creation in Christ. The whole process had taken less than an hour.

I was on cloud nine. God had begun to answer my prayer. He had kept his promise! Nothing was too hard for Him. I began to meet with Gene regularly, teaching him some of the principles of Christian living. We would do this while sitting in my car, eating our lunches.

Perhaps a week later, I was walking toward my car in the campus parking lot when I saw two students seated in my car. In those days, you could leave your car unlocked! I was a bit surprised, but as I approached I was relieved to see that one of the students was my new friend Gene. When I got into my car, he greeted me quickly, then said, "Chuck, this is Hans. Hans, this is Chuck. Now, give him the works!"

Chuck nodded, his face serious: "Yes, let me have it."

This certainly was the direct approach, one I had never encountered before or since in quite the same way. Obviously, Gene had talked with Chuck before, and had now brought him to me to share the same Good News with him.

I did, and within a half hour's time, Chuck bowed his head and asked Christ to come into his life. He beamed with his newfound faith. I thought, *Sarah was only promised one son. I already have two!*

This was just the beginning of one of the most fruitful periods of my life. Campus Crusade for Christ, under Bill Bright's leadership, had just come into existence. Bill Bright had targeted UCLA as their first campus and soon was making strong inroads into the lives of students. They focused initially on fraternities and sororities through in-house student contacts. Meetings were arranged in these houses in which Christian students shared their personal stories of discovering life's purpose in Christ. The meetings ended with a concise presentation of the gospel. This led to more personal interactions that night, as well as appointments to meet at a later date.

I was privileged to participate in many of these meetings, both on the UCLA campus and at other colleges. It was sometimes amusing for me to be teamed with some of the star athletes of the football team, like giant All-American UCLA center and linebacker Donn Moomaw. Size-wise, I probably would have had a hard time making it on the football team as water boy! But those meetings allowed me to develop skills in sharing the gospel. It was also here that I first became acquainted with Daniel Fuller, son of famed Christian radio preacher Charles Fuller of the *Old Fashioned Revival Hour*.

One particular experience stands out in my mind. Bill Bright had asked me to join a Campus Crusade team for a weekend conference in a Presbyterian church in Fillmore, California. During one of the meetings I shared my personal testimony. After the meeting, a couple of high school kids approached me, a guy and a gal. They looked troubled and said they needed to talk, so we sat down and I asked how I could help.

They told me their story. They were two teenagers, madly in love. One night, things had gone too far, and now she was pregnant. They were afraid to tell anyone. With a puzzled look on his face, the young man said, "I cannot understand how this could have happened." You have to remember that this was the early 1950s. Kids apparently were not as smart then as they are now! The clincher was when he said, "I cannot understand how this could have happened, since we prayed together before it."

I asked them what they had prayed about. His answer was, "We asked God to show us if what we were doing was right or wrong." I told them that there are some things you do not even have to pray about, especially since God has already given us clear instructions in His Word.

This convinced me more than ever that in order to obey Him, we needed to know His Word. Here was a case of a couple of confused teenagers stumbling in the dark because they had not taken time to listen to or seek instructions from the Scriptures.

A statement ascribed to the famed evangelist Dwight L. Moody reads, "The Scriptures were not given to increase our knowledge but to change our lives."[5] It is not so much what we know that counts, but what we apply in our daily life. Experiences like this one helped solidify in my mind the purpose of seeking Him and His Word with all of my heart and then applying these truths to my everyday life by being obedient to Him.

Along with my Campus Crusade experiences, I also spent many Saturday mornings with some collegians who had determined to follow Christ. We met in the home of Henrietta Mears, the renowned Christian education authority from Hollywood Presbyterian Church. I recall many one-on-one sessions with Bob Davenport, UCLA's All-American fullback, who found the Lord during those days.

There is no question in my mind that my final year of studies was my most fruitful year on campus, and it all dated back to that cry of desperation to God and asking Him to bless me. He had given me a promise and I had claimed it for myself, much like Abraham and Sarah. God had been faithful to His Word, and I had seen spiritual offspring!

In the movie *Chariots of Fire*, Eric Liddell, Olympic runner and gold medalist who became a missionary to China, said, "I believe God made me for a purpose, but He also made me fast. And when I run, I feel His pleasure."

This might not fit me exactly, but I too came to believe that God made me for a purpose. And I was beginning to discover God's purpose for my life. It began to unfold during that last year at UCLA, and for that I will always be grateful.

19

I WANT TO GET OUT OF HERE

November 1953

Los Angeles, California

"Hans, what is it that you wanted to see me about?"

The question was from Dawson Trotman. He was behind the wheel, with me sitting next to him, as we drove down the Pasadena freeway toward the Los Angeles airport.

"I want to get out of here," I blurted, without really thinking about how this might sound. When Daws asked me to repeat it, I knew I was in trouble. I also knew that I could not change my story, so I meekly responded, "Daws, I want to get out of the office."

I'd graduated from UCLA in the summer of 1953 and was now ready for my next chapter. I knew after my Colorado experience that God had called me to give myself to the ministry here for now, but eventually overseas.

I attended college with a 2-S draft classification. The Navigators encouraged me to write to my draft board and request a reclassification on the grounds that I was involved in ministry, "regularly preaching and teaching the gospel of Jesus Christ." However, they warned me not to be surprised if I was turned down. In fact, they had never heard of anyone who had succeeded in doing this.

I wrote my letter and within a short time received word that my request had been granted. I took this as a further confirmation of God's purpose for my life. Without doubt, He had worked this out and I could now proceed.

Interestingly, several others, seeing my success with the draft board, took my letter, copied it, and submitted their own letters. All were turned down, and they were promptly requested to report for induction.

Again, I thanked God for directing my steps.

My initial assignment with the Navigators was to assist in their headquarters operations in Eagle Rock, near Pasadena. My days were spent in shipping and supplies. Daily runs to the post office, preparing literature and other printed supplies for mailing, and stapling booklets provided me with ample variety. There was a genuine camaraderie among the staff and great times of fun and fellowship.

I could not, however, see myself continuing in this type of work indefinitely. I was restless to move forward in the direction God had indicated.

I asked for an appointment to meet with Dawson Trotman. Daws was traveling most of the time, especially since Billy Graham had asked him to develop and then oversee the follow-up program for his evangelistic crusades in the States and overseas. Obviously, his time was limited whenever he was home, and I was just hoping to catch him for a few minutes.

I was therefore happily surprised when his secretary told me that Daws would be available to spend time with me on his way to the airport, and that he'd asked me to ride along with him. When I stepped into the car that morning, I was taken aback, as two of his secretaries were in the backseat. He explained that he wanted to finish some dictation and other business first, and that we would talk after that.

Sure enough, once he had finished his work, Daws turned to me and asked his fateful question. My answer must have shocked him. He turned to his secretaries behind us and exclaimed, "Did you hear what he said? He wants to get out of here."

What followed was a dressing down unlike any I had experienced in my life. Daws lit into me, telling me he had received reports that my attitude in the office had not been good, my heart had not been in my work, that he had personally noticed it for a couple of years, that I had been a disappointment to him, and on and on.

As he talked, I sank deeper and deeper in my seat. To hear what Daws had to say was bad enough. But to hear him say it in front of these two secretaries was humiliating. I would have loved to open the door and make my exit, but we were traveling at more than fifty miles an hour.

I was trapped—and devastated.

After some time, Daws relented and asked, "Hans, what do you really want to do?"

Quietly, I replied, "Daws, all I wanted was for you to give me an opportunity to become involved in hands-on ministry rather than spend my time working in an office." Before we reached the airport, Daws said that he would give this some thought and let me know.

Once Daws left, it was my sad privilege to drive the car back in the company of the two gals who had witnessed this encounter. Before I could say anything, one of them quickly encouraged me. "We understand how you feel," she said. "We've gone through situations like this too."

I cannot remember what we talked about the rest of the hour in the car. My head was in a blur and I was glad when I finally got home to Pasadena.

The first thing I did was seek out a close friend, Rod, who also worked at the Navigator office. As we walked the streets that evening, I poured out my heart to him. I related my encounter with Daws, tears streaming down my face.

I was crushed and humiliated. I had hit rock bottom.

Rod let me talk until it all came out. Then he asked me a simple question.

"Was it true? Was it true what Daws said to you?"

This jolted me. I thought for a moment and replied, "Of course it was true." This made it hurt all the more.

Then I heard some of the best advice I have ever received. Rod told me to write a letter to Daws and share my heart with him.

The next night, after work, I wrote Daws a one-page letter. I admitted that what he'd said about me was true, and I begged him to give me another chance to make good at the office and *not* send me on the assignment I'd requested. I knew I could not leave as a failure and feel assured of success by going somewhere else. I asked him for a second chance.

I also told him I was sad about something else he had said. "Daws," I wrote, "why did you wait two years to tell me of the weaknesses you had seen in my life? Why didn't you tell me sooner? I could have worked on those all this time."

Once I mailed the letter, a sense of peace settled in my soul. I decided to dedicate myself wholly to the work given to me. I desired to make good on my commitment and did not have to wait for a reply to my letter.

I never received a letter back from Dawson. I got something better.

A couple of weeks later, I helped drive a big moving truck from Los Angeles to Colorado Springs, where the Navigators had purchased a castle and property known as Glen Eyrie. It was to be their permanent international headquarters. We were hauling office furnishings on this trip and drove nonstop to our destination.

We arrived late in the afternoon, dead tired. After a quick

bite to eat, I decided to turn in early and was already in bed when a knock sounded at the door. It was Daws.

I invited him in, and he sat on the side of the bed. He thanked me for my help with the move and then asked how I felt after the trip. We chatted a while. Then, just before leaving, Daws reached into his back pocket and pulled out his wallet. From it he removed a folded piece of yellow paper. It was the letter I had written him two weeks earlier.

With a smile, he said, "Remember this? I have carried it with me ever since I received it. I want to thank you for writing this letter to me."

And with that he was gone.

Later, I learned from my friend Rod that this letter, more than anything else, convinced Daws that I was ready for an overseas assignment.

I had nearly blown it, but the Lord protected me. Others who had similar encounters with Daws either rebelled against him, refused to accept his counsel, or defended themselves. God had allowed Rod to counsel me wisely and had given me an open heart to accept his advice and so discover God's purposes. What could have become a stumbling block in my life, God used to make a stepping stone.

Luis Palau used to say, "Big doors turn on little hinges." This was a little hinge that would open a big door in my life. I did not know it at the time. All I knew was that I had to respond to the Lord's molding process in my life. I was content to leave the future up to Him.

20

REUNION WITH
MY GERMAN SISTERS

Christmas 1953

Scottsbluff, Nebraska

As soon as my sisters reunited in Germany, they applied to the American consulate in Frankfurt to obtain entrance visas to the United States. But this was easier said than done. The wheels of bureaucracy move slowly, sometimes very slowly.

After waiting and more waiting, word came that even though her parents and siblings lived in the U.S., Eva did not qualify for an immigration visa. You can imagine the shock of receiving this news for the rest of our family. The reason given was that she had been born in China, and since China was now a Communist country, no visas were issued to anyone born there. This convoluted reasoning did not make sense—but that is what the law said.

Appeals needed to be made to higher authorities. Of course, we believed that God was ultimately in charge and so we redoubled our prayer efforts on behalf of Eva and Anita. Where else could we turn?

Papa, who at this time served as pastor of a bilingual German/English congregation in Scottsbluff, Nebraska, was advised to enlist the aid of the U.S. chief of chaplains. This got the ball rolling again. Then U.S. Representative Roman Hruska of Nebraska lent his voice to cut through the red tape. Nearly three years later, the visas were granted.

It was on March 19, 1953, that the S.S. *United States*, carrying "precious cargo," passed the Statue of Liberty and entered New York Harbor of Hudson Bay. Among the masses of people awaiting the arrival of loved ones and friends stood my mother, looking to find two daughters she had not seen for many years—twelve in Eva's case, eighteen in Anita's. You can imagine the joy, the hugs, and the tears of that reunion!

I had graduated from UCLA in August 1953, but had to wait till Christmas before I could meet my sisters. I could hardly wait. I hitchhiked from Pasadena to Denver and from there hopped a bus to Cheyenne, Wyoming, where Papa and my sisters were to meet me. As soon as I arrived, I slipped into a restroom to freshen up. I was excited and a little nervous. I wanted to look my best when I met my family.

When I stepped out, there they were—Papa and my long lost sisters. Mutti had made summer dresses for her daughters. I remember Anita's was pink and plaid, sleeveless and fitted. I reached out to hug them both. We shared a long embrace, and the tears flowed from each of us.

I too had not seen Eva for twelve years. She had grown into a beautiful young woman of twenty-four. Yet we had so many shared memories that we were able to pick up where we left off.

With Anita, however, I was starting from scratch. She'd been separated from our family since she was three. Now she was an attractive young lady of twenty-one, and I basically had no memories of her. As we talked, we found some difficulty connecting because our lives had taken such different directions.

Slowly, however, our family bond began to bridge the years of separation. Anita had never had a big brother before, and I could tell that she was proud to finally meet him.

I too was proud, and thankful, to have my two sisters back again. You cannot imagine the time we had driving the hundred miles from Cheyenne to Scottsbluff!

We had planned to make this Christmas a special time when the whole Wilhelm family, parents and six children, would be united in one place for the first time ever. This had been a lifelong dream. Now that we had everyone in the same country for the first time, it seemed to be the ideal time and place.

Alas, it was not to be. My sister Esther, in nursing school in Chicago, was not able to get time off. We were the whole family minus one! We all were disappointed, of course, but we enjoyed our time nevertheless. It was so good to be together as a family.

As I reflected on what this meant for my parents, I marveled again at God's sustaining grace to them over the years of separation. I never heard my parents complain that they had been robbed of two of their children for the sake of the gospel. I know that they grieved in their souls, but outwardly they only reminded us of Anita and Eva as often as possible, praying for them every single day. When we built a little mud-brick summer cottage in the mountains of China to escape the unbearable summer heat, my dad suggested that we call this house "Anita."

During our war years in China we basically lost everything we owned. But that was little in comparison to the much bigger sacrifice our family experienced in being separated from two of our members.

If there is one passage in Scripture that brought comfort to my parents, it was the response of Jesus to Peter's statement in Mark 10:28–30:

> Peter said to him, "We have left everything to
> follow you!" "I tell you the truth," Jesus replied,
> "no one who has left home or brothers or sisters

or mother or father or children or fields for me and the gospel will fail to receive a hundred times as much in this present age (homes, brothers, sisters, mothers, children and fields—and with them, persecutions) and in the age to come, eternal life."

"For me and the gospel"—this, finally, was the underlying motivation that allowed my parents to make this sacrifice. Even though it went contrary to all they humanly felt and desired, they accepted it in obedience to their Savior's call to follow Him. They were buoyed by the hope that He who had called had also promised a hundredfold reward.

21

I Will Never Go There

January 1954

Pasadena, California

Early one morning, I sat in the basement of Lorne Sanny's home in Pasadena for my daily devotion. My reading that day took me to Galatians 1. Here Paul spells out his call into the ministry. The following verses seemed to connect with me in a special way that day:

> "But when God, who set me apart from birth and called me by His grace, was pleased to reveal his Son in me so that I might preach him among the Gentiles, I did not consult any man, nor did I go up to Jerusalem to see those who were apostles before I was, but I went immediately..." (Galatians 1:15–17)

Several things struck me. I recognized once more that God had a purpose for my life which dated back to my very beginning. Not only had God set me apart from birth, but also I knew that my parents had dedicated me to Him for His service when I was born in the mountains of Guizhou.

He had not only set me apart, but He had also called me by His grace. I recalled that night in Shanghai, when I did not want to go to the Free Christian Church and attend the special evangelistic youth rally. It took my father's "persuasion" to get me out of the house and attend that service. It was there that the Word of God spoke so directly to me so that I could not resist the marvelous grace of God drawing me to Himself. He had called me into a relationship with the living God through His grace—totally undeserved!

I also was reminded, as I meditated on the Galatians passage, that before I could proclaim Him to others I needed to have Christ revealed in me. His likeness and character needed to take root in my life so that my life would become my message. Only as I walked the walk could there be authenticity and authority to what I was preaching to others.

I rejoiced in all of this that morning. But there was one other thing that hit me between the eyes. It was the single word *obedience*. Though not included in the text I was reading, it was powerfully implied.

As soon as Paul was aware of God's calling in his life, he immediately obeyed. He was so convinced that he had heard God's voice that he did not need to consult any man for a second opinion. He knew God had spoken and there was no other option but to obey, and to obey unconditionally.

I remember jotting down the phrase "unconditional obedience." It was something that appealed to my German background as well, and before long I whispered to the Lord, "I want to be unconditionally obedient to you, like Paul was." The thought of emulating Paul gave me a new sense of excitement. I desired to be an obedient soldier of Jesus Christ more than anything else.

I should have known that whenever you make a commitment

to God, He puts you to the test. And indeed, it did not take long for my commitment to be tested.

As I was praying and meditating, the though suddenly struck me: *What if God calls you to be a missionary in Africa?*

I didn't remember ever having viewed ministry in Africa as an option for my life. I had a strong desire to return to Germany and share the Good News with my own people. A few months earlier, the Navigators had considered sending me to Germany, but the timing was not right. However, my desire to return there for ministry never left me. Therefore, the thought that God might want to call me to service on the African continent caught me totally by surprise.

"But Lord," I prayed, "You could not possibly send me to Africa when you know Germany is where I want to go."

The inner voice instantly responded.

> Didn't you just say that you would be unconditionally obedient?

"Yes, Lord. But this does not make sense. Germany is where I need to be. I am a German, I speak German, I have a heart to minister there."

> So, you did not mean it when you said "unconditional obedience"?

"No, I really did. But…"

The struggle went back and forth until, finally, I surrendered. "Lord," I prayed, "I do want to obey You unconditionally. If You really want me to go to Africa, I will indeed go there." Yet I added this P.S. to my prayer: "But please send me to Germany."

The thought about going to Africa disappeared immediately and was supplanted by another: *What if God wants you to go somewhere in South America?*

Incredulously, I pondered the idea of going to a continent where I had to learn Spanish to communicate the gospel. "Lord, You cannot be serious about sending me to South America?"

There was a replay of the struggle I had just gone through with Africa. How could God do this to me? Wasn't Germany the place He had prepared me for throughout all of my early years of upbringing and education? Yet the commitment to unconditional obedience again gnawed at my conscience. If this was the place God had for me, then I could do nothing but obey.

"Lord," I prayed, "if You really want me to go to South America, I will go there. Once again, however, I added the same P.S. to my prayer: "But please send me to Germany."

There was one more test coming. This one shook me to the core.

> What if I want to send you back to work with the Chinese?

This time, my response was swift and unequivocal: "That is one place I will not go!" I had spent seventeen years in China already. I knew what life over there was all about. Having lived as a "foreigner" in that country had built up an insatiable desire to be among people of my own kind. Besides, we had left Communist China just a few years ago. I was not willing to go back and work among its people.

"Lord, I will go anyplace you send me—anyplace except China!" I said it with a note of finality that surprised me. Anyplace—but China? Never.

Yet I could not dismiss God's voice that easily. His Spirit quietly, gently, yet firmly kept probing the commitment of my own spirit. Was I really fully surrendered to Him? Was unconditional obedience just a matter of words or did I really mean it?

There was a huge storm in my heart. Was I willing to give in to the one I called Lord and Master?

The breakthrough came. I bowed before Him, my heart broken. "Lord, not my will, but Your will be done. If You want me to go back to the Chinese, then I am willing to go."

This time there was no P.S. I had learned that you do not play games or bargain with God.

Then the unexpected happened.

It was a mere two hours later. I had just arrived at the Navigators office when I was summoned to see Dawson Trotman. I wondered what I had done that would prompt such an unexpected invitation. I made a quick mental check to make sure I was up to date on my memory verses. You never knew when Daws might check on your memory work.

I entered his office. After a quick greeting, Daws came right to the point.

"I have had a call from your friend Dick Hillis on Formosa [now known as Taiwan]," he said. "Dick asked me, 'Do you have someone on your staff you could send to work with us in evangelism with military officers and in our discipleship program?'"

Daws looked at me intently. With a smile playing around his lips, he continued: "As I have reviewed who we have that is available to fill this job, I have concluded that you are the only one who fits the bill. Your Chinese background, your training, and your friendship with Dick Hillis make you the best candidate for this job. Are you ready to go?"

I could hardly believe my ears. It had hardly been two hours since that fierce struggle in the basement. Now when the call came, none of that mattered anymore.

"Of course I am," I said. There was no iota of doubt in my mind that God had prepared me that morning for what was to follow. I was thrilled with the assignment!

Once again, a gracious God had allowed me to experience His sovereign wisdom and power to work out His purposes in my life. It was just a simple step of obedience, but it became another major stepping stone that would determine my future.

A few days later I called my folks at their home in Nebraska. In those days we stayed in touch mostly by weekly letters. Telephone calls were reserved for emergencies or important matters.

What I needed to communicate to them that day was extremely important. I was happy to hear my mother pick up the phone. My dad was gone for a meeting, so the two of us had a chance to talk.

I described to her the events leading up to my new assignment. "Mutti," I said, "the Lord has called me to go to Formosa. What do you think?"

As soon as the words left my mouth I realized what a shock this would be to my dear mother. It had not dawned upon me before, but now I sensed the full impact of my words.

If my mother and father had one unfulfilled dream, it was to be united with all six of their children at least once. We had come close a couple of months earlier with our reunion in Scottsbluff—minus Esther. I knew my mother longed for the day that all of us could be together.

Now my phone call was dashing my mother's hopes. I wished I could take my words back. I did not want to hurt my mother.

Yet I quickly learned how little I knew my own mother and her inward faith and strength. "Son," she said, "if God has called you to go to Formosa, you not only have my permission, but you have my blessing!"

Here was a woman who walked with God, a woman who was able to set aside her own desires no matter how legitimate they were in order to respond to God's claim on her son's life. Her response was instantaneous, not a labored or agonizing acquiescence to the inevitable. There was a serene trust on her part that God, who had saved her and then called her to serve Him in China, could be trusted in everything.

My mother left this legacy for all of us—and we are deeply grateful.

22

FORMOSA, THE BEAUTIFUL ISLAND

August 24, 1954

San Francisco Bay

It was on a sunny summer afternoon that a little freighter carrying all of six passengers sailed out of San Francisco harbor and passed under the Golden Gate Bridge. Gradually the faint outline of the California coast vanished as I stood by a railing on the deck of the M.V. *Lightning* of the American President Lines. A little over four years before, I had arrived in the United States for the first time. Now I was taking a last look at my adopted country—I was Formosa-bound!

The past few months had gone by in a whirl. When Dawson Trotman called me into his office and said, "Formosa needs another man, are you ready to go?" wheels had been set into motion that left me spinning until the moment of my departure.

The very night I said yes to this new assignment, a young man came to me and asked who would take my place in the Navigator office. He was burdened about it. So we started praying. Within a short time, he realized that he was the answer to our prayer and he started work there.

Sharing my vision and financial needs in churches was a new experience, but even here I saw God's hand at work. Through contacts my dad had with Back to the Bible Broadcast, I was invited to attend their annual summer conference. When the missionary arm of this organization heard about my new assignment in Formosa, they promptly offered to assume more than half of my missionary support. I was overwhelmed by God's goodness and grace.

The renowned Oswald J. Smith of the People's Church in Toronto was the special speaker at this conference. His church's missionary vision and support of hundreds of missionaries had become legendary not only in North America but all over the world. I will never forget the day he asked me to come to the platform and laid his hands on me, setting me apart for missionary labor.

What impacted me more than anything else, however, was the message spoken by my father at that meeting. Dr. Smith had asked him to say a few words. In his straightforward manner, my dad said, "Since I cannot return to the mission field myself, I am sending a substitute. But more than a substitute, I am sending my own son."

The affirmation of my godly parents, the blessing from my mother and this commission by my father, became a constant source of strength and encouragement and continued to be that as long as they lived. My missionary parents provided nearly all of my necessary outgoing equipment.

I had made a list of fifteen prayer requests that needed to be answered before leaving the country. Every one of them was answered beyond my asking and thinking. God had not only called me to obey, but He had also provided all the resources needed to fulfill His command. Nothing could ever thwart the purposes of God!

Later, my ship docked in Yokohama, the port city near

Tokyo. I waited for friends to meet me. While standing there with my luggage, I spied a dockworker that looked more Chinese to me than Japanese. I drew closer. My senses had not misled me; he was indeed from China. I remember the occasion only too well, since I tried to share the gospel with him in Chinese. My language skills were a bit rusty after several years away from China—but inwardly I rejoiced at the privilege of reaching out spiritually to the Chinese.

After a stopover in Japan and a visit with Navigator staff ministering in that country, the day finally arrived for me to make the last leg of my journey to Formosa, or "Ilha Formosa" (Beautiful Island). This is what a Dutch navigator on a Portuguese ship exclaimed in 1590 when they first discovered it. It became the island's name for the next four hundred years.

On an early morning flight in late September, I finally laid eyes on the place I had long anticipated seeing. Seeing the green rice terraces scattered throughout the countryside gave witness to its current name: Taiwan, the land of ten thousand terraces. As my flight approached Taipei, I bowed my head and asked Him to bless my ministry in this place in a special way.

Dick Hillis and other members of his One Challenge missionary team, along with Navigator staff members, greeted me warmly. They all made up the team I would be joining. It did not take long before I began feeling right at home. I lived with another missionary family that had a small room they turned over to me. It was just big enough to accommodate a bed, a small table, and a dresser of drawers. I was thrilled.

Dick had a profound impact on my life as a teenager back in Shanghai. He and I carved out time on Sunday afternoons to study the Scriptures together, play ping pong, or learn about baseball, something totally strange to me. He also encouraged me to consider college in the States. After my arrival in California, Dick maintained our friendship. On more than one occasion, he asked when I would come out to Formosa and join him in ministry there. I thought he was kidding, but he told me even then he was dead serious. Now I was actually here!

Shortly after returning to the States in 1950, Dick responded to an invitation from Madame Chiang Kai-shek through Bob Pierce, who later founded World Vision, to come to Formosa. Though Formosa faced an imminent invasion on the part of Red China, her assessment of the situation was right on. "Our primary need is not military aid, not economic support, and not political backing," she said. "Our basic need is spiritual. We need your help."

Even her husband, President Chiang Kai-shek, acknowledged this. When asked why China had fallen into the hands of the Communists, he said, "We lost because it was basically a spiritual conflict, and we fought it as if it were merely a physical war."

Though Dick Hillis had vowed not to return to China ministry after his turbulent experiences under the Communists in China, he could not refuse such a Macedonian call for help. He launched a short-term ministry in Formosa which later developed into the full-fledged missionary organization now known as OC (One Challenge) International.

Army camps all over Formosa allowed teams to come in and present the gospel message to thousands of troops at a time. Gospels of John were distributed and applications for a Bible correspondence course were offered, resulting in thousands of troops beginning to study the Scriptures. The same occurred with middle and high schools across the island. It was a time for harvest.

One of the most convincing door-openers given to our young team of missionaries in Formosa was a card bearing the seal of the "Office of the President," in which President Chiang Kai-shek made the following statement:

> "I delight very much in encouraging people
> to read and study the Bible, because the Bible
> is the voice of the Holy Spirit unfolding God's

righteousness and His love. It tells how Jesus Christ, the world's Savior, gave His life and shed His blood to save all that believe on Him. His righteousness exalts a nation. Christ is the rock of all freedom, and His love covers all sin. All who believe in Jesus shall have eternal life."

Such a ringing endorsement from the leader of Free China was a godsend to Dick Hillis. He found plenty of use for it.

It did not take long for me to plunge into active ministry. With my Navigator background, I was given the opportunity to disciple young men and conduct training seminars in personal evangelism. I also became actively engaged in village evangelism across the island.

Other opportunities to teach in an officers' language school in Taipei, the capital city, provided for many personal encounters in which the gospel could be shared. I had the joy of leading many of these officers to a relationship with the Savior.

There was also a special ministry to American teenagers both from military and missionary families. This would bring me into contact with a very special person!

23

THE VOW OF A
SEVENTEEN-YEAR-OLD

September 1954

Formosa

Not long after my arrival in Formosa in September 1954, I met a young lady who served as secretary to our mission director. Alice Bell was a twenty-three-year-old Canadian whose parents had immigrated to Canada from Scotland. Through her association with the Navigators, she had responded to an invitation to serve as a short-term missionary in Formosa. After completing her two years, however, she had a strong conviction to stay there indefinitely, even at the risk of living the rest of her life as a missionary old maid. She later said, "I didn't mind being a single old-lady missionary, but I sure didn't want to look like one!"

When I arrived, Alice was in Hong Kong on mission business. She returned a couple of weeks later with precious food supplies, which were unavailable in Formosa.

I confess that the first time I saw Alice, I was smitten. She was just five feet tall, with long brown hair that bounced as she walked. When she came through the gate to the mission compound, I greeted her with a big smile and said, "Welcome back!" Alice returned my smile, but hurried into her house, leaving me standing there. Her cool response disappointed me.

Much later I found out why she'd left me standing there. She too was smitten, and wanted to hide her feelings. Thinking she was committed to a single life, Alice felt convinced this was a testing of her commitment and that she had to resist this "temptation from the devil" (her words, not mine!).

Things soon took a turn for the better. We both worked in the mission office, and we began to relate in a normal way. Her warm and friendly spirit made me forget her early coolness. I began looking forward to going to the office. Whenever I heard the clicking of Alice's heels approaching my house in the morning, I timed my exit so that we could walk to the office together. The shortcut took us through a busy and smelly open fish market filled with wooden tubs of coagulated blood, live chickens hanging by their feet, and many noisy hawkers peddling their wares. I was mostly oblivious to all this, however. I'd grown up in the interior of China, where these were common sights. And now I was in the company of a pretty secretary.

In those days, with funds limited, the mission tried to economize wherever possible. Desk lamps were scarce, so the solution was to push two desks together and place the lamp in the middle, thus killing two birds with one stone. The only problem with this arrangement was that my desk partner was Alice. Whenever I looked up from my work, I would see her brown eyes twinkling back at me. It would not be truthful to say that I did not enjoy this.

One morning, however, the day of reckoning came. Alice told me in no uncertain terms that she would prefer I treat her a bit more "businesslike," whatever that meant.

I reluctantly obliged. After that, I spoke with her only when it was absolutely necessary. I wanted to show her that I could act in a businesslike manner. Her request did surprise me, since I had no serious intentions at the time. In fact, my hands were tied—but then, how was she to know?

* * * * *

In the summer of 1948, when I was seventeen, my family visited Kuling, in the province of Jiangxi in central China. Kuling was a mountain resort, frequented by missionaries who sought escape from the intolerable heat and humidity of Shanghai. This was long before air conditioners were known. Kuling also was the location of the China Inland Mission School for missionary kids. My brother and two sisters had been studying there for some time, and it was good to spend time with them.

I was nearing the end of my studies at the Shanghai British School, which I had attended for the previous couple of years since the close of our German school. I had brought my textbooks with me to cram for my Cambridge certificate exam, which would enable me to enter university. Geometry was not my favorite subject and I had to work hard to memorize all those theorems I was required to know.

However, there was also plenty of time for recreation.

I remember one afternoon when I walked alone through some bamboo forests. The narrow path was barely two feet wide. All of a sudden, I stood face to face with a man I'd never met, but whose face was most familiar to me and millions of others. It was none other than Generalissimo Chiang Kai-shek, the president of China. He also had a summer home in these mountains and had been out on a walk through the same bamboo groves. The president wore a cap and was dressed informally, in a typical Chinese gray gown. He used a walking stick and was closely followed by several bodyguards who immediately crowded around him.

At the sudden intrusion of this foreign teenager into his tranquility, however, he smiled kindly. We exchanged no words except his mumbled "*Hao, hao*" greeting as he stepped off the path and waved me through. This act of kindness and humility by a man who ruled the most populous nation in the world has indelibly imprinted itself on my mind.

But there was something else that occurred that summer in the mountains of Kuling—something that would have a profound influence on my life.

There were a large number of teenagers, most of them missionary kids, spending their vacation up there as well. Since our family stayed for several weeks, we teens had plenty of opportunities to get quite well acquainted. Jean and Mary Kay were daughters of a good missionary friend of ours and we all enjoyed each other's company during those days. It was Jean, the outgoing, vivacious type, who soon became the favorite of several of us guys.

I remember one afternoon, returning from a fun group outing, when a thought struck me. Could it be that a friendship with a girl at this time in my life might prevent me from accomplishing God's purposes in my life?

It was less than three years since I had committed myself to Christ and to following Him. I was serious in my dedication and wanted nothing to interfere with His claims on my life. I felt that some of my closest friends, who had found Christ about the same time, had compromised their commitment. Their point of departure had come through relationships with girlfriends that had taken them on a detour spiritually. If it could happen to them, then it could also happen to me, I realized. I was not prepared to see this happen in my life.

What to do?

I prayed about it. "Lord," I said, "I am making a vow to you today, that I will not get involved with a girl until I am twenty-five years old."

I was seventeen at the time. Why twenty-five? I don't know. But I knew that whatever it would cost, I was prepared to let this vow be a wall of protection around my life. I did not want anything to hinder me from attaining what God had purposed for me.

I redoubled my efforts to spend time in the Word. It was during this time that I developed my close friendship with Dick Hillis, then a missionary with the China Inland Mission. One day he threw out a challenge to me. He told me that he would memorize the book of Philippians that summer, and dared me to do it also. "But," he added, "I don't believe that you will."

This was the wrong thing to say to me (or perhaps the right thing). It made me all the more determined to do it. Before the summer was up, I had memorized all 104 verses of this New Testament book. In fact, I reviewed it faithfully every day for fifty days after I had memorized it.

A couple years later, I arrived in the States and enrolled at UCLA. Never in my life had I seen so many girls! Here they were on the college campus by the thousands. It was nothing like China. There were blondes, brunettes, and redheads, and girls with blue eyes, brown eyes, and hazel eyes, in all sizes and forms. It was a huge field to choose from! Then the Lord graciously reminded me of the vow I had made.

But Lord, I thought, *You can't hold me to that now. I was only seventeen and I was not aware of what lay ahead of me. Please, let me off the hook.*

The answer came back, gentle yet firm:

> I did not ask you to make that vow. That was your idea; you voluntarily made that commitment to Me. You did not want anything to interfere with My purpose for your life. Don't you remember that?

Yes, Lord, but...

No matter what I said and how hard I tried, I always came back to what God's Word had taught me about making a vow to the Lord. I remembered so clearly what it said in Deuteronomy 23:21, 23: "If you make a vow to the LORD your God, do not be slow to pay it, for the LORD your God will certainly demand it of you and you will be guilty of sin…Whatever your lips utter you must be sure to do, because you made your vow freely to the LORD your God with your own mouth."

I had enough fear of the Word of God in my life that I did not want to take the risk of disobeying it. Today, I firmly believe that it was this commitment that protected me throughout my college years from becoming entangled in a relationship that would hinder me from being available to Him.

I was twenty-three when I sailed for Formosa…two years to go!

* * * *

Of course, Alice had no way of knowing all this.

The aloof nature of our relationship was resolved after someone told Dick Hillis, our mission director, that I hadn't eaten for two weeks—an exaggeration, but I *was* troubled. Dick had already observed the strain in my conversations with Alice. He asked to speak privately with Alice, and she expressed her uncertainty about our relationship. We were the only single young missionaries in our mission and worked in close proximity. She admitted to an attraction to me. But would it be different if she were in a normal setting with other young men around? She needed time to sort through her feelings. She feared that things were developing too quickly.

Dick listened and then gave Alice some wise counsel: "Don't fight your feelings, but let God work things out—and act naturally."

I had a similar talk with Dick. I told him about my vow, and he encouraged me to share this with Alice.

So I wasted no time in telling Alice that my hands were tied until I was twenty-five. I could see she was visibly relieved. It took the pressure off everything. We were able to relate to one another in a friendly and free manner and involve ourselves in the ministry without distraction.

We were both involved in working with teenagers in Taipei. They were principally kids from the American business and military community, as well as missionary teens. However, among them were also a number of youth of distinguished Chinese families, both political and military. We saw many of them come to Christ and grow in their Christian lives. It was a special time when Alice and I experienced a shared ministry— something which would also mark our future lives.

I vividly remember a July morning about six months before my twenty-fifth birthday. I was taking some time off to study my Bible. My reading was in Isaiah 28, and as I came to the last verse of this chapter, it jumped out at me with such force that I could hardly believe my eyes. Here in black and white was the confirmation I had been looking for in regards to a future life partner.

I read, "All this comes from the LORD Almighty, wonderful in counsel and magnificent in wisdom" (Isaiah 28:29).

Here was a message from the Lord to me personally. I was seeking and listening to Him to find His personal direction for my life concerning Alice as my future life partner, and God led me to this obscure passage in the Old Testament to give me the reassurance I needed. It is always risky for someone to say, "The Lord told me." But in this case, I just *knew* He was telling me that Alice was the one He had selected for me.

A peace and confidence flooded my soul. Even though I could not make a commitment at that time, I knew we were on the right course.

Over the next few months, severe testing would challenge this direction. What made it hard was that it came from close friends. I sought the counsel of respected friends, coworkers, and my own father. In the end, I had to conclude that the only counsel that was "wonderful" came from the Lord. I was assured that He would work things out in accordance with His "magnificent wisdom."

24

THE BODY IN THE STATION WAGON

Fall 1955

Taipei, Formosa

It was a dark, rainy Saturday night in Taipei, the kind of night to stay home and huddle around a cozy fireplace. The only problem was that none of our homes on the mission compound had fireplaces. If you wanted to stay warm, you either went to bed or huddled on a couch with a blanket.

This night was different, however, because we had our regular Young Life Club meeting scheduled for that evening. A group of teenagers had already braved the weather and shown up. Just as we were about to begin our activities, the phone rang. An unfamiliar voice requested to speak to me. The caller said that a German missionary lady had suddenly passed away and had left my name as a contact point. Would I be able to come immediately and take charge of the situation?

Of course, this did not leave me with any options. I briefly explained the situation to our youth group and then made arrangements to borrow a station wagon from a fellow missionary so I could drive to the little village, which was two hours away. I invited Alice and Peter, a Chinese high school boy, to join me.

We set out in pouring rain, which seemed to get worse the farther we went. As long as the roads were paved, we managed fine, but soon we turned onto dirt roads which were muddy and slippery.

As we drove, I explained my connection with the missionary lady. Her name was Rosa Kocher and she had come to China from Germany about the same time that my parents were there. In fact, she was stationed not far from our little village and often stopped by to visit with our family.

After World War II, Rosa went home to Germany for a brief time, but then felt a need to return to work with her "beloved Chinese." The mission agency did not want to send her due to her age and health factors. But she insisted and her determination finally won the day.

Rosa had arrived in Formosa just a few weeks before. We welcomed her, and soon she was on her way to a remote little village where she wanted to establish a church and new ministry. In fact, the opening of the new little chapel was scheduled for the next day. And now she was gone.

It was late in the evening when we finally pulled into this out-of-the-way place. I realized that our first stop needed to be at the local police station so we could obtain permission to transport Rosa's body to Taipei for funeral arrangements.

The police were not used to foreign visitors. We were greeted politely and asked the reason for our coming. We explained that we had come to take charge of the body of the deceased missionary and transport it back to Taipei. They had already heard of her death but wanted to know our relationship to her. Were we members of her family? I told them that she did not have any relatives in this country.

In that case, the police captain replied, he could not give us authorization to take her. Even when I tried to explain that her only relatives lived in Germany, he remained adamant. Shrugging his shoulders, he said that he was only following instructions.

At this impasse, we resorted to the familiar "cup of tea" routine. They told us to make ourselves comfortable and drink some hot tea with them. We were only too happy to oblige after the long, wet drive. As we sat there, they were eager to reopen negotiations with us. Did we belong to the same organization as Rosa Kocher? If we did, that might provide a way out. Again, I had to answer "no," and further informed them that she was here independently. We were not getting anywhere, so more tea was poured.

As the night drug by, I realized that this event provided the police officials with a welcome change in their daily routine and that they were none too eager to find a rapid solution. One asked where I had learned to speak Chinese. This question provided me with an opening to tell them about my background in China, that I had been born there, and that my parents had been missionaries there for twenty-seven years. In fact, I said, that is where we had first made contact with Rosa Kocher.

The policemen sat in up in their chairs. Noticing their interest, I added that when I was born, Rosa had been the midwife who assisted my mother at my birth.

I must have hit the right button, because the captain immediately wanted to verify what I had said. "She was the midwife when you were born?" he asked. When I affirmed that, he sat back and solemnly declared, "Then she is officially related to you! You should have told me that earlier. This qualifies you to take her body since you are her relative."

Without further ado, he signed a slip of paper authorizing us to take her body with us.

We quickly made our way to the place Rosa had rented and where she was planning to hold her first church service the next morning. A young helper greeted us warmly and then began to recount to us her last hours.

Rosa had been full of excitement waiting for Sunday to come.

It was to be the beginning of a new ministry for her. She had spent time readying the place and arranging chairs. Everything was fully prepared for Sunday.

Feeling a bit tired, she had wanted to stretch out a bit and relax that afternoon. Suddenly, Rosa called her helper and explained that she was about to leave and see Jesus. She gave him a few more instructions and then with a glow and radiance on her face quietly told him, "I can now see Jesus. I am going."

We entered Rosa's room. She lay on her bed, fully dressed, with eyes wide open and a serene smile on her face. A picture of total peace and joy!

Her Chinese helper, who had called to give us the news of her passing, told us that Rosa's last words were, "I see Him coming for me."

I stepped to the bed, gently leaned over, and closed her eyes. Her smile remained. What a way to go!

After a brief prayer, we now had to tackle the task of moving her to our car. She was a very large lady, and it was impossible for me, Alice, and the helper to lift her. Peter stood back and watched us struggle. He had never seen a dead body in his life, let alone touched one.

"I need your help, Peter," I said. And he rose to the occasion. We took hold of the bed sheets on all four corners and gently lowered her body from the bed to the floor. Then we dragged her out of her bedroom and down a narrow hallway, making several tight turns, to the front door.

It was still raining as I backed up the car as close to the front of the house as possible. I opened the back of the station wagon, and we pulled, dragged, and lifted—I still don't remember how we did it—until Rosa was in the back of the car. The only problem was that her legs still stuck out! After some gentle pushing, shoving, and bending, we finally managed to close the back of the station wagon. I guess this is not how the professionals do it, but we had no other way to transport her body back to the city.

It was already midnight when we set off on our return trip. A couple of hours later, we arrived in Taipei and headed straight for a funeral home. When we got there, the place was dark, and the big iron gate at its entrance was locked. On a weekend at 2 A.M., this was no surprise. It was time for all sane people to be in bed.

Yet we banged at the gate, hollered, and shouted, and soon aroused the dogs in the neighborhood, which began to chime in with us. Finally, a light came on and a man slowly staggered out to talk to us through the gate.

"What do you want?" he said. We explained that we had a body in the back of our car, which we needed to deliver. He reminded us gruffly that they were closed and that we should come back in the morning.

"But that is impossible," I replied. "We can't just park the car on the street in front of our home with a dead body inside!" This did not seem to concern the funeral home keeper much. He seemed more interested in getting back to his warm bed than in standing in the rain, talking to us.

Again we endured back and forth negotiating, similar to what we had encountered at the police station a few hours earlier. This time there was no hot tea.

After what seemed a long, wearisome process, the funeral home official agreed that we could leave the body, provided we were willing to pay for an embalming treatment and return in the morning with the necessary medical documentation to comply with their procedures. We accepted this offer with profuse thanks and finally arrived home about 4 A.M.

The next few days kept us busy. Telegrams to mission headquarters in Germany were the first item on the agenda. After that we set out to obtain the needed medical death certificates. But how could you obtain that, since no doctor was present when she died? We pleaded our cause with a missionary doctor in Taipei who had spent many years in China. He took note of our dilemma and said that even though he had not examined the body, he would sign a death certificate for us.

We began to make funeral arrangements, arrange for a

service, schedule a speaker, and get the word out to the missionary community. But where to bury her? Rosa Kocher was German, but there was no German consular representation in Formosa at the time. The American consulate was not able to help us either. Finally, the Canadians agreed to help. Since Alice was a Canadian citizen at the time, she sweet-talked them into making a plot available in Tamsui, a suburb of Taipei, where a Canadian cemetery was located.

Then we received a phone call. On the other end was the secretary of Madame Chiang Kai-shek, wife of the president. The Madame, a committed Christian, had seen our announcement in the local newspaper and had expressed her desire to attend the funeral service. With the Madame coming, we now had to go on a telephone-calling spree to missionaries in the community, urging them to come even though they did not know Rosa, so that the service would be acceptably attended.

The service went smoothly, and at the close, Madame Chiang was the first to pass by the open coffin to pay her final respects to this German missionary whose final wish, when leaving Germany, was to die in China.

However, the incident was not complete.

It poured rain as a number of cars followed the hearse for the interment at the Tamsui cemetery. The last stretch of the road was up a muddy incline. Somehow, the hearse got stuck, with wheels spinning and scattering mud on everyone following behind. After several unsuccessful attempts to get it out of the ever-deepening ruts, several of us lifted the heavy coffin out of the hearse and transferred it to the back of the station wagon I was driving. Finally, we made it to the top.

Several men at the gravesite were in the final stages of digging a hole deep enough to embed the coffin. By this time, however, it was already half filled with water. After a very brief service, the coffin was lowered in and nearly covered with water. We threw some clumps of mud on it and bid our final farewell to this brave and dedicated missionary soul.

Two reflections worth noting:

One, it was one of those unique experiences in life granted by God. Rosa assisted my mother in bringing me into this earthly life. Now I'd been granted the privilege to help usher her out of this life. Twenty-four years had passed between these two events, and we both had changed much during this time. Yet the God who gave life and now took it had never changed. He could be trusted fully to the end. Rosa Kocher was eminently ready for her day when it came in that little village in Formosa.

Two, about a year and a half later, I addressed a crowd of several thousand people who had gathered in a small town of southern Germany. This town was the headquarters of the mission Rosa Kocher belonged to. The meetings were held under a huge tent, and I had been asked to recount the home-going of this valiant missionary. As I concluded my story, I closed with a final challenge: "Who will take Rosa Kocher's place?" She had given her life so that men and women could hear the Good News of Jesus Christ. Since many more needed to hear this story, others were needed to continue in this ministry.

Several responded to this call and later found themselves on the mission field serving God.

> Only one life, 'twill soon be past—Only what's done for Christ will last.[6]

25

The Man Will Not Rest

September 1955

Taipei, Formosa

As the first anniversary of my arrival in Formosa came around, I was able to reflect with a great sense of joy on all that I had been privileged to experience in those twelve months.

I was accommodated in bachelor quarters—a simple room with a bed, dresser drawers, desk, and chair—in the home of another missionary family on the compound made up of three houses occupied by three families. But I did not spend much time in the room apart from sleeping and meals with my host family. I was busy in the office, having inherited the dubious honor of being mission treasurer and bookkeeper. It was often a time-consuming duty.

Beyond that, I was actively involved in a discipling ministry among some of our Chinese coworkers in the office and a number of university students. I found in them a hunger and spiritual responsiveness to grow in their Christian life, and was able to pass on what I had received during my years of training with the Navigators.

On Friday nights, I taught a large Bible class to Chinese military officers in the Officers Language School. They came from all branches of the armed forces and were there to learn or improve their ability to speak English. What irony: Here was a German teaching Chinese how to speak English!

The textbook for my language training was the Gospel of John, and in the process of teaching them to read and speak English and to learn basic grammatical principles, it was also quite natural to tie in principles from God's Word. I maintained my involvement with officers there for all my years in Formosa and saw scores of them come to know Christ. Later, we had classes for them in our home and saw abundant fruit from these labors. Out of one class of fifty political officers, seventeen found the Savior. Most of them were colonels in rank.

On two occasions, I invited Madame Chiang Kai-shek to speak to our class. While we generally had about three hundred officers in attendance, on those two nights about five hundred officers came to hear Free China's First Lady. It was my privilege to serve as master of ceremonies at these meetings and introduce her. I will never forget the first time she spoke. She simply shared what she had read in her quiet time, which was Psalm 143:8–10:

> Let the morning bring me word of your
> unfailing love,
> For I have put my trust in you.
> Show me the way I should go,
> For to you I lift up my soul.
> Rescue me from my enemies, O Lord,
> For I hide myself in you.
> Teach me to do your will,
> For you are my God;
> May your good Spirit
> Lead me on level ground.

The next time she spoke was in celebration of the tenth anniversary of our weekly Bible study. She took her text from Romans 12:2: "Be transformed by the renewing of your mind." In both instances, Madame Chiang gave a clear message that was founded on her genuine belief that the Bible was the Word of God.

My mission work was not the only thing I had on my mind in those months. On Saturday night, January 7, 1956, I helped host our regular Young Life meeting. After the kids left, I chatted briefly with Alice, who wore a beautiful new white angora sweater and black skirt. She seemed to glow with a special radiance that evening. My twenty-fifth birthday was just a couple of hours away.

Unbeknown to me, Alice was already a step ahead. I did not realize at the time that women have a unique, sixth sense for gauging people and situations. Her feelings toward me had grown over the past year, and she knew that a wedding might be around the corner once my vow was completed. So on an earlier business trip to Hong Kong, she'd done a little shopping. On Nathan Road, she came across a bridal store. At that time, Taiwan did not have these available. Result: She came out with a beautiful, laced wedding gown. All of this before I had even proposed to her! At any rate, she made sure she was ready.

Alice was expecting something that Saturday night, January 7. She knew we Germans have to do things by the book, and that I would not discuss marriage before my twenty-fifth birthday the next day. But she thought I might pop the question one minute after midnight!

I disappointed her. Instead of a marriage proposal, I asked her to go out with me for breakfast at the Grand Hotel.

In the morning, I picked up Alice and drove in the old mission vehicle to the hotel. After dropping her off in the lobby, I excused myself and hustled over to a missionary friend who had promised me to loan me his new station wagon for the day.

I drove back to the hotel and without telling Alice where I

had been the past twenty minutes, escorted her to the dining room for a nice breakfast. Afterward, her eyes grew big when I showed her the car and told her that we would go off for a little ride up into the mountains above Taipei city.

As we drove, we chatted amiably about all sorts of things, but the higher we climbed, the more the temperature dropped. In those days there were no heaters in cars, and Alice began to shiver. She begged me a couple of times to find a place to stop, but I drove on. Then the snow gently began to fall.

We found a secluded spot and I pulled over.

I had never proposed to a girl before. I wanted to make sure that I did it the right way and felt that I needed to set a spiritual tone to the whole thing. I pulled out my Bible and told Alice that I wanted to share something from the book of Ruth in the Old Testament. As I read the account, I interspersed it from time to time with what I considered "salient" comments. I doubt they impressed her.

Yet I went on. Chapter one. Chapter two. Chapter three. I'm sure she thought I would never stop. And she was freezing. "Hurry," she said. "I am so cold, and there is so much I want to tell you."

Finally, I came to the verse that I had in mind all along, at the end of chapter three:

> "For the man will not rest until the matter is settled today." (Ruth 3:18)

I expressed my deep love to Alice for the first time, though she must have sensed it during the past months. I told her that this was the day I had been waiting for since I was seventeen. I thought it would never come, but here it was! God had used my vow to save and protect me for her alone all these years. I had never loved or kissed a girl before. I had saved it all for her.

I reminded Alice that the year before, during a special Young Life banquet bearing a *TIME* magazine theme, she had given me a subscription to the publication on behalf of the group.

"Today," I said, "I would like to give you a subscription for *LIFE*. Will you marry me?"

With a glow on her face, she accepted with a resounding "yes!" I had not anticipated anything else. It was then that I kissed her for the first time. Later, Alice told me she knew immediately that I'd never kissed a girl before!

A couple of months earlier, I had asked a friend to pick up an engagement ring in Hong Kong on his way to Formosa. He'd selected a beautiful, sparkling diamond, which I now placed on Alice's hand. She was absolutely stunned, never thinking that I, a poor missionary, could afford to give her a ring like that. But I had saved up for it and money was never put to better use.

Alice in turn had a present to give to me. After all, January 8 was my birthday. She reached to the backseat and pulled out a package containing a beautiful blue cashmere sweater. I later teased her that this was a bribe so that I would ask her to marry me.

We returned to the city and the Grand Hotel, where we enjoyed a special Chinese dinner together. Even our waiter was impressed when Alice showed him her new ring. She was just glowing!

I have always believed in long courtships and short engagements. We decided on March 10 for our wedding. In the meantime, lots needed to be done.

First, there was that important phone call to Canada and Alice's dad, David Bell. He hailed from Scotland and still spoke with a pronounced Scottish brogue. Phone calls in those days were rare, and expensive. I never called my parents during the ten years we lived in Formosa—all communication was through the weekly letters that flew across the Pacific.

The phone connection was not the greatest, but I finally did manage to get her dad on the line. I did not know how I was supposed to ask my future father-in-law for permission to marry Alice. I mumbled something about asking him for the hand of his daughter. I had read that somewhere in a book and thought this was the way to do it. He feigned misunderstanding, and after a couple of unsuccessful tries, he finally said, "Speak up young man, what is it you want?"

"I want to marry your daughter!" was all I could blurt out.

"Oh, is that all you want?" he said. "Go right ahead." This was not the only affirmation I received from David Bell. Shortly thereafter, a check for $25 arrived in the mail. For a Scotsman, this was something special.

The second thing that occupied our time was the planning for a Billy Graham Crusade scheduled for February. Billy Graham and his team had responded to an invitation from the churches in Formosa to hold a special series of meetings. OC was responsible for setting it up and making all the arrangements. Of course, both Alice and I were deeply involved as well.

The meetings went well and it was thrilling to see the multitudes make first-time decisions to follow Christ. During my first year at UCLA in 1951, I had participated in a Billy Graham Crusade in the Hollywood Bowl and had served as a counselor. Here in Formosa, four years later, the same gospel was producing the same results. Indeed, as Paul wrote, the gospel is the power of God unto salvation, no matter where and when it is proclaimed.

After an evening service, Bob Pierce, founder of World Vision, pulled me aside and asked me to come to his hotel room. I had met Bob as a teenager in Shanghai and he remembered. On one of his previous trips to Formosa, he'd learned that a Christian radio station in the United States, which had promised to underwrite Alice's missionary support, had suddenly dropped her. Apparently, he knew the people at this radio station and was incensed to hear this news. Spontaneously, he promised that World Vision would take care of her needs. And it did, even with a few extras (such as a couple of vacation trips). Bob had a big heart, and now I was going to experience just how big it really was.

"How much will your honeymoon cost?" was his direct question.

"Bob, I really don't know," was my honest reply. "I've never been on a honeymoon before, so I can't really answer that question."

"Well buddy (he called everyone buddy), I want you to do it right, not like I did it. We eloped in a Model T, but you can't do that. I want you to do it right." With that he pulled out his checkbook and wrote me a check for $400, more than three months of my missionary salary. "Is that enough?"

I swallowed hard and thanked him for this unexpected and undeserved demonstration of love. Of course, as I walked out, I thanked our Lord, the giver of every good and perfect gift. I was on cloud nine—this marriage was being confirmed so graciously by our Lord.

When the crusade was over and we were saying goodbye to the whole Billy Graham team at the Taipei Sungshan airport, I had an interesting encounter with a man named John Bolten. John, a German businessman and entrepreneur, once had personal dealings with Hitler. When he became disenchanted with Hitler, John left Nazi Germany and settled in America. Knowing of our common ancestry, John chatted with me at the airline counter. He'd heard that Alice and I were to marry in a couple of weeks. In a previous conversation, Cliff Barrows, Billy Graham's longtime associate, had asked Alice where we were planning to spend our honeymoon. Jokingly she'd replied, "The airline has given me a free airline ticket to Hong Kong. That's where I'm going, but I'm not sure about Hans!"

John had heard that comment and no doubt felt sorry for his German compatriot. As we stood there at the counter, he wrote me a check for $50, which nearly covered my round trip to Hong Kong.

Seeing this, Billy Graham pulled me aside and with a smile said, "I wonder what you've got that I haven't got. I've asked John to accompany me all around the world in my meetings and he hasn't given me a dime. And here you are, and he writes you a check!" Of course, I had no answer for this, but I told Billy that we did have something in common. When he asked me what that was, I said, "You married a Ruth Bell and I am marrying an Alice Bell."

Perhaps this is where any comparison of me with Billy Graham ends.

26

A Honeymoon Like No Other

March 1956

Hong Kong

Our wedding was literally the talk of the whole missionary community. Missionary weddings did not occur frequently, so everyone wanted to witness this joyous occasion. People from other parts of the island arranged a visit to Taipei just to be there. Even some overseas guests from Japan came to celebrate with us. A lot of our Chinese friends crashed the party and the crowd of merrymakers grew to several hundred. Everyone shared in our excitement. Of course, we missed our parents terribly, but we realized that this was part of the cost of serving Him in faraway places. Alice's dad called it "Godforsaken" places! But that is exactly why we were here, to present the Good News that God had not forgotten His people, but loved them.

Dick Hillis did the honors, and I am glad he kept the sermon short. Norman and Muriel Cook stood up with us and the special music was great. But on that day, I had eyes only for my beloved. She was absolutely gorgeous on the outside and radiating an inner beauty from the inside. Veteran China missionary Dr. James Graham stood in as father of the bride. It was interesting to see them both navigating down the aisle, with him occupying three-quarters of it!

Alice had meticulously organized everything down to a "t" and it all ran as smooth as clockwork. Well, nearly all—the wedding cake precisely ordered turned into a banana cake on delivery. But who cared? I sure didn't.

Just as the wedding started, it began to rain, to the great delight of our Chinese friends. "Rain means blessing," they told us.

I had made arrangements with our famous Grand Hotel to get the private, detached VIP suite for our honeymoon night before we would fly to Hong Kong the next morning. I was excited about this special little extra on our first night.

Then a few hours before the wedding I received an urgent telephone message from the hotel. John Foster Dulles, the U.S. secretary of state at that time, had unexpectedly arrived. The hotel was calling to apologize that "our" suite had been assigned to him and that they had made other arrangements for us. I swallowed hard, but then decided not to mention anything to Alice until after she had said "yes" at the altar. Not that I was afraid she might back out of it, but I felt that this was one pressure she could do without.

There was one moment during the ceremony as we were standing together, however, that the tears started to flow down her cheeks. For a split-second I panicked. Had she changed her mind? She later reassured me that these were just tears of joy. Guess there was a lot about women I did not know!

The next morning we boarded a Civil Air Transport for our flight to Hong Kong. Quite a few friends came to the airport to see us off, but we hustled through quickly to take our seats. When we arrived in Hong Kong, some American friends and a businessman from Formosa whom we knew well met us. He insisted on taking us out for dinner immediately.

After dinner, we were faced with another surprise: our hotel reservation had again been given away! Who was it this time? "Marlon Brando is in town," said the officious British clerk. "Didn't you know?"

One of my good-humored American friends turned to the clerk who had just sought to impress us with this bit of information and asked, "And who is she?"

This was met with an icy stare of incredulity. "Marlon Brando is a world famous actor, not a she!" Apparently there was little sense of humor among the Brits when it came to these uneducated Americans.

We did finally manage to find lodging at the Fourseas Hotel on Waterloo Road in Kowloon, where we also received a generous missionary discount. Hong Kong with all of its scenic beauty—the harbor, the Peak (the city's famous mountain landmark), and the surrounding islands—was an ideal place for a honeymoon. So much to see, good restaurants of all varieties to enjoy. We also enjoyed renewing relationships with old friends.

Yet for all the joys a young couple experiences in their first days of married life, there was also a time of testing and of sensing the reality of our life here on earth.

We had been in Hong Kong less than a week when Alice began to have symptoms that caused us to call for a British missionary doctor. Those were the days when house calls were still common practice. The doctor and his wife came to our hotel room, and after his examination gave his first diagnosis: an early pregnancy.

"Impossible," we both exclaimed, "we've just been married a week!"

That seemed to make sense to the doctor. Then he gave his second verdict, and this one was as grim as it could be. "The diagnosis," he said, "is not good. Either she has TB [tuberculosis] or cancer. In either case, my advice for you is to return to America as quickly as possible."

With those words still ringing in our ears, he bid a hasty farewell and Godspeed and was out of the door.

Numb with pain, I remember falling on my knees at Alice's bedside and weeping, "I have only had you for such a short time. Must I lose you now?" The whole thing seemed so incredible. Was it just a dream? Would I really lose my bride after a week of marriage?

Reeling from this disastrous news, we decided the next day to seek additional medical advice. I took Alice to a local hospital, where a Chinese doctor took x-rays and examined her carefully. After what seemed hours to me, he emerged holding one of the x-ray films in his hand. With a smile, he simply said, "Well, if she has TB or cancer, then so do I!"

He quickly assured us that all Alice had was a minor infection. He prescribed some tablets and in a few days my bride was back to normal. We were glad that in this case, our Chinese doctor had been right and our British doctor friend had been wrong!

One of the special times with friends still stands out in my mind. We'd been invited to join a couple for a picnic on one of the islands within the Hong Kong territorial waters. We'd rented a small boat with an even smaller outboard motor to get us there. It was a lovely day and we enjoyed the open waters taking us to the island.

I suddenly spotted a large motorized Chinese junk—a Communist boat with a big red flag fluttering in the breeze. As an avid photographer, this was too much of a temptation for me to resist. I had just acquired a new camera (thanks to Bob Pierce's generosity!) and was already zooming in on the boat. But I wanted to get a bit closer. I requested that our boatman move in for a better shot. That's when it happened.

With my camera trained on the ship, the crew began scurrying about, frantically waving and screaming at us. Then it changed course and trained its guns on our little boat. This frightened our boatman. He shouted that we needed to get out of there. He turned our boat around and, at full throttle, tried to get away from the Communist ship, which gave chase and rapidly gained on us.

We were no match for the gunboat. With the crew shouting at us to stop and "pull over," we began to realize the danger we were in. The memory of a recent incident in these same waters, when the Chinese Communists picked up two American journalists, was too fresh for us to ignore. If the same were to happen to us, this surely would become an unforgettable honeymoon!

Soon only fifty yards separated us from the gunboat. We had lost the race.

All of a sudden, from nowhere, a British police vessel appeared. Running at top speed, it pulled alongside the gunboat. The British ordered the Communists to halt, then the British Harbor Police boarded the vessel. It had infringed on British waters and the British would have none of it.

At this point we breathed a silent prayer of thanks. Our little boat with its put-put engine left the other vessels behind and found its way to our little island. There we gratefully enjoyed a rather anticlimactic picnic.

When we returned to our hotel room that evening, the reality of what we'd just encountered really hit us. How close we had come towards making a gigantic turn in our lives, had it not been for the intervention of the British gunboat! And all of that after what we had just gone through with Alice's medical history. It made us thankful beyond words to our loving Lord who had protected us. He had other plans for our lives. His purposes would prevail.

> "For I know the plans I have for you, declares the Lord, plans to prosper you and not to harm you, plans to give you hope and a future." (Jeremiah 29:11)

27

A FISHERMAN CALLED
MR. SABBATH

April 1956

Hong Kong

A telegram from Dick Hillis, our mission director, called an end
to our blissful yet eventful honeymoon. It simply stated that
meetings had been scheduled for me and that I was to return as
quickly as possible. Dutifully we marched to the airline offices,
only to discover that all flights were booked up. In the meantime,
some of our missionary colleagues in Formosa persuaded Dick to
give us a few more days of grace. The meetings were postponed
for a week.

Back in Taipei, the mission had moved to a new compound
consisting of four single homes. We were given a new home
furnished by what was available in some of the other homes. The
one thing we lacked was a stove. For the first few weeks, Alice
had to use a little camp stove to cook our meals. Our first dinner

turned out to be a "burnt offering," but we were in love and that was all that mattered.

Then I was off to the Pescadores Islands, located in the Taiwan Straits, midway between Formosa and the mainland of China. They consist of a group of sixty-four small islands, many of them uninhabited. Portuguese colonists had given them the name Pescadores, or fishermen's islands, in the sixteenth century. China ceded them in 1895 to Japan after the First Sino-Japanese War, and they were returned to China after World War II.

With a team of Chinese coworkers, I set out on this two-week mission trip. In a letter to Alice, I wrote:

> We had a good trip here…and a total of nineteen meetings in three days. This meant splitting up our team, which enabled us to cover quite a bit more ground. We rented a boat and several church members came along too, making thirteen people in the group. Most everywhere we met very receptive people who listened well. It really is hard to do much on one visit. They hardly ever hear the gospel. What is needed is people from the churches to go back again and again to warn and teach these poor folk.

Two days later, I wrote again:

> We have had a full and busy day, but praise God for the privilege of preaching His gospel. We left this morning on bicycles and have done quite a bit of riding over hot, dusty roads, uphill and downhill all the way. When Mr. Tsao, one of our team members, started speaking, the crowd was small and some fellows started to mimic him. They told the crowd not to listen.
>
> Since this is a very superstitious place, and people cling to their idols, many stood offside trying

to stop the meeting. When I started speaking, they naturally came to see me as a "foreigner," and I sang to them in German before giving the message comparing our wonderful God to their idols. Pretty soon, some crazy guys in the back started throwing firecrackers to stop us—but I kept right on preaching. Bill Lee (another team member) said later that I should have thanked them for "welcoming us so kindly!" There were a number who listened well, thank God…

As I see the tremendous needs here on the Pescadores my heart is stirred. Sometimes I even sense frustration—so many souls, so much superstition, so much indifference—yet also so much hunger and desire to hear more. Yesterday afternoon three women turned to the Lord. But what are they among so many?

I was again and again reminded of the apostle Paul's missionary journeys where he encountered both positive and negative responses to the preaching of God's Good News. Even in Rome, Paul received a mixed reception, but some believed.

There was one event on the islands that made an indelible impression on my mind. We had visited another one of those scattered islands to have meetings. Someone suggested that we make every effort to go there, since outsiders rarely, if ever, visited. While there, I heard a story from a village elder, a story I had never heard before or since.

In answer to the question of how the gospel first came to this little island, he told us a fascinating account about a fisherman who later became known as "Mr. Sabbath." Prior to this, no missionary had ever set foot on this island—it had been totally isolated from any contact with the Christian faith.

This simple fisherman had a dream one night. In the dream, God appeared to him and gave him a personal message about

Himself as the only true God. What was so striking was that God also gave him a list of the Ten Commandments. These needed to be followed, and he urged this fisherman to make them known to everyone on this island.

Of all the commandments, the one that stood out to them was the command to honor the Sabbath. This was a radically new concept. And so this fisherman soon became known all over the island as "Mr. Sabbath." He strictly adhered to this new set of rules for their lives. When it came to the Sabbath, or Sunday, this fisherman refused to go about this business, even though all the other fishermen did.

Then one Sabbath, he violated this command. He went out to fish and encountered a terrific storm. He went down with his boat, but his death caused shock waves across the island. "He violated God's commandment and God punished him" was the unequivocal opinion of everyone.

Several years later, when the first missionary arrived on that island and began preaching, he was amazed to find these people—without a Bible or biblical texts—already aware of the Ten Commandments and the consequences of disobeying God.

Many times over the years, I have been asked, "What about those who have never heard the gospel? Will they be saved?" Here is a striking example of God's ability to reveal Himself in a supernatural way even in the remotest of places and to respond to any heart that seeks after Him. Indeed, it is His desire for all men to be saved and to come to a knowledge of the truth. That is His purpose for every human life. It is our responsibility as believers to make Him known—the rest is up to God.

I had been invited to speak at a week's conference for tribal workers high in the mountains of Formosa. They belonged to the Bunun people, one of the aboriginal tribes. Since I did not speak their language, I spoke in Chinese, which was translated for them. They were most appreciative of what they were receiving and I enjoyed this opportunity to minister to a new people group.

At the conclusion of our meetings, we were invited to visit a neighboring village and conduct a service. The way took us along narrow and steep mountain paths. Fortunately, it was a moonlit night that made lanterns or flashlights unnecessary.

After all these years, I do not remember much of the service, except for a question I was asked after the meeting. The reason I remember the question is because I did not have an answer, at least not a good answer. An elderly tribal man approached after I had finished preaching and said, "How long have you had this Good News?" Without waiting for a reply, he asked a follow-up question: "What has taken you so long to bring it to us?"

I was taken aback and struggled with an answer. I cannot remember my feeble attempt to respond to this old man, but the question stuck with me. Do we owe it to those who have never heard the gospel to hear this question too?

Before coming to Formosa, I attended a meeting in which Oswald J. Smith, pastor of the People's Church in Toronto, spoke on the subject of world evangelism. He used the illustration of Jesus feeding the five thousand and asking his disciples to begin distributing to those sitting in the first row. When they finished, Jesus asked them to go back and feed them again and again, while those sitting behind them went without food.

Then Dr. Smith asked this pertinent question: "Why should anyone hear the gospel twice, when there are so many who have not even heard it once?"

Yet when I was confronted by this Bunun elder, I stumbled to search for an answer. The real answer should have been to admit our failure after nearly two thousand years to obey His command to preach the gospel to every creature. It is and must continue to be the mission of the church.

Jesus had told His disciples in John 10:16, "I have other sheep that are not of this sheep pen. I must bring them also." "Others" certainly included those who had never heard the gospel.

Dietrich Bonhoeffer, the dynamic German pastor martyred in 1945 by the Nazis shortly before the end of World War II, wrote: "The church is the church only when it exists for others."[7]

The purpose of the church and my personal purpose in life had intersected. I had to keep going until His command was fulfilled.

28

I'm Sorry, I Don't Have Time

1957

Tainan, Formosa

In those early years, OC was involved in a special cooperative agreement with the Presbyterian Church of Formosa. Its goal was to double the number of churches on the island. We covered one district after another, doing open-air evangelism in hundreds of villages. We had two trucks equipped with loud-speaking systems. Standing in the truck bed, we preached to villagers and townspeople. Most were not believers.

To attract a crowd was easy in those days. The presence of foreign faces still was an attention-getter. We often started out by singing "Old MacDonald had a farm, E-I-E-I-O." Kids would rush towards the truck, and soon their elders would drop what they were doing and join them. We might act out a little drama, which would lead into a gospel presentation. Then we invited them to enroll in our Bible correspondence course. If some responded to the invitation to come to Christ, a team of local church members helped answer their questions. Those interested became the nucleus of a new church in their village. Then we moved on to the next place and repeated the program.

In this manner, we were able to cover four or five villages a day. These efforts indeed paid off; during that ten-year period the number of churches doubled.

One afternoon in the city of Tainan, on the southern part of the island, we concluded our last meeting in the outskirts. I remember preaching from Psalm 135 about idols made by man's hands.

> They have mouths, but cannot speak, eyes, but they cannot see; they have ears, but cannot hear, nor is there breath in their mouths. (Psalm 135:16–17)

I'd sensed an unusual freedom in preaching this message and afterwards thanked God for this opportunity to reveal Christ as the only answer and hope to their needs. We returned to the pastor's simple home where we were staying, tired but happy.

We were up early the next day for our 6 A.M. prayer meeting at the church. After the meeting, we asked for God's blessing on our lives as we set out once again to proclaim Christ to those who had never heard. As we were leaving the church to get into our truck, I noticed a young man standing on the curb, leaning on his bike. I had never seen him before, but before I knew it, his face brightened and he exclaimed, "I am so glad that I found you!"

The young man said he had heard me preach the night before and that he had been deeply moved and needed to talk with me. He had not been able to sleep all night, but had peddled through the town looking for our truck. "If I only can find this truck," he said, "I knew that I could find you. You don't know how glad I am that I have finally found you!"

I greeted him cordially and thanked him for coming. Then I did something incredibly wrong. I looked at my watch and explained to him that we were scheduled to be in another village within thirty minutes and that I just did not have time to talk to him then. I would try and talk to him later that night.

"But you don't understand," was his shocked reply. "I have been looking for you all night and now I have found you. You must help me find God."

Equally shocking was my response. "I really would like to talk with you, but I really can't right now." I said. "We have this meeting scheduled and we can't be late. Please, give me your address and I will get in touch with you."

I can still visualize the look of despair on this man's face. Finally, with a shrug of his shoulders, he said, "Well, then you are too busy for me." At my insistence, he quickly scribbled an address on a slip of paper and watched us as we hopped into our truck and drove off.

The day was a disaster for me. My agony over leaving a searching soul standing on the street increased with each passing hour. It was misery all the way. Had we not just finished praying together that God would lead us to open and prepared hearts? Here we had met one, and I just left him standing there.

As soon as we got back from the day's task, I begged the pastor to help me find this man. Alas, the address he had given proved to be inaccurate. We could not locate him.

You can't imagine the anguish of my soul, the torture of my spirit, and the pangs of guilt which flooded over me. I had miserably failed this man and had miserably failed our Lord! Tears of confession and repentance did not bring relief for a long time. My only hope and prayer was that God in His mercy would bring someone else into his life that would be more faithful in leading this man to Him. Right then and there I made a new commitment to never let an opportunity like this pass, to never say "I don't have time" when eternal issues are at stake.

29

DRIED FISH, TREE FUNGUS, AND TWO PIGS

1958

Taiwan

When Alice and I returned to Taiwan from our first furlough in the States in 1958, we came back as U.S. citizens. I had actually asked her to adopt German citizenship, and she had countered by asking me to become a Canadian! A happy compromise was drawn on February 26, 1958, when we became naturalized American citizens at the U.S. District Court in Omaha, Nebraska.

Our hearts thumped when we arrived in Taipei on May 12 and were greeted by a host of Chinese friends and coworkers. Forty-eight hours later, I was on my way to Orchid Island, about forty miles off the east coast of Taiwan. Here is what I wrote to some of my friends:

> We battled through rough seas in a little motorized junk for ten hours, and some of our team suffered acute seasickness. But finally, around midnight,

we set foot on the little island, populated by the Yami tribe, 1,600 strong, one of the aboriginal tribes. The people eat only raw fish and sweet potatoes, and live in grass huts under very primitive conditions. It has been dubbed "Death Island" due to many deaths caused by a strange insect. I was bitten on my leg by something and was in bed several days after we returned, but evidently it wasn't the same bug!

Just six years ago, a young tribesman from Taiwan went to this forsaken island to preach the gospel. One month later, he saw the first convert, and after three years there were twelve baptized believers and four preaching points. Then he returned to Taiwan to attend seminary.

When we arrived, we found the people very friendly. Since hotels were unheard of and money was of no value, we were fortunate to receive permission to sleep in a schoolhouse on the cement floor (and it felt mighty good after a long hot day). We quickly got used to eating fish, canned beef, and rice, which we had taken along for our three daily meals for two weeks. But we ran out of food, due to a typhoon, which delayed our boat from picking us up. Then we received help from an unexpected source. The schoolmaster rounded up his students and sent them on a frog hunt. Soon they returned with forty good-sized frogs, which looked more like toads. They were delicious!

Often walking four to five hours a day across coral-strewn beaches, or crossing steep mountain paths, we were able to visit each village and preach in twenty-six different meetings during those two weeks. Wherever we went, people seemed hungry for the message. I preached in a little church one Sunday afternoon, hardly big enough for a person to stand up straight. People squatted on the mud floor, while I had a hard time from bumping my head on the roof.

After one evening meeting, they requested another message, and then a third before they would go home. And over and over again they asked, "When are you coming back? Why don't you come more often?"

We promised the believers there that we would tell others of their need. Overjoyed, they took their offerings (dried fish and tree fungus) and traded it in for two female pigs. With these they bought a wonderful piece of property right in the heart of "Redhead Village," where they wanted to construct their church. Amazing what a couple of sows can mean to the kingdom of God.

On a subsequent trip to Orchid Island the following year, we took along cement and showed the villagers how to dig ditches and lay the foundation for their new church. A carpenter and a mason came with us to oversee the construction and guide them.

Shortly after our first trip, while we were sitting at our breakfast table, a sudden thud-like explosion interrupted our conversation. We couldn't imagine what had happened, but soon discovered that a Chinese Air Force plane had missed our compound by about seven hundred yards and crashed into four Chinese homes two blocks away, killing two and injuring fourteen. We realized afresh that "the angel of the Lord encamps around those that fear Him."

The political situation in Taiwan, in the meantime, began to darken. Newspaper reports warned every day of a massive troop buildup in Communist China and rumors of an imminent invasion of Taiwan were rampant. One news report stated that the Communists were ready to strike in this area while the West's attention was focused on the Middle East. All leaves and furloughs of Nationalist soldiers were cancelled, but life in this capital city went on as usual. However, we received word from the American Embassy that we should have our things packed if there should be a sudden evacuation of American citizens.

Sometimes Alice and I wondered about bringing a child into a dangerous world like this. Yet at the same time there was a deep sense of trust that our lives were in the hands of a sovereign Lord. We both wanted children and to build a family.

On October 6, 1958, Hans-Martin Wilhelm Jr. (Marty) made his long-expected and overdue appearance. Watching the miracle of birth unfold before my eyes was an unforgettable experience, only to be repeated a couple of years later on July 22, 1960, when Elita Marie (Lita) was born. As I look back, I thank God for both of our children and I am grateful to them for the many lessons they taught us during the years they were in our home, and in later years.

One of these came just prior to our second furlough.

My father, Max Wilhelm age 19, served in World War I
as a sergeant in the German army

My parents, Max and Anna Wilhelm, Eva, and baby Hans
in Guizhou, China, 1931

My birthplace at the mission home in Jinping

Big sister Eva taking care of me

Age 4

College freshman at St. John's University in Shanghai, age 18

Preaching in the villages of Taiwan in the early 50's led to the planting of many new churches. Crowds gathered around the sound truck as we presented the gospel using visual charts, drama, and music

"Bringing the Word on Wheels" with a team to villages inaccessible by trucks

As a news correspondent, I interviewed Lt. Liu Cheng-ssu after his defection from Communist China in his Mig-15 fighter jet

Introducing Madame Chiang Kai Shek to my weekly Bible class at the Officers Language School in Taipei

Madame Chiang Kai Shek encouraged several hundred officers to follow Christ. (L-R Muriel Cook, center Madame Chiang with two aides, the commandant, Alice, and Margaret Hillis)

With my bride Alice, dressed in tribal costume at
Sun Moon Lake in Taiwan

This bundle of frogs became our dinner while
stranded and hungry on Orchid Island

With both of our children "Made in Taiwan" – 1963

Sharing our first Christmas in Brazil with Maria and her daughter at her "home" in 1966

Brazil team meeting at the beach (1972)
(L-R Larry Keyes, Jim Kemp, John Quam, Paul McKaughan, Bill Keyes, Hans, Paul Landrey, and Ary Velloso – Marty Wilhelm, front)

Zambia, Africa 2006 – Leaders Conference (L-R Pastor Henry, interpreter, Marty, Hans – David Bulger in front)

With Bishop Robertson Nonde in Zambia

"Walking on eggs" (ostrich) in South Africa

"Volksmarching" in Germany in the 80's

Taking a much needed lunch break

I revisited the exact same seat in a Shanghai church, scene of
a pivotal experience in my life 50 years earlier

Teaching in a seminary in China in the 90's

With Dick Hillis, Founder of OC International and one
of my principal mentors

1965 Family Reunion in Scottsbluff, Nebraska – the only picture ever taken of our family together (L-R Esther, Anita, Eva, Hans, Fred, Peggy with my parents)

Our son Marty and family (Mark, Kari, Karl, Heidi, Karen and Marty)

Our daughter Lita with her husband Will Lott

Alice and I enjoying our "Golden Years" in Arnold, California

30

FOREIGN CORRESPONDENT

March 3, 1962

Taiwan

There was excitement and euphoria on the streets of Taipei. Second Lieutenant Liu Cheng-ssu of the Communist Chinese Air Force had defected from mainland China and landed his MiG-15 fighter jet in Taiwan. He had become a hero overnight and was already a household word to millions living on the island. He was given a wild reception and celebrated by old and young alike.

A couple of years earlier, OC had launched the Far East News Service to bring news of religious significance to the American public. I had been assigned as the Taiwan correspondent. With pertinent letters in hand, I went to the Ministry of Foreign Affairs and received full press credentials. This enabled me to have access to many new areas that were generally "out of bounds" for missionaries. I enjoyed the same privileges accorded to Associated Press, UPI, and *Time/Life* correspondents. Besides it opened up some wonderful opportunities for personal contact with government and military officials as well as Chinese and foreign press representatives.

When Lieutenant Liu made his historic escape to Free China, I immediately approached the Ministry of Defense and requested an interview with him. The department complied and arranged an appointment for me to meet with Liu. My primary interest was to inquire and get his take on the religious situation in Communist China. Specifically, I questioned him on the wellbeing of the Christian church there.

I learned several things from Liu. Even though he had no personal contact with Christianity, he admitted that all religions in China were suppressed. The government had no use for religion and had further abolished Sunday as a special day. Every day was a workday, seven days a week, 365 days a year! When I asked him what he thought of the vast difference between an atheistic Mao Zedong and a strongly professing Christian President Chiang Kai-shek, he smiled and said that he was not able to speak to this.

At the end of our interview, I was able to give Liu a brief word of personal witness, to my knowledge the only one he had ever received. I also handed him a booklet in Chinese, entitled *On Being a Real Christian,* by G. Christian Weiss, and encouraged him to read it and find out for himself the truth concerning God. This he promised me to do.

Subsequently, I learned that Liu indeed had attended President Chiang's private chapel services. Only eternity will reveal the outcome of this encounter.

I experienced more exciting adventures as a member of the press corps. I regularly received press credentials for major events, including high-level military maneuvers which were conducted in Taiwan, many times in the presence of President Chiang and top government and military officers. When U.S. President Dwight D. Eisenhower, Vice President Lyndon B. Johnson, Senator Bobby Kennedy, and other notable visitors came to visit the island, I had the opportunity to photograph them from just a few feet away.

In addition, I had access to military flights from Taiwan to the famous "offshore islands" of Quemoy (Jinmen) and Matsu, which received major international attention during the Nixon-Kennedy debates in the 1960 presidential campaign. These were a group of four small islands located within a few miles of the China mainland but held by Taiwan and its local garrisons stationed there.

In 1954 and again in 1958, China initiated regular shelling against the islands. Perhaps it was only President Eisenhower's veiled threat of nuclear intervention that prevented an open outbreak of hostilities between China and Taiwan.

On a number of occasions, I had the privilege of taking several visitors to the islands, including Larry Ward of Food for the Hungry and Ken Anderson of Gospel Films. Another of these visits stands out in my mind, however.

I believe it was 1960 when Al Sanders, vice president of Biola College (now Biola University) in Los Angeles, was in Taiwan and expressed interest in visiting the islands. I arranged a trip to Quemoy through the Department of the Chinese Air Force. Shelling of these offshore islands had ceased for a period, then resumed on an every-other-day basis. So we decided to fly out on an "off" day and come back the third day.

The trip across was probably the bumpiest ride I ever had on a plane. Faces started to take on a yellowish complexion, followed by a fleeting smile and the inevitable trip to the back of the plane, where a bucket was handy for those who could not cope with the situation any longer. When we came close to Quemoy Island our military plane dropped to approximately fifty feet above sea level to avoid enemy radar detection. As soon as it landed, it was wheeled into safety in a massive shelter carved out of the mountain. Al and I were greeted by local military officials, loaded into two separate jeeps, and rushed off for a tour of the island. A fine drizzle came down.

Al was in the lead jeep when it happened. His driver must have skidded on the muddy road and lost control. He veered off and careened into a ditch, which shattered the windshield. As soon as I saw what had happened, I asked my driver to pull alongside. I jumped out and managed to pull Al out of his jeep. His head had smashed against the windshield and was bleeding profusely. We rushed off to the nearest emergency military hospital.

It was a primitive place, and Al seemed truly puzzled as he sat surrounded by medics dressed in battle fatigues instead of the standard white worn by doctors. As they bent over him to attend to his wounds, he inquired, "Which of these is the doctor?"

"They all are, Al," I replied, "and don't worry, they will take good care of you."

He had a big gash on the top of his head reaching right into his beautiful shock of black hair. We thought it required stitches, and this raised another concern in Al's mind. "Hans, don't let them shave off my hair," he pleaded.

Fortunately, they were just surface lacerations and no stitches were required. They took care of closing the cut without doing what Al feared most.

After receiving first aid, Al was wheeled into a recovery room. Looking around at the walls and ceiling, he noticed the pockmarks and holes. "What are these?" he wanted to know. I calmly informed him that there was still regular shelling of the island, but that he did not need to worry. I am not sure he believed me at that point.

While Al recuperated, I made a quick trip into town to visit the pastor of the local church. I was told he was busy in the church. I walked over, looked in, and saw about fifteen people kneeling on the floor, praying out loud. I could not resist, I had to have a picture. Here, on one of Free China's outposts, the world's front line of defense, I had found a praying church!

Back at the hospital, Al was watched and attended to meticulously. A beautiful Chinese military "nurse," who looked more like a movie star and had been sent at the request of the admiral, entered the room to provide "comfort" for this special patient. I am sure she had won some beauty pageant and never attended nursing school. It was the military's way of trying to make amends for the accident that had occurred. When I returned, she was reading a book entitled *Cerebral Hemorrhages*. I asked her to pose for a picture. She obliged, but when I asked her to take Al's pulse while I shot a picture, she demurred and said quietly in Chinese, "You embarrass me."

A bit later, the commanding general of the island's garrison arrived to express his personal regrets and to invite us to have dinner with him after Al had recovered a bit. He was able to do so very quickly, and the pretty nurse, no doubt, contributed to his speedy recovery!

We were ushered to special underground facilities for our dinner. It was probably several stories below the surface and absolutely safe from a massive bomb attack. Again, the general greeted us warmly. Interestingly enough, he was no stranger to me, since I had been in his home on several occasions and Alice had led his son to the Lord several years earlier while he attended the Taipei American school. Again, deep apologies were made by our host, along with offers to make our visit as comfortable as possible.

Due to the circumstances, we were not able to return to Taiwan on our scheduled flight, nor did we have a chance to contact our family members in Taipei. When we did arrive, we were a day late.

The Air Force provided us with transportation to our home, where Margaret Sanders and Alice anxiously waited for us. They knew of the regular shelling of Quemoy and were beginning to wonder whether this had interfered with our return. As we got out of the car, I told Al that we should have a little fun with all that had happened.

My beige overcoat was bloody from pulling Al out his jeep, and his entire head was still wrapped with a huge white bandage. I decided to pull one of my arms out of the sleeve and let the loose sleeve dangle. When Alice and Margaret spotted Al and me, they rushed out to welcome us. Seeing Al's head and only one of my arms, their smiles quickly turned to consternation. Simultaneously, both said, "What happened?"

Putting on a brave demeanor, I calmly answered, "Never mind. Just thank the Lord that we're alive!"

We were able to have a good laugh afterwards, although our women did not think this was very funny at the time. They were probably right.

I continued as Taiwan correspondent for the Far East News Service until 1963. I was able to meet government officials and news reporters I never would have had the opportunity of meeting otherwise. I remember meetings with one of the reporters of the Chinese News Agency who loved classical music. I would hang out with him at a special coffee bar where all they played was "long-hair" music. While I liked some of it, I was even more intent on establishing personal friendships and relationships. Many of these led to a personal sharing of the Good News and in-depth discussions on the purpose of life.

Sometimes, God allows us to sow the seed. Other times He calls us to water and nurture what others have sown. At still other times, He provides opportunities to reap. No matter which of these comes our way, it is God who is at work in the lives of people. It has been my privilege to experience that again and again.

31

FRANK'S $7,000 CHECK

1962

Taipei

I had never met Frank before, but his brother, who was closely connected with OC, had shared with him that a missionary family in Taiwan needed regular financial support. Frank was a businessman in the States and he responded to his brother's challenge. We were the missionary family he began to support. A couple of years later, Frank showed up in Taipei and we got acquainted.

The two of us immediately clicked. I was able to help him with an important contact for his business and this sealed our friendship. Frank had an exuberant personality, always on the go and talking a mile a minute. There never was a dull moment around him and we enjoyed our time together. Although he had been raised with a Christian background, I wondered even then whether he really had a personal relationship with God.

One day, while driving together through Taipei dodging bicycles and pedicabs, Frank suddenly turned to me and asked,

"When did you have your last vacation?" I told him that it was some time ago. "Where would you like to go?" he asked next. My reply was that we had been invited to go to Japan by some missionary friends, but that this was really out of the question due to the travel costs involved.

"No need to worry about that, I'll take care of it," was Frank's instant response. With that, he pulled out a pen and wrote a check which covered all our expenses. I was flabbergasted and thrilled.

Alice and I immediately got busy and made the necessary travel arrangements for us, Marty, and Lita. What a totally unexpected gift from heaven this was.

The night before leaving, Frank called from Tokyo to verify our flight arrival and say he would be there to meet us. Just before hanging up, he said, "By the way, Tammy will be with me. She's a really nice girl and you'll really like her." I thought, *this is going to be an interesting trip.*

When we landed in Tokyo, sure enough, Frank was there. With him was Tammy, a young and attractive Japanese gal. They rushed us to their nice apartment in downtown Tokyo and wanted us to feel right at home. Tammy brought a pair of slippers, served tea, and then asked me whether I would like a bath and massage. Alice was quick to respond: "No, he doesn't need one, but I would love one."

While Alice was getting her massage, Frank proceeded to fill me in on the relationship he enjoyed with Tammy. He said he'd met her in a bar where she worked as a geisha, providing for all the comforts of the customers. She had been forced into this type of work to provide an income for her family. Frank had "rescued" her from this lifestyle, bought the apartment, and now provided for her and her family as well. I did not bring up the fact that Frank was married. Obviously, his wife in the States did not know anything about these acts of "compassion."

Later, Frank and Tammy showed us around their apartment, including their bedroom. He drew special attention to a Bible on the nightstand. "We read this Bible together every night before we go to bed. Tammy has already made real progress in becoming a Christian—she's quit smoking."

Alice and I both gulped inwardly. We realized that the Lord must have brought us here for a special purpose.

The next day, Frank took us to the movie *Gone with the Wind* and treated us to a huge banquet in a fancy restaurant. Since it was summertime, hot and humid, he made arrangements for a private taxi to take us that night on our eight-hour ride to Lake Nojiri, the destination for our vacation. Before saying goodbye, he promised that he and Tammy would come and join us for a couple of days in the next couple of weeks.

True to his word, they did come. Alice and I found ourselves in a quandary. We had two bedrooms, one for us and one for the children. We arranged to put the kids in our bedroom and prepared the other for Frank and Tammy. Fortunately, we thought, there were two beds available for them.

"This is great," Frank said enthusiastically when he saw the room. "This bed is for us, and the other for our suitcases." And with that he threw their luggage on the bed.

We went swimming together, played tennis, ate, and had a good time. The evenings provided us with stimulating conversations. One thing I discovered was that Frank was quite well versed in the Scriptures. He obviously realized I had some serious questions about his lifestyle and was quick to acquaint me with his theology. He believed that once a person had been saved, he would always be saved, and that nothing he did would deprive him of eternal life. He was able to proof-text this belief by citing various Bible verses.

While his theology was correct, Frank had missed the truth that new life in Christ demanded a revolutionary change in value system and lifestyle. If that didn't happen, it raised serious doubt whether one was truly saved. I chose not to make an issue of this at the time, because my main concern was to keep the door open and to reassure him of my personal friendship and love for him. Of course, prayer for him was an integral part of this. I believed the day would come when God would open his eyes to the truth.

As the years passed, Frank continued to stand behind us financially, and we met from time to time. He brought Tammy down to stay with us in Taiwan so we could help her become "a better Christian." We were on the way to helping her when, unfortunately, she made contact with another missionary who started "making eyes" at her. This was not at all helpful, so we thought it better for that visit to come to a close.

Frank did not give up on Tammy. When we were on furlough in Glendale, California in 1964, he brought her to the States and asked whether we might be able to host her for a period of time while he went home to take care of his business and saw his wife. I was attending classes at Fuller Theological Seminary, which kept me very busy, so the burden was on Alice to take care of Tammy.

One day, Alice and Tammy decided to visit Forest Lawn Memorial Park in Glendale, located near where we were staying. At the conclusion of their visit, they went to view the magnificent picture of the Crucifixion painted by the noted Polish artist Jan Styka. This picture, displayed on a screen that is 195 feet by 45 feet, describes the scenes surrounding the death of Christ. It is a breathtaking experience in every sense of the word.

After Alice and Tammy left the auditorium, they sat for quite a while in the car, during which Alice again related the basic elements of the gospel and how to develop a personal relationship with Jesus Christ. Tammy nodded her head, deeply moved by what she had seen and heard.

When Alice finally asked her whether she was willing to invite Christ into her life, Tammy opened her purse. Slowly she pulled out a check for seven thousand dollars, an enormous amount in 1963. She mentioned that Frank had given this to her to use in case anything happened to him. Quietly, she said, "If I ask Jesus to come into my heart, then I would have to give this up." After a few more moments, she added, "I just can't do that."

Tammy realized the cost that was involved in becoming a follower of Christ. She'd decided the price was too high.

As the years passed, I stayed in touch with Frank. Whenever I came back to the States for a brief visit, I called him or we got together. He considered me a close friend and shared things with me concerning his business that he even kept from his own family. In fact, his son called me every now and then to ask what his father was up to.

A few years after Tammy's visit to Glendale, Frank separated from her. He befriended a young lady from Korea after helping her come to the States. Frank had divorced his wife, and though this woman was fifty years younger, she and Frank eventually married. In fact, Frank fathered two sons after he was seventy-five years old!

It was on one of my visits to the States that I saw Frank again. I had just finished a Sunday morning service and he invited me to come to his home for lunch. That afternoon, as we sat around the pool, he told me a story which I will never forget.

Frank had recently joined a Nazarene church. The preacher had given a "hellfire and brimstone" sermon and it had really gotten to him. Frank went forward at the invitation after the sermon, repented of his sin, and asked Christ to come into his life.

"You don't know, Hans, what kind of a guy I have been," Frank said. I responded that I had something of an idea of his lifestyle. Then he began to unpack his tragic story.

Frank's son had been a missionary leader in Southeast Asia and was happily married, with a number of children. Frank invited the son to visit him in Japan. There, Frank introduced him to a prostitute. This Christian leader fell, and he fell hard. It led to the breakup of his marriage and the end of his missionary career.

As Frank told me this, I could see his heart was broken.

"How," he asked, "could God ever forgive me for what I've done?" Yet that Sunday in the Nazarene church, he had confessed his sin and received a new understanding of the grace of God. He'd experienced forgiveness for all he had done. "I am free of all guilt," Frank said, "because God loved me and the Lord Jesus paid the penalty when He died for me on the cross."

This event changed Frank's life. He was an old man, but he became a new man. Now he could not get enough of the Bible. He told me, "I have one in every room in my house, even in the bathroom!" He taught his two young boys to memorize Bible verses and had them quote them to me on subsequent visits. Every now and then, Frank called me and asked, "Have you read your Bible today?"

You cannot imagine my joy to see this transformed life, a real trophy of God's grace.

When Frank was hospitalized for a time, I went to see him and asked point blank, "Frank, are you ready to meet God?"

With a radiant glow on his face, he responded, "You bet I am, because Jesus is my Savior."

When I later heard that Frank had passed into eternity, I went to his memorial service. I wanted to be there when my old friend was given his final farewell. I had not intended to say anything at the service, but his brother, knowing of our close relationship, asked me to speak. Many of Frank's old cronies from his earlier life had gathered to pay their final respects, and I felt here was my chance to let them know about the transformation that had occurred.

"Many of you have known Frank for a long time," I began. "But today, I want to tell you about the Frank you never knew." I shared the story of our friendship over many years, and then talked about the change that had taken place in his life. I closed with these thoughts: "Frank would have only one wish for all of you, that you too would discover real purpose in life by coming to know Jesus Christ in a personal way—before it is too late."

Frank's story is the wonderful account of a faithful God who pursued him until his old age, never giving up on him because He wanted him to share in the glories of heaven. Frank had pursued heaven on earth by every means he could, but none of the pleasures that this life afforded were enough to satisfy the longing and thirst of his heart.

God had stepped in and revealed Himself to him. This encounter was so powerful that Frank became "a new creation" through Christ—all of it thanks to the mercy of a loving God. Yes, there was a purpose to Frank's life. His only regret was that it took so long for him to discover it.

32

PREPARE TO BURY YOUR DAUGHTER

1963

Taipei

Someone knocked at our front door—it was Dr. Donald Dale, our family doctor. The news he brought was not good. It concerned our daughter Lita, then almost three years old. We were preparing to go back to the States for our furlough and planned to travel via Germany to visit my parents for a short time. The doctor knew this when he made the statement, "You really should make preparations to bury your daughter in Germany, since she has only three months to live."

You can imagine the bombshell this was.

But let me allow you to read the story from Lita herself in a letter she wrote in November 1978:

> This month I want to share with you something about myself.
>
> I was born in Taiwan (Nationalist China) because my parents were missionaries there. I lived there

until I was three years old. I don't remember Taiwan at all (nor do I speak Chinese), but my mother used to tell me a story about a family who lived there at the same time we did.

This family was a happy one. They had two children—a son and a daughter, ages five and three. The kids were full of life and very happy. One day the mother noticed that the little girl hadn't been feeling her normal happy self for a few weeks, so she took her daughter to the doctor to have a checkup. About a week or so later, the results came back. The little girl had leukemia. This cancer had affected 85 percent of her blood, and she was only expected to live for another three months.

As you can imagine, this news came as quite a blow to the parents. They never dreamed that this was the problem with their little girl. However, there was a strange peace in their hearts, because just before this news had come to them the parents felt that God wanted them to completely give their daughter to Him. So, whatever He had in store for her life was His will. The mother proceeded to give away all her daughter's clothing because in a short while the girl would not need them anymore.

In this same city lived a woman with great faith in God. She believed that God would cure this little girl completely and she went off to collect all the clothes the little girl's mother had given away. She also started a prayer chain over the complete island of Taiwan. So there were people praying that the family didn't even know. The girl was taken in for more exams. And to the doctors' surprise, the results were negative! God had answered the prayers of His people.

As proof that God answers prayer, I am here today—I am that girl! It has been fifteen years since this happened. Just recently I have learned to recognize and appreciate what God has done, because my life is a present from Him!

"But watch out! Be very careful never to forget what you have seen God doing for you. May his miracles have a deep and permanent effect upon your lives! Tell your children and your grandchildren about the glorious miracles he did (Deuteronomy 4:9 TLB)."

This is a miracle that God has done in my life. My mother and father passed this story on to me and I hope to pass it on to my children some day. God is doing these things in our every day lives. Let me just challenge you to think about what God is doing in your life and to pass it on to others so that they might give the glory to Him."

I think Lita has captured the essence of the story well. As we look back, we are grateful for experiences such as this one. We have had the privilege again and again to encounter His miracles in our lives. His purposes stand firm, and whether it is by life or by death, He is the one in full control. We are glad that in this instance, He preserved Lita's life. It has become another, lifelong reason for being grateful to Him.

33

FULLER THEOLOGICAL SEMINARY

1963

Pasadena, California

After five years in the field, it was time to return to the States. We arrived in the summer of 1963, and I immediately enrolled at Fuller Theological Seminary in Pasadena, California. Why seminary after nearly ten years of missionary work?

The answer is simple. Our opportunities for ministry in Taiwan had shifted from direct evangelism to church-related ministries. Thousands in army schools and high schools had made the decision to follow Christ, and a Bible correspondence course had been established to guide them. To further assist them in the growth of their faith, a simple course had been written by Roy Robertson of the Navigators, and thousands had enrolled to study it by correspondence. Our office staff of nearly thirty handled the applications that poured in.

As soon as these students completed a lesson, they returned it to our office. It was then corrected and mailed back with the next lesson. This process continued until they had finished at least eight lessons. It was a huge undertaking for us, especially since we probably had several hundred thousand people enrolled in the course. They came from every part of the island. We were able to supply names of these students to any missionary interested in church planting in practically every area.

But this soon led to another concern. Churches were not able to integrate these students into their congregations. Why? The church leaders lacked the know-how. They had never been trained themselves. Our emphasis began to shift to a more church-related ministry and to assist pastors in building up their flocks.

There was a problem connected with this new approach. Pastors often asked me, "Are you an ordained minister?" I had to tell them no. This was often followed by a second question: "Where did you go to seminary?" Again, I had to admit I had never attended seminary. To add insult to injury, they would look at me and ask, "How old are you?"

For this reason, I felt I should attend seminary for at least a year and seek ordination. The question of age, given time, would resolve itself.

I chose Fuller Theological Seminary since a number of my friends had attended in the past and others were enrolled at the time. I had met Dr. Charles E. Fuller, the renowned speaker of the *Old Fashioned Revival Hour,* who had cofounded the school along with Dr. Harold Ockenga from Boston, when I helped with counseling after his radio broadcast originating from Long Beach, California. Dan Fuller, his son and now dean of the faculty at Fuller Seminary, and I had teamed up together during my time at UCLA in Campus Crusade ministries. So I felt good about going there.

I did have one apprehension, however. At age thirty-two and having been out of the world of academia for ten years, how could I keep up with all these young students? I soon discovered, however, that this was not a problem. I began to enjoy each class I took. I registered as a "special student" since I wanted to pick the topics most pertinent to my ministry in Taiwan and get the most out of the one year I was on furlough. I selected courses in systematic theology, church history, Greek, ethics, and biblical studies. I was challenged not only by the study materials, but also by the godly qualities of the professors who taught us. Among these, Everett F. Harrison, Clarence Roddy, Gleason Archer, Paul Jewett, Geoffrey Bromily, Allan Tippet, and David A. Hubbard stood out. Some of their prayers before their lectures blessed me as much as what they presented to us, because they were a reflection of the inner man.

These disciplined studies opened up a new world for me. But the more I got involved, the more I wondered whether I had made the right choice. I was beginning to see the advantages of completing my whole seminary program leading to a degree, instead of just picking and choosing. This conviction grew in my heart, and I approached the mission leadership about extending my furlough to allow me to finish my training. They responded favorably, with the added request that I finish as quickly as possible in order to return to the field. This I promised to do, and I started to double up on courses. As a matter of fact, I finished nearly all of the three-year program in two years.

But this intensive study program was not without serious shortcomings. While I enjoyed my studies immensely, I gradually began to neglect family relationships. In addition, I had been asked to teach a large adult Sunday class at Glendale Presbyterian Church which further ate into my time schedule. And then there were the regular missionary speaking commitments and missionary conferences. Much, much later, when I looked over my calendar of appointments for those years, I commented to Alice that I must have been insane.

Yet then, I was totally oblivious to it all.

One day, Alice, who was longing for some kind of personal communication and interaction, asked me to share with her what I was studying at the time. I said, "You wouldn't understand it if I told you. Here's the book, you can read it for yourself." To make things worse, this particular book dealt with a course on marriage counseling.

At another time in the early fall, Alice asked when we could sit down together and talk over some important issues. I looked at my calendar and said I could carve out some time around Thanksgiving! Looking back to that time, and even writing about it at this stage, leaves me stunned by my insensitivity and loss of priorities. Yes, I did well in school, but in the process nearly lost my family and marriage. A year or so later, the full impact of this hit me. Once the pressures and priorities of studies were over, our separate paths merged once again. It was only the grace and mercy of God that protected us from disaster.

During these years at Fuller, my wife took the full brunt of all the work at home, the upbringing of our children, and just keeping things going. Without her, I could not have made it. All marriages are made in heaven, so the saying goes. I know that this one was and I am eternally grateful for the faithful, supporting, and loving wife the Lord gave to me, who put up with all my foolish ways.

Later on, I realized that many seminary students experienced the same struggles, and some marriages did not survive.

I was finishing my second year at Fuller and had completed all of my classes, with the exception of a couple reading courses. I hoped to graduate that summer. To my surprise, however, the registrar informed me that my graduation application had been turned down. No one had finished the whole degree program in two years before, I was told. It would not make the seminary look very good if they allowed this, so I was asked to return to school in the fall of 1965 to finish off. I was stunned, because I was anxious to return to the field. I realized God must have had a purpose in all of this. I wondered what it was.

In the meantime, something which puzzled me was slowly taking root in my life. It did not make sense to me, but that would soon change.

34

LORD, IT DOESN'T MAKE SENSE

May 6, 1965

Fuller Theological Seminary, Pasadena

It was my last class in homiletics. Due to my missionary experience, a number of preaching sessions had been waived, but here I was with one more opportunity to speak to students of the senior class. They would soon head out into a world of reality after having been involved in academia for several years.

The text which had been assigned to me was Acts 8:26–40, the story of Philip the evangelist and the Ethiopian eunuch. God had directed him to leave an exciting field of ministry in Samaria, where a revival had broken out, and go into the desert where God wanted him to pursue one man who needed help. When I prepared my message, I asked God to allow me to have a special word for the graduating students that would help them discover God's place for them in the ministry.

As I spoke that morning, I challenged them to consider the basic criteria for determining God's will for their lives. In Philip's case, God's direction for him was not where the opportunity was the greatest or the need the most severe. It is so easy to think God wants us to serve Him where we have the greatest potential to accomplish great things for Him. Or, if that is not the case, to go where people need Him the most. Neither case applied to Philip when he left the revival in Samaria and attached himself to a lonely traveler in the desert.

What was the criterion that forced him to make that decision? Simply to listen to God's voice and then obey it. I told the students, "It might not make sense to you. Humanly speaking, it might be a waste. However, if God has spoken, there is no other option but to obey and follow His direction!"

The words were no sooner out of my mouth than I sensed God's hand on my shoulder and His whisper in my ear:

> Well said! That's what I have been trying to tell you all these weeks.

I knew immediately what this meant and it came as a shock.

For the previous couple of months, I had awakened each morning with a strange burden for Brazil on my heart. Where it came from, I did not know. But it seemed to increase steadily. I would pick up a magazine, and Brazil would stare me in the face. I would listen to a news report, and there was Brazil once again. I would bump into people who had just gone or were going to Brazil. Was God trying to say something to me about that country? Impossible.

But the more I tried to put it out of my mind, the more it seemed to bore its way into my heart. Did God have a change of direction in mind for us? I could not imagine it and therefore did not even want to broach the subject to my wife. Here I was, born and raised in China, speaking Chinese, and loving the ministry God had given us in Taiwan. How could God with all of this now change directions in my life and send me to Brazil, an unknown country with an unknown language?

Lord, it just doesn't make sense, I thought.

And now I found myself preaching to the class of 1965

at Fuller Theological Seminary about how to discover God's direction for their lives. This is where God spoke loudly and clearly. I am not sure how I finished my sermon or what grade I received. But I knew that I had heard a sermon that was directed to my own heart and had come through my own lips.

When I got home that afternoon, I said to Alice, "I need to share something very important with you, Honey. You better sit down." Then, trying to stay as calm as possible, I said, "I don't think we'll be returning to Taiwan."

Alice matched my calmness and replied, "I have known that for some time. In fact, it has been quite a while. When we packed to come home last year, I packed our things so that they could be shipped to us."

Now came the second blow. Briefly, I recounted what I had been experiencing the past few weeks concerning Brazil. It had seemed so illogical to me that I had not even wanted to burden her with it. "But," I said, "God spoke powerfully to me as I was preaching. It was too big to miss. There is no question in my mind now—He wants us to go to Brazil."

Alice's reply totally stunned me: "I have known this too, because the Lord has been talking to me about Brazil as well."

Now it was my turn to sit down! I could not believe it. Both of us, independently, had come to the same conviction that God was directing us along a new path. We did not understand all that this entailed, but we were sure that we were discerning His will and purpose for our lives.

Three days later I was involved in a missions conference with Dick Hillis, our mission director. I did not get a chance to speak to him, but before slipping out for another engagement, I handed him a note that read, "Dick, I really need to talk with you about something important."

A few days later, I met Dick in the living room of a friend in Hesperia, California. Alice went with me for this important rendezvous. It was one thing for a missionary to be convinced of what he felt God's will was, but to get the mission to agree to it was another thing. As we sat down, Dick asked me to share what was on my mind.

I began to rehearse God's dealings with me and my struggles to understand what He meant by all that I was experiencing. I expected Dick to interrupt me momentarily, but he didn't. He just let me talk and quietly sat there listening.

After I finished, there was a long silence. This surprised me, because it was totally out of character for Dick. He usually was two jumps ahead, and was what we call "a fast mover."

Finally, Dick spoke. And when he did, it was deliberate and to the point.

"Hans, you might never believe this," he said. "For the past few months I have had a deep conviction that the Wilhelms need to be in Brazil. But I was afraid to talk to you about this, because I knew that you loved the Chinese people and I just was not sure that I could do this to you."

Then a big smile rose in his cheeks. "But since you've brought it up, we can talk about it now," he said. "I know it doesn't make sense, but if God has directed you, and has told me the same thing that He told you and Alice, then I know He is in this."

Alice and I drove back to our home in Glendale, our hearts filled with a deep sense of peace. Dick's affirmation of God's leading brought new light to Matthew 18:19: "Again, I tell you that if two of you on earth agree about anything you ask for, it will be done for you by my Father in heaven." Three of us, independently, had come to agree that this was from God. There was no longer any doubt that we were moving forward in His will.

Dick had mentioned that he needed to consult the board on this important decision. The answer came quickly. The letter from the secretary of the board stated that while this shift in our assignment did not make sense humanly speaking, there was an unshakable conviction among the board members that God was in this. They gave a big green light to proceed.

Twelve years earlier, the Lord had pointed my attention

toward South America. At that time, I still had Germany on my mind. I'd said, "Lord, you cannot be serious about sending me to South America."

There was a struggle in my heart, but my commitment to unconditional obedience had finally won out and I had yielded to Him: "Lord, if you really want me to go to South America, I will go there."

God, however, had sent me to work among the Chinese instead, and we had ten challenging and satisfying years in Taiwan. Now He was cashing in on my promise. Even though it did not make sense, I was filled with new confidence that the Lord was fulfilling His purposes in mysterious and wonderful ways.

35

Delta Flight 824

1965

Pasadena

Since Fuller Seminary had requested that I finish my degree program in the fall of 1965, I scheduled a fairly heavy load of missionary meetings and conferences in preparation for our upcoming ministry in Brazil. Again and again, I saw God open up doors and opportunities beyond my wildest dreams.

One of these doors involved a trip to Indiana, where I was scheduled to speak in two meetings. The Lord brought me in touch with a carpet salesman, Jim Jorges, who invited me to come to Chattanooga, Tennessee. During my week in Tennessee, Jim arranged for me to speak at twenty meetings, and I had great opportunities to present the vision and burden God had given us for Brazil.

All in all, I spoke at sixty meetings during the forty days I was gone from home. I loved every minute of it, except that I really missed Alice and the family.

In November, I was invited to return to Chattanooga to

speak at a missionary conference of First Presbyterian Church. Before taking off for the week, I had to turn in an important paper for one of my classes at Fuller. The topic was "Literary Techniques of the Prophets." I had not done any research for this and so was facing a real deadline when the invitation to go to Chattanooga reached me. The day before leaving on my flight, I went to the library and picked up a half dozen German volumes which were collecting dust in the vaults. To my surprise, they were exactly what I was looking for. What an advantage I had over my fellow students who were not able to make use of these excellent resources.

I worked all night on my paper and was able to finish it by daybreak. I rushed it to a friend who'd promised to deliver it to my professor. After a quick shower, I headed for the airport and boarded Delta Flight 824 to Atlanta, which would connect to a flight to Chattanooga.

As I settled down in my seat, a heavy weariness settled on me. All I wanted to do was sleep. Since the seat next to me was empty, I shot up a quick prayer: "Lord, don't let anyone sit here, please." To make my point, I laid my coat on the empty seat. I was tired and not in the mood to talk to anyone, let alone a stranger.

As passengers entered, they took a look at the seat next to me and passed on. I viewed each pass as an answer to prayer. Finally, the plane was full and they closed the door. I settled back in my seat with a grateful heart.

Then there was a slight delay, the door was reopened, and one more passenger was admitted. Since the seat next to me was the only one left on the plane, I quickly removed my coat, and he took the coveted seat. After a quick nod to greet him, I pulled out a pillow and tried to sleep. I felt that this would give him a signal not to engage me in a conversation.

Shortly after takeoff, breakfast was served. As I pulled out my tray and started to eat, I had a change of heart. I felt it would be rude to not engage in some small talk.

"Hi, where are you headed?" I asked. His reply affirmed

the obvious: Atlanta. _What a dumb question,_ I thought. Equally lacking was my response: "So am I." Where else could I be going on this nonstop flight, unless I planned to exit the plane in midair?

After this intelligent start, we began to exchange more pertinent information. He was an engineer from New York and was headed back there. He had immigrated to the United States from South Africa, where his Jewish parents had found refuge after fleeing Nazi Germany before World War II. In fact, he told me that most of his relatives had died in German concentration camps during the war.

Then it happened. I am not sure just what prompted me to say it, but I turned to him and blurted out, "I am a German, and during the war years, I was a proud member of the Hitler Youth movement and greatly admired Adolf Hitler."

The look on this Jewish man's face was as if a bolt of lightning had struck him. I have learned that rule number one when sharing something important is to capture the other person's attention. Mission accomplished!

Quickly, I assured the man that my life was no longer the same, that I had experienced a tremendous transformation. When he asked what had caused this change in my life, I knew why God had seated me with this man. All weariness of mind and body suddenly disappeared. I immediately came to the point: "My life totally changed when I met Jesus Christ and came to know God in a personal way." He listened intently as I shared my personal journey and how I had come to faith as a teenager in Shanghai.

I sensed relief sweep over him as I told him about my pilgrimage in search for the truth. I asked where _he_ stood spiritually. His family, he said, was of orthodox Jewish background, but he was more liberal and not so well versed in the Scriptures. Of course, by that he meant the Old Testament.

I had recently read a book by Martin Buber, one of the foremost Jewish theologians. I asked whether he had ever heard of Buber. He replied affirmatively, and so to build a connection with him, I mentioned what Buber had emphatically stated, that the greatest contribution of Judaism was not just the concept of a monotheistic God in a polytheistic world, but rather that God was a personal God, one who had a name, and one who could be known by us personally.

He admitted that he had never heard of this, but the statement intrigued him. I knew what was coming next. "Just how," he said, "does a person come to know God personally?"

This was the question I wanted to answer more than any in the world. One of the verses I related was John 1:18: "No one has ever seen God, but God the One and Only, who is at the Father's side, has made him known." For the next few hours we had all the time we needed to go into detail on how to move into a personal relationship with the Lord.

When our flight landed in Atlanta, I had to move quickly to catch my connecting flight to Chattanooga. My Jewish friend insisted on accompanying me to my gate. Before taking his leave, he embraced me and said, "I want to thank you for sharing Christ with me. The first thing I will do when I get to New York is to buy a New Testament." And then he was gone.

I have often regretted not getting this man's address or phone number. Only eternity will reveal the outcome of the seed that was sown on that Delta flight. I have thanked God many times for the opportunity to share His Son with this son of Israel. I arrived in Chattanooga with my adrenaline still pumping through my veins. There was not a trace of tiredness even though I had not slept for thirty-six hours! Indeed, it had been a flight with a purpose, even though I had nearly missed the opportunity He had provided.

The Lord also blessed my efforts on the paper I'd turned in before my flight. It apparently surprised my professor, who happened to be the president of Fuller Theological Seminary. He gave me an "A" and wrote in the margin, "This is an excellent paper. Thanks for calling my attention to some of these German works which I haven't had a chance to look up. When you come back on your next furlough with Portuguese under your belt, you will have even better linguistic equipment! As a technical study, this is the best paper yet turned in for this course."

36

Donald McGavran, Missionary Giant

Fall 1965

Pasadena

Little did I understand the workings of God when the faculty of Fuller Theological Seminary denied me early graduation. He had some special things in store for me which I could not begin to imagine.

In the fall of 1965, Fuller launched its new School of World Mission. Dr. Donald McGavran was appointed as its first dean and senior professor of mission, church growth, and South Asian studies. He had grown up in India as the son of missionary parents. As a missionary himself, he had spent much of his life trying to overcome social barriers to Christian conversion.

McGavran, known as the father of the church growth movement, developed his church growth principles after rejecting the popular view that mission was "philanthropy, education, medicine, famine relief, evangelism, and world friendship." He became convinced that good deeds, while necessary, "must never replace the essential task of mission, discipling the peoples of the earth."

There is no doubt that McGavran ranks along with William Carey, Hudson Taylor, and Cameron Townsend as one of the key pioneers of the modern missionary movement. To have had the opportunity to claim Donald McGavran as one of my mentors is a unique privilege I will always treasure.

When I returned to Fuller to complete a couple of courses, this coincided with the beginnings of the School of World Mission, and I was privileged to be in Dr. McGavran's first class. Since we were only about a dozen students, most of us with missionary experience, we were able to develop close personal relationships with him and the other members of the new faculty.

A special bonus was a class on church growth in Brazil taught by William Read, a veteran missionary from that country. I could not have had a better introduction into ministry in that country. Not only was I able to read and study about fifty books on Brazil, but I also had mentors who could bring perspective to the unprecedented growth there.

Shortly before leaving for Brazil, I needed to complete one more matter before returning to the mission field: ordination. What an honor, therefore, to have two outstanding leaders participate in this event. Rev. Norman L. Cummings, home director of OC at that time, gave the ordination address and Dr. Donald McGavran came to deliver the charge to me as the candidate.

His words profoundly moved me that day, and still move me every time I read them:

> Brother Hans Wilhelm, at the conclusion of these
> years of your theological and missionary training,
> as you are being ordained for the lifelong ministry
> of the church, and as you set out to Brazil as a
> missionary of the gospel, it is my happy privilege

to give you the charge; that is, to adjure you in the most solemn way possible, to perform your high calling as a messenger of God.

I charge you, remember, in the presence of God and Jesus Christ. He is witness to these proceedings. What I say and what you hear, that is all known to God. So I must speak with care. Nothing light or of secondary importance must occupy my time. You must listen with attention and do with diligence, for Scripture declares that He in whose presence we now stand, "is to judge the living and the dead." We shall give answer to Him.

I charge you, first, give yourself without stint to the ministry of reconciliation. As God was in Christ, reconciling the world to Himself, so He has entrusted to you the message of reconciliation. You are an ambassador for Christ, God making His appeal through you. The reconciliation of which the Scriptures speak here is not horizontal reconciliation, but vertical reconciliation; not that of man to man, but of man to God. Devote yourself then, without stint, to announcing that the King is just and merciful, and does not desire that any should be lost. Plead with men to make Him their Savior who will be their judge.

I charge you secondly, to preach the gospel, the amazing Good News that God has opened a way to forgiveness through the atonement of His Son on Calvary. Preach the atonement. Preach the gospel. Never substitute the many good and true and beautiful things in the Christian way for the Good News of Jesus Christ. Let your consciousness of its grace and glory grow in you day by day and year by year. The gospel is the power of God to salvation. Always be proud of it.

As you go to Brazil, I charge you specifically to master the Portuguese language so that you can preach the gospel in beautiful Portuguese. God has granted you ability in languages. Use it unfailingly as a vehicle without parallel for the Good New of His Son our Savior.

Preach the gospel in confident expectation that through it multitudes will be brought to conviction of sin, repentance, and belief into life eternal. Attempt great things for God through your preaching and expect great things from God. Refuse to be discouraged by the first few months or, it may be, years, when you feel hampered by a foreign language. You are a missionary of the gospel. Continue to preach till the liberating message sings itself from your lips and wings its way to many a heart. Preach for decision. Preach for a verdict. Preach before judgment, that you may rejoice not weep at judgment.

Thirdly, I charge you, who are being ordained as a missionary of the gospel of Christ in these troublous times, to take your share of suffering for the gospel's sake as a good soldier of Jesus Christ. We must enter the Kingdom of God through many tribulations. Count yourself fortunate when you are counted worthy to share His sufferings. I charge you then to become an active member of that band of disciples who bear about in their bodies and their spirits the marks of the Lord Jesus. There is no cheap entrance ticket to the redemptive society. The way is daily to deny yourself and take up your cross and follow Him. I commend to you the words of Jacob Riis who, when all his comrades had died on the west coast of Africa a hundred years ago and when he was commanded by his board to give up the mission and return to Germany his homeland, replied, "Africa must be won for Christ, though a thousand perish."

Finally, I charge you, as Paul did Timothy, to take heed to yourself. Christ's minister must look to himself. Be conscious that you are a minister of Christ by command of God, and live every hour in that consciousness. You bring a rich heritage to your ministry. Your missionary parents, your godly forbears, and your God Himself are all witnesses this day. Be much in prayer. Be well versed in His Word. Spend your time as befits God's ambassador. Choose your amusements as one on the King's business. Determine the main emphases of the years of labor God grants you, knowing that we shall all account for our stewardship to the Righteous Judge. Among the multitudinous field of labor in Brazil, determine where you will spend your life, not according to your wishes, but according to His will. Take heed to yourself, man of God, every day of every year, and every moment of every day, be a man in Christ.

These words from this missionary giant and world statesman are a sacred treasure which will accompany the rest of my life. I felt as I was standing in the presence of one of the early apostles. Donald McGavran, the "apostle of church growth," bared his soul and commitment to the gospel in these profound words. They shall never be forgotten.

For many years, Dr. McGavran, or "Dr. Mac" as we used to call him, served on the board of directors of OC. Even while in the field, I received letters and notes from him. When there was opportunity, I looked him up in his office at Fuller Seminary. I always walked away refreshed and challenged by the faith and vision of this man.

One more remembrance sticks with me.

"Gentlemen, what is the time of day?" the white-haired Dr. McGavran, then seventy-seven, said as he looked around the OC boardroom, his keen, alert eyes penetrating every single individual. "Many mistakes are being made in missions today because too many think it is May when it is September! This is not the time for sowing; it is the time for reaping. This is harvest season."

Dr. McGavran concluded his remarks by saying that the "holy, unprecedented receptivity" to the gospel in many parts of the world at that time demanded an unflagging commitment to Christ's Great Commission of "discipling the nations."

There is no doubt that Donald McGavran left a legacy and an indelible imprint upon the growth and development of the missionary enterprise worldwide. He also left an imprint on my life in sharpening my focus. I became more determined than ever to fulfill His purpose for my life.

37

Together at Last

December 1965

Scottsbluff, Nebraska

It was one of the most unforgettable experiences of our lives.

In December 1965, a few months before my parents celebrated their seventieth birthdays, God allowed our whole family to meet and be together for the very first time. He literally brought us together from all over the world: My brother, Fred, traveled from Portland, Oregon. My oldest sister, Eva, came from Germany. Peggy flew in from Washington D.C., and Esther and her family drove in from Chicago. Alice and I flew in with our children from California. We all came to join my sister Anita and my parents in Scottsbluff, Nebraska, for a few days as a complete family!

You can imagine the thrill of being united as a family here on earth. We had come close twelve years earlier during the reunion that Esther missed. Then we were scattered again to different parts of the world. But this time, finally, all had worked out.

There was so much to catch up on, and we really burned the

midnight oil. The laughter, the joy, the stories, the kidding of siblings with each other—all the things we'd never been able to do before, we now had a chance to experience. We loved every moment!

The days passed only too quickly and soon we were dispersed once more. But my mother's prayer had been answered—God was good to us. We had learned that we could never out-give God! He always gives us much more than we ever can realize.

A special thrill was to have our family picture taken. It was the very first one of all of us—and the only one.

We called it our first family reunion. None of us realized it also would be the last. A little over a year later, Esther died suddenly from cancer, leaving three little girls. Esther was just a couple of years younger than I and we had shared many experiences together. Yet I had often ignored her, being too preoccupied with my own friends and agenda. Looking back, I truly regret this. In later adult years, however, I learned to treasure her love and friendship. There was a spiritual kinship I felt with her and this made me sense her loss all the more. We were in Brazil when the sad news reached us, yet it was a tremendous comfort to know that she was with the Lord, in a place far better.

Nine months after that, Papa collapsed and died while going through immigration at the airport in New York. He was returning from his last visit to Germany. News reached us in Brazil a few days later. While the telegram had been sent to us immediately, it had been held at the telegraph office because of some snafu. It was a shock! I had seen my dad just a few months earlier while on a quick trip to the States for board meetings. I never dreamed that this would be my last time to see him.

I had always enjoyed the times we had been together in ministry. Whenever I visited in Nebraska, he asked me to preach in his church. He often set up other meetings for me and always accompanied me to those speaking engagements.

I remember when he came to visit us in Taiwan. I took him to a remote area, where that morning I preached. He was asked to speak as well, but since he had not used Chinese for many years, he asked me to interpret for him. What an honor! Once he caught me on my translation and corrected me in Chinese, to the great delight of the congregation.

Papa was strict, no question about that. Once he disciplined me for something for which I was innocent. But when he found out the truth, he came and asked for my forgiveness. That impressed me!

He also had a great sense of humor, more so outside of the family than within. But we loved his stories.

Now that he was gone, the questions came. If only I could have asked him about this or that. There were so many more things I wished I could have learned about him, his life, his ministry. Now that opportunity was gone for good. All the more reason for me to leave a record behind.

My mother passed away in 1974 in Schooleys Mountain, New Jersey. Mutti had spent the last couple of years in the U.S. home of the Liebenzell Mission. We did not have too much contact with her until she fell ill. Several of us gathered at her bedside and it was a great comfort to her to see several of her children expressing their love for her and for each other.

Three years earlier, I had paid tribute to my mother in a newsletter written to my friends:

> Today is my mother's birthday.
>
> Today she is seventy-five. That is why this day is extra special for all of us and only right that we share it with you, too. Allow me, as a son, to pray tribute to my mother:
>
> I will never forget hearing my mother and father pray for each of us children by name night after night. Often, I saw my mother with her tear-stained face emerging from her bedroom where

she had brought us and our needs before her heavenly Father.

I will never forget the joyful hours my mother sought to give us, whether it was a birthday, Christmas, or some holiday. She made our childhood happy.

I will never forget her response when God called me to leave home and serve Him in Taiwan, even though this would spoil a mother's dream of having her whole family united just once: "If God has called you, I will gladly give you my blessing."

Mutti's life has been full, beginning with her years of service as a deaconess of the Friedenshort with Mother Eva von Thiele-Winkler in Germany, her twenty-six years as a missionary in China, and her years as a pastor's wife in America. And yet, all these years only produced a growing sweetness and gentleness of character that make her a saint indeed. I love it whenever someone asks Alice about her mother-in-law. I love it, because I always know what her answer is. It is, "Mutti is an angel!"

As a family, we give thanks today to God for a mother like this.

"She is a woman of strength and dignity, and has no fear of old age…Her children stand and bless her…a woman who fears and reverences God shall be greatly praised." (Proverbs 31:25, 28, 30, *Living Proverbs*)

And then my brother left us in 2004. Fred did not have an

easy life. The cultural change from China to America during his high school years was traumatic for him. He got into some bad company and after finishing school and an attempt at college, he joined the U.S. Air Force. Again, he went through ups and downs, until he experienced a new spiritual awakening. This was something which my parents did not live to see.

Fred died with an open Bible on his lap. Late in life, he'd been fascinated by the events surrounding our Lord's return and read extensively on this subject. Was it then a surprise to find his Bible opened to Matthew 25, where Jesus spoke of the end times, when Fred entered His presence?

Earthly reunions mean little without the hope and expectation of a heavenly one. Our fervent hope is that God will grant us this eternal reunion.

Without question, one of the shaping influences on our family was the impact of the sacrifice of separation from two of my sisters during the duration of World War II. There was always the fervent hope that in a few years things would change and that we would be reunited as a family. But the wars in China, the Japan-China conflict, and World War II made this impossible.

In retrospect, there are many unanswered questions. For Anita the haunting question throughout her life must have been, "Why was I the one to be left behind?" It could just as easily been one of the rest of us siblings. Why was her life impacted in such a horrendous way?

A letter my dad sent to his sister in Germany shortly after our return to China in 1935 gives a glimpse into the heart of my parents and the obvious pain they bore throughout these many years of separation. He wrote:

> We miss our little sweet Anita very much, and have decided that, if we had to do it over again, we would not leave her behind. It is very hard for us, because we realize that Anita will never have a true and close relationship and contact with her

parents and her siblings. We brought this sacrifice
for Jesus and we pray that He will bless our little
daughter in abundance.

As a family we are thankful that when Anita came to the States she was able to settle in Scottsbluff and be near our parents for the rest of their lives. Nothing could ever make up for the years lost, but it was a small comfort that she was given these years with Mutti and Papa. Anita is grateful that Papa's predictions concerning her relationships with her brothers and sisters did not come true. We are richer for each member of the family God gave us.

If we believe that God has a purpose for our lives, then we can take comfort in the fact that even in this event He had a sovereign plan, though it might be totally outside our ability to comprehend it on this side of eternity. In his 1981 book, *When Bad Things Happen to Good People,* Harold S. Kushner raises this question that has plagued so many people through the ages. However, my conclusion does not coincide with the author's. I am convinced that no matter what happens to us, our God is a God of love as well as an all-powerful, sovereign Lord. He is able to use every circumstance in our lives to accomplish His purposes, as Romans 8:28 states: "And we know that in all things God works for the good of those who love him, who have been called according to His purpose."

This truth of God's sovereign control over all circumstances, including those which touched our family at its core, has been deeply etched into my life.

38

BRAZIL: THE LAND OF "WOW"

April 1966

Atlantic Ocean

Slowly turning south along the northeast coast of South America, the Japanese liner *Argentina Maru* brought us closer and closer to our destination: Brazil, or as a recent National Geographic article described it, "The Land of Wow!" It was a place of unprecedented opportunities, potential, and resources. What it held physically we were also to experience spiritually. The church there was beginning to grow and the response to the gospel was exciting.

Soon we disembarked in Santos, the harbor city for São Paulo, went through customs, met our fellow missionaries, and settled into our new home in São Paulo, a city of fifteen million people. A new chapter in our lives had begun.

While aboard ship, I read from the biography of J. O. Fraser, the great apostle to the Lisu tribe in western China. In one of his earliest letters to friends at home in England, he wrote:

> I am feeling more and more that it is, after all,
> just the prayers of God's people that call down

blessing upon the work, whether they are directly engaged in it or not. Paul may plant and Apollos water, but it is God who gives the increase; and this increase can be brought down from heaven by believing prayer, whether offered in China or in the homeland…Solid lasting missionary work is done on our knees. What I covet more than anything else is earnest, believing prayer.[8]

Leaving Los Angeles once more brought to our hearts the close friendships and relationships which had been forged during our time in California. We were overwhelmed by the love shown us by those who helped us pack our belongings, cleaned our house, provided transportation, and gave gifts. One of the special farewell surprises the Lord gave us came in the way of a check for seven hundred dollars from a sweet Christian friend who did not want to be identified. "Investing it in the Lord's work," she said, "is better than keeping it in the bank." Friends like these committed themselves to pray for us and to keep us financially supported while on the field.

We immediately jumped into the task of learning Portuguese. Despite our past experience, absorbing a new language still required a great deal of discipline and patience. Someone who had gone before expressed it this way:

"You are faced by a mountain, it is called the (*Portuguese, my insertion*) language. It is very steep at first, but gradually seems easier as you go up. Then, just when you feel you are getting on, another peak comes into view, rising higher than the first, but all part of the same mountain. This also has to be climbed. It is called (Brazilian) thought and mode of expression. You had been told about it before you began to scramble up the first mountain, but you did not see it then. And the first glimpse shows how far it is above you."

Even with German, Chinese, and English under my belt, it was a formidable challenge. You can imagine, therefore, the special joy I felt when I was invited to preach in a church in São Paulo—a Chinese church! We discovered that there were four Chinese churches in the city and I thoroughly enjoyed the opportunity of ministering again in Chinese, the language of my birth. The warm-heartedness of our Chinese friends brought back many memories of our time in Taiwan and we thanked God for the opportunity to minister to Chinese in a strange land.

Two weeks after that invitation, I attended services in a German-speaking congregation a few blocks from our home. It never ceases to amaze me how God orchestrates events in our lives and bring them to us just when we need them the most.

Of course, there were funny stories that reflected our struggles with the language. Like the time when I went to a pharmacy and asked for onions, when I really was looking for aspirin tablets.

Our language deficiencies sometimes led to more serious consequences. One afternoon, I received an urgent telephone call from Alice while I was in the office in downtown São Paulo. "You better come home quickly," she said. "Something terrible has happened to all of your books."

I have always loved books and been fond of my library. As soon as I heard this, I raced home in the pouring rain. When I walked into our courtyard, I could hardly believe my eyes. There were all of my precious books, spread out across the driveway, face up, and it was just pouring cats and dogs. I couldn't believe it! Who could have done this to me?

What had happened was that our Brazilian helper had misunderstood my wife's Portuguese. Alice intended to ask her to dust off my books. Instead, our helper took them all out of the house to be sunned and aired. When a sudden tropical rainstorm struck, the books were not "dry cleaned" but went through the laundry instead.

You can imagine that I was not too happy about this. But our helper was totally nonplussed about the whole thing. She felt that this was not really her fault, but God's, since He was the one who had sent the rain. Now that many years have passed, I can laugh about it, but it was no laughing matter then.

Then there was Maria, another woman who came to help Alice in our home. The image of a maid is usually one of someone in a crisp uniform, efficiently running a household. But our Maria was different. All her life she had lived in a humble shack. No electricity, no running water.

About two years before our arrival she had become a follower of Christ. With new motivation, she started working as a maid in other people's homes. Since she could not read or write, this was all she could do. Then she discovered she had a tumor. She sold what little furniture she had to try to pay for her operation. Then she lost most of her front teeth. They were still missing when we met her, since she could not afford to replace them. All this made her dependence on the Lord all the more real.

To make things worse, Maria's husband turned against her. He was quite a character, fathering eleven children, each with different mothers. God spared Maria's life when he tried to kill her with a knife a few weeks after she came to our home to work. Each morning after that, we were glad to see her walk into our home alive.

On our first Christmas in Brazil, we decided to take some presents to Maria's home. She lived on the outskirts of the city. It had rained the night before and we had to drive through muddy alleys to finally get to her "home," if that is what you could call it. It was not much more than a shack, primitively built with throw-away lumber, along with a barely shingled roof and supported by plastic covers.

What touched our children the most was Maria's bed. She had a sheet of plastic and one thin cover. The plastic was to keep the bed dry when it rained through the roof at night. The nights could be cold, with the temperature dropping to the low forties. We gave her a blanket along with the few presents we'd brought.

As we held a modest Christmas celebration, Maria told us her story. She had first heard the gospel in a little Pentecostal church in the neighborhood and decided to follow Jesus. Then she had felt the urge to share her faith with others and opened her home to be used as a meeting place. The bed, a table, and a couple of chairs were about all the furniture she had. She would move these outside and then sweep the dirt floor so that people could sit there.

When I asked who the preacher was for this little home church, she confidently looked at me and said, "I am." She told me that she would go to church on Sunday morning and then come home for the afternoon meeting, teaching her guests the songs she'd learned and repeating the sermon as best as she could remember. What an inspiring example!

Maria further mentioned that she also hosted a Wednesday night prayer meeting. She'd been asking God for some bricks because the sideboards of her house were decaying. This was about the most different church I'd ever seen.

But I saw much more than a leaky roof and decaying walls. I learned from Maria something about the effect of the gospel on her spirit. Instead of complaining about the difficulties and problems in her life, she recognized that her service to God was not dependent on material possessions, but rather on commitment. That, she had—and it put all of us to shame.

Here was a beautiful illustration of the life of Paul, the great missionary apostle. He had gone through his share of suffering, but as he neared the end of his ministry and wrote from a Roman prison cell, he said this to his friends in Philippi:

> "I have learned to be content whatever the circumstances. I know what it is to be in need, and I know what it is to have plenty. I have learned the secret of being content in any and every situation, whether well fed or hungry, whether living in plenty or in want. I can do everything through him who gives me strength." (Philippians 4:11–13)

What had motivated the apostle also motivated Maria. She had discovered the secret of living a life of purpose—the purpose of glorifying God in every circumstance.

Thank you, Maria! You have taught me and blessed me.

39

I HAD A FRIEND

May 1968

Brooklin, São Paulo

This morning, Alice and I went to a friend's funeral. We saw the casket lowered into the ground and massive cement slabs placed over it. Workmen shoveled a dirty cement mixture on top of it, sealing the edges. Then they filled it in with dirt.

No hymn was sung. No Scripture read. His brother turned to me: "Will you say a prayer?" I did.

Many friends came to the home for the viewing of his body. All night they stood in silent grief as four tall candles burned near his head. Their mourning was deep. They carried no hope or expectation of seeing him again.

When we laid his body in the casket, we hardly felt the weight. More than fifteen months of cruel suffering had reduced a once powerful body to a mere specter of its former self. He had endured pain as few others had.

Only one hundred days had passed since I first met him. A few months earlier, an ambulance had brought him when his family moved across the street from us. We learned to love his family. His friends became ours too. Now he was gone.

But I will see him again!

Jesus said: "I am the resurrection and the life. He who believes in me…will never die" (John 11:25–26). Yes, my friend Hany died—and yet he lives. He lives because he heard the message of the Son of God. He not only heard it, he believed it.

How well I remember the first time I told him the story—the only story. "The most beautiful story," he called it. "Why didn't I hear it before?"

Now his thirty-eight-year-old body, bearing all the marks of his dreaded disease, lies in the grave. But he is with Him, and all is well. And we can smile through our tears and thank Him.

I had a friend. He died yesterday. But thank God, he lives!

40

BRAZIL, LOVE IT OR LEAVE IT?

1967

São Paulo

It was a Good Friday service in São Paulo. I'd arrived right on time and the place was already jammed—at least five thousand people by a conservative estimate. The service ran longer than I had anticipated, a full three hours. This did not in the least inhibit the Pentecostal congregation. With worship, music, a message centered on the Cross, and a communion service, the service did not lag. Everyone kept involved.

At the close of the service, I introduced myself to the pastor and commented on the size of the congregation and church. "What church?" was his immediate reply. Noticing my perplexed look, he waved his hand at the huge hall where we'd gathered. "This isn't our church," he said. "We're still building it. This is just the foyer of our new church!" Gripping me by the arm, he then led me behind the hall, where huge pillars were already pointing skyward over an area that could have accommodated over a hundred homes. "This," he said, "is one day going to be our church, and it is all to the glory of God." When I inquired how many this place would seat, he answered, "Twenty-five thousand."

I was blown away.

This pastor, a man all of five feet tall but with a dynamic personality and vision, was Manoel de Mello, the founder of Brasil para Cristo (Brazil for Christ). He was a bricklayer by profession with only primary school education. When he became a follower of Christ, all of the energy in his compact body exploded into total surrender to Him. Brazil for Christ was his goal and he fearlessly began his witness in the streets of São Paulo. The response to his down-to-earth preaching was not slow in coming. A congregation emerged, and soon another, and yet another. In just a few years he became one of the key Christian leaders in the country, with a nationwide radio ministry and a network of over 130 churches in São Paulo alone. The church membership in the city was well over one hundred thousand people.

Our meeting marked the beginning of a fruitful relationship and friendship. It wasn't long before I received a letter from him asking whether we could provide a special speaker for a series of meetings. Bob Harrison, an evangelist and singer working with OC at that time, seemed to fit the bill. When he arrived, he really connected with Manoel and his people.

It was at the close of these meetings that Manoel invited me publicly to train his youth in principles of spiritual growth. I was excited, but then nothing seemed to come of it.

Then I received a phone call from Manoel. "I have changed my mind," he began, and my spirit sank. "I do not want you to come and teach my young people. I want you to come and teach all of my pastors and leaders. They need it more!" This was the second time he had blown me away.

And so on a weekly basis, he gathered well over one hundred pastors, and along with Paul McKaughan, a member of our team, we taught them basic principles of spiritual growth. It was an unforgettable experience.

One more experience with Manoel de Mello stands out in my mind. I had been invited to an evening service at one of their churches. According to custom, I was requested to sit on the platform along with Manoel and other pastors. During the service, at the time for prayer, everyone stood and began to pray out loud. I felt a strong grip on both of my hands, as Manoel on one side and another pastor on the other got hold of me. Up went our arms in true Pentecostal fashion. Then they started praying in tongues.

I had never prayed in tongues before, though many friends had. I honored them for this, but it was not a gift I had received. As I stood there, I wondered what I should do. I couldn't stay silent. Then an idea entered my mind. I began praying out loud with all the fervor I possessed—in Chinese. Immediately, I felt the pressure of Manoel's hand on mine, as if to say, "I was not quite sure about this guy, but he really does speak in tongues." In a way, I had.

Within a year of our arrival and while still engaged in our study of Portuguese, there was a major shift on our team. Those who had been there for the past four years decided to return to the States or elsewhere and continue their ministries there. A whole new team of missionaries came to the field. I was asked to be field director.

They were an exceptional group of gifted men and women. Later on, most of them developed into key mission leaders and statesmen in their own right. However, in their early years of missionary life, it was a formidable task and challenge to form them into an effective team working side by side to develop ministry and strategy for Brazil.

In the process, there were the periods of confrontation, disagreement, and discouragement. Early in our time, there were moments when we wondered what we were doing there. But it was the firm conviction that God had brought us to Brazil and that He had a purpose for our being there which always won out in the end.

The breakthrough arrived when we learned something about the biblical principle of the functioning of the body. Each of us was gifted by God to contribute to the needs of the body—the church. And each gift was necessary for the health of the body. When we learned to value each other from this vantage point, a real team concept emerged. Each person contributed his gift for the good of all. There came a bonding and molding together which I have never experienced since. We enjoyed working together, eating together, laughing and crying together—just being together! Though our paths have gone in different directions, these team members have remained close personal friends for the past forty years.

From a personal perspective, Alice and I were immensely blessed by a special missionary conference held in 1972 when Larry Coy, a longtime associate of Bill Gothard, presented a Design for Successful Living seminar patterned much after the Basic Life Conflicts seminars. The help we received not only gave us new handles on day-to-day issues, but in a personal way gave us a new perspective of the Word. We stayed in close touch with Larry over the years until his premature passing, and will be forever indebted to him.

One morning in 1972, I woke up early and stood looking out of our bedroom window. An incredible sense of gratitude to God overwhelmed me. I began thanking Him for sending me to Brazil and for the privilege of these past six years working side by side with this committed team of godly men and women. We were launching a number of new ministries and the excitement of all of this was truly exhilarating. The tough years of preparation and laying the groundwork were behind us; we were beginning to step out as a team and see our dreams and vision realized. There was no greater place to be than just where I found myself.

I thought of the bumper sticker I'd seen on many cars: "Brazil, Love It or Leave It." We as a family loved living here and would not trade it for anything in the world.

Then it happened.

I went to the office a couple of hours later. While sorting the mail, which just had arrived, I gravitated towards a rather thick envelope from OC headquarters in Palo Alto, California. A strange foreboding entered my mind as I opened the letter. Could it be?

It was a lengthy epistle written by our executive director. As I skipped through the first few paragraphs, I impulsively turned to the last paragraph on page six. It was what I had feared in my premonition. I was asked to return to headquarters and serve as a special assistant to Norm Cummings, OC's executive director.

I sat there, stunned and speechless. Slowly, I read the letter in its entirety. I read it again, then again. Yes, the message was clear—my contribution in Brazil had reached its end and another opportunity beckoned. Of course, I could have said no. But deep in my heart was that still, small voice:

Yes, this is My plan for you.

Brazil, love it or leave it. Of course we loved it. Why should we leave? Then came that ever-so-gentle rebuke in my spirit:

You are getting too comfortable here. I have some
new challenges for you.

Needless to say, we endured a few sleepless nights. But I recognized that I had no other option. It was not easy for the family, and both of our children were not thrilled with the prospect of moving back to the States, at least when they first heard about it. But then the unmistakable peace of God settled in our hearts and gave us confidence to make the decision.

Our team members also went through some personal spiritual exercises in adjusting to this new development, but they too concluded that this was from the Lord and gave us their blessing.

Once the decision was made, a new excitement gripped me. I am sure that it was the new challenges that faced me and the uncertainties that go with them. To work with Norm Cummings was something I looked forward to. I had gotten my share of "brutally honest" letters from him in days gone by, but I had learned to look past them and see the man behind them. Yes, there were those who prior to his field visits called him "Storm-am-coming," but I'd gotten to know Norm more personally just six months earlier when I'd roomed with him during OC's first leadership conference in July 1971.

During long conversations, Norm shared from his heart. I found him not only a deeply spiritual man who was committed to the Lord and His Word, but also a man who was deeply committed to the men and women in the mission. OC was going through leadership struggles at that time and the board had to deal with them. It was not unknown to them that I had been on the receiving side of some very "candid and honest" letters. They wanted to know how I and other field personnel were responding to these letters. Was Norm Cummings the man who could step into Dick Hillis' shoes as chief executive, since Dick was wrestling with some severe physical limitations?

I could, of course, only speak for myself. I instantly recalled some of the lessons Daws Trotman taught me right out of college. He also had confronted me very strongly, but out of sincere love and care for me. It was the same once again. To the utter surprise of most board members, I was able to speak from my heart and give a ringing endorsement of Norm's leadership and personal love and care for the mission family. At the end of these important board meetings, Norm was appointed to serve as CEO and executive director of the mission.

Whether this had anything to do with Norm now turning to me and asking me to assist him in his momentous task as CEO, I don't know. I never mentioned anything to him regarding the meeting with the board. However, a genuine kinship and friendship began developing between the two of us from that point on. Norm became my mentor in the truest sense of the word and I have always considered those years of working with him a great privilege and honor.

Again, a new chapter lay ahead of us—much like when we'd arrived in Brazil six years earlier. And again, it was with the firm conviction that God was working out His purposes in our lives that we once again packed our bags and returned for our new assignment in the U.S.A.

41

SINK OR SWIM

1972

Cupertino, California

We had barely unpacked our suitcases in California and I was on my way to speak at a summer conference when the urgent phone message reached me. It crisply stated that Norm Cummings was hospitalized with a massive heart attack. I immediately rushed back to our new home in Cupertino, wondering what this would mean for the mission.

Within a few days, Norm's condition had stabilized, but the doctors said he'd be out of commission for several months. I was asked to take over his office and told bluntly, "The mission is your baby now."

I had been back for too short a period to be briefed by Norm for my new role as his assistant. Now he was unable to provide me with any orientation. It was a sink or swim situation. Two thoughts came to mind: One, this was definitely out of my comfort zone. Had the Lord not warned me that I was getting too comfortable in Brazil? Secondly, since all this was so new to me, I really had to lean hard on the Lord. Wasn't that exactly what He had wanted me to do in the first place?

Norm had not just one huge desk, but two. Each was covered by stacks of documents and letters. I made a quick decision. I instructed my secretary to pack up everything on those two desks in cardboard boxes and put them in storage. I figured that if they contained important materials, someone would sooner or later ask for them. In the meantime, I wanted to start with a blank slate. A daring move, but it worked.

Personnel issues arguably were the most difficult ones to handle and we were not spared the pains of these encounters. I often felt myself caught in the middle and sometimes wondered why I was there. But I realized again and again that God had directed my steps and that there were important lessons I needed to learn. One of my early decisions was not to bring these issues home at the conclusion of a day in the office. I did not feel it wise to burden my wife with some of these matters, especially as they related to people and fellow missionaries she knew. In retrospect, I still believe this was the right move.

A natural break from this sometimes arduous routine was getting involved whenever possible in activities with our two teenagers. As a family, we backpacked in the Sierras for a week at a time during the summer months. We also skied in the winter. I had never been on skis, skates, or rollerblades before, and found learning to ski in my forties far more difficult than anticipated. In fact, I was ready to give it up, resign myself to driving the family to ski resorts, and sit with a book in the lodge. But a little wager with our son, Marty, finally provided the beginning of a most enjoyable experience for me.

Marty had received a barely passing grade in algebra. Along with his teacher, I sought to encourage him to give it another shot. He was reluctant. In desperation, I finally told him, "If you get an A in algebra, I will learn how to ski."

"But skiing is easy, Dad," was his retort. Eventually we agreed to the deal. Marty did come up with his A, so the pressure was on me to hold up my end of the bargain.

We went to the Sugar Bowl ski resort in the Lake Tahoe area. I asked for a class for beginners to get started. I struggled until at a break in the action, I ran across a young Austrian skier who happened to be the coach of the American national team. He volunteered to take me up the mountain and show me how easy skiing really was. He did!

The young coach led me to the very top of the ski area. I thought I would never make it down the hill. But the coach said *"Locker, locker,"* which in German means to stay relaxed, and told me to ski after him. He spent two hours with me without charging a dime, and when we were finally done, I thought there was nothing to skiing. I have skied ever since.

If there was anything that kept my compass straight in those days, it was a regular adult Sunday school class I taught at Los Gatos Christian Church (now Venture Christian Church). LGCC was one of the largest churches in San Jose, with a combined worship attendance of over five thousand in several services each Sunday. I was asked to teach a class of about thirty-five. Over the next few years, it grew to 350 people! This is what I looked forward to each weekend. It was just fun to teach the Word, and it kept me in the Word as well.

It was in that class that I stated my basic purpose for ministry. I wanted to leave a twofold legacy:

1. Growth in spiritual life through a new love
   for the Scriptures.

2. A vision to participate in the Great
   Commission.

I encouraged them to read the Word of God regularly. One year I made it a project to read with the class through the entire Bible. Each week, I shared some specific truth or application from what everyone had read. How thrilling to come to the end of the year with about seventy who read through the whole Bible for the first time and got started on a regular intake of Scripture.

I also knew that we needed to build global awareness by sharing specifically what God was doing around the world. I am not sure who learned more in the process, me or the class. But it became a lifesaver for me and a welcome change from the world of administration and management.

But God was not through with me yet. There were still tough lessons I needed to learn. Some were rather painful.

I was on a flight to the Midwest to speak at a missionary conference when, seemingly out of nowhere, a sense of guilt and shame flooded my soul. I tried to suppress the pangs of conscience, but they only grew worse. The roots for this attack were planted ten years earlier while I studied at Fuller Seminary. I had been assigned to exegete a passage from Psalm 51 in Hebrew and had made use of some "outside" help. I'd totally forgotten about this, but now the Spirit of God in His faithfulness brought it back to my mind. Here I was headed to speak at a missions conference, and now this. How could I serve our Lord as an unclean vessel?

Of course, I immediately confessed this as sin to the Lord. But there was more that He wanted me to do. He wanted me to get in touch with the professor and confess it to him as well! I struggled with this while riding on the plane, but found no rest until I came to the firm conviction that I had to clear my conscience. I surrendered to the Lord. I had no idea of where to contact this man since he had left Fuller Seminary years ago, but I said, "Lord, if I can find him, I will make this right with him."

Upon arrival at my destination, I was met by my host who took me to his home. Since we had some time to spare before the first meeting, I sat down to relax in his living room. I picked up a magazine on the coffee table in front of me and started leafing through it. Suddenly, there it was—the name of my former professor, along with his address, staring me in my face. I blinked, and then blinked again. Could this be? It was.

I wrote the letter which needed to be written. The minute I

finished it, a huge burden was lifted. I felt free and my conscience was clear. But more than that, there was a deep thankfulness in my heart that welled up to my Father in heaven who had been so faithful and gracious in allowing me to go through this experience and learn from it.

Later, I received a most gracious response letter from the professor. It not only reflected the Savior's forgiveness, but also that of a godly person who had learned the value of forgiving others and restoring them to complete fellowship.

There would be more lessons that needed to be learned, more valleys and rivers to be crossed, and more mountains to be climbed. But I had been obedient to the voice of the Spirit and that renewed my desire to live for His glory.

42

BUT DAD, YOU PROMISED

1980

Cupertino

I was excited. This was one of those special occasions, I believed, that come just once in a lifetime. I eagerly shared it with my Sunday school class one morning.

OC International had received an invitation to send a basketball team to China and now was inviting me as an "old China hand" to go with them. China was just emerging from its Cultural Revolution and the Bamboo Curtain was lifting for contact with the outside world. It had been over thirty years since we had left China, so I jumped when the invitation came. "There are some things you don't have to pray about" had been my boisterous and spontaneous response.

As I expressed my excitement with my class, it was not long before they shared in my enthusiasm. They all agreed that this was an opportunity I could not let pass.

But it was a different story when I shared this new venture with my family at the dinner table after church. Somehow my enthusiasm failed to ignite our two children, Marty and Lita. Even the most enthusiastic picture I painted was met by a very stoic response. No one said anything.

Finally, Lita burst out, "But Dad, you promised to go backpacking with us then. You can't break your promise." In my excitement, I had totally blocked this date out of my mind. When she reminded me, I immediately tried to convince everyone how special this China assignment was. We could go backpacking any time, but this was an opportunity I might never have again.

Try as hard as I could, I was not able to shake them in their conviction. "Dad, you promised, and you can't break your promise!" This was the trump card they played, and I knew that they had me beat. Yes, I had promised, and there was no way out. I was reminded of once making a promise to the Lord when I was a teenager—a vow that had protected me through all my school years until I met Alice in Taiwan. Now I was faced with another "promise tester."

The following Sunday, I had a special announcement for my class: "I will not be making the China trip because I have made a prior commitment to my family and I must keep my word, my promise."

There was a moment of stunned silence. Then, to my amazement, there was applause. In that decision, I believe I taught my class more than I could have by delivering the best Bible study on spiritual truth. I had demonstrated to them an important lesson from my own life.

Paul once wrote to the believers in Philippi, "Whatever you have learned or received or heard from me, or seen in me—put it into practice" (Philippians 4:9). Today I am grateful to my children for reminding me of my promise and teaching me the importance of keeping my word. It was hard at the time, but a lesson well worth learning.

God will never shortchange anyone who is committed to Him. Little did I know then all that God had in store for me—especially as it related to the land of China.

43

WHEN A MAN'S WAYS ARE PLEASING TO THE LORD

1979

Los Gatos, California

My years in the States were anything but boring. Various assignments within the mission kept me moving. I had come home from Brazil in 1972 to serve as assistant to Norm Cummings. He had carried a heavy load and his heart attack alerted the mission that major organizational restructuring was called for. Three associate executive directors were appointed to deal with the areas of personnel, overseas fields, and administration.

Norm Cook was asked to head up the personnel responsibilities. We had worked in Taiwan together and he and his wife, Muriel, stood up with us at our wedding. They were treasured old friends and we were blessed to work together once again. Norm's gregarious spirit made him ideal to work with people and to recruit others to the mission.

Ed Murphy, the new associate executive director for our field ministries, had served the mission in Latin America. We first met in 1957 before he went to the field. Through the years, we too had developed a bond of friendship and respect. Ed was a gifted teacher and communicator and able to articulate the mission of OC as well as give clear leadership to our field ministries.

My responsibilities were to provide administrative oversight of the mission and deal with the myriad tasks connected with it. Endless committee meetings seemed to sap a lot of our energy, but it helped us develop strong team relationships and friendships which have remained to the present day.

In 1974, Norm Cummings resigned as CEO and executive director of the mission for health reasons and we once again reorganized. Dick Hillis resumed his role as president and asked me to assist him as executive vice president. This continued through the two-year stint when evangelist Luis Palau served as president. When Luis left to pursue his evangelistic calling, I served for a brief period as CEO and carried a huge share of the leadership of the mission.

Clyde Cook, former missionary with OC in the Philippines and then director of missions at Biola College (now BIOLA University), became OC's new president in 1979. Very graciously, he asked me to continue in my present position, and I assured him that I would be happy to work in any capacity he wanted to use me. Besides, where would I go?

I had just returned to the States from an overseas trip when I received a call from Marvin Rickard, senior pastor of Los Gatos Christian Church. He invited me to come to a staff retreat for their church leadership and share the Word during those days. Though I was a bit tired, I agreed to go.

It was during this retreat that I sensed a new stirring in my heart. I felt a change was imminent for us. I was not sure what this meant, but God evidently was preparing me for a new venture of faith. The previous seven years at OC headquarters had allowed me to settle into a routine which I knew well. But again, as during my closing days in Brazil, there was that little voice—"you are getting too comfortable"—which kept poking me.

That is why, when I received the phone call from Pastor Rickard, it caught me by surprise in one sense—and in another sense it didn't. He asked me to join the staff of LGCC as pastor of discipleship and Christian education and told me that the entire pastoral staff and elders were unanimous in extending this invitation. Before giving him an answer, I needed some time to seek the Lord. Also, I had to be absolutely sure that I had the blessing of the mission in making such a move.

The assurance came quickly. I ran across Proverbs 16:7 and it jumped out at me:

> When a man's ways are pleasing to the LORD, he
> makes even his enemies live at peace with him.

My desire was to please Him, but I also wanted to live in a right relationship with those who had been my partners in ministry in OC. If He could do this with enemies, how much more could He do it with those who were friends? Both Alice and I took this as clear direction from Him. My Bible is still marked at that passage with this note: 5/16/79 re leaving OC and joining LGCC.

When I shared this new development with Clyde Cook and the mission leadership, there was an overwhelming sense expressed by all that the Lord was directing our steps. They were ready to let us go with their full blessing. They did request that I continue my involvement with the mission by serving on the board of directors. I was honored and naturally accepted this offer.

Obviously, leaving OC after twenty-five years was not easy—but it was the right thing to do, and that is what counted.

My time at Los Gatos Christian Church was marked by several highlights. First, I welcomed the change and shift from the many administrative responsibilities I had carried over the previous seven years. I relished the new opportunities to preach and teach the Word on a full-time basis. This in turn forced me into a deeper study of the Scriptures.

Second, much of the staff of the church was made up of younger ministers, and many of them began to look to me as a mentor. Often it was the informal breakfasts or luncheons together which provided the best venues for heart-to-heart sharing. Close bonds of friendship and fellowship grew from these times together.

Third, nothing was more exciting than touching lives where it really counted. Let me tell you about three of them. One day, a young college student introduced me to his father, who had recently become a Christian. "Will you help him grow spiritually?" was his simple request. The moment I shook Chuck's hand, I could tell that here was a man who had spent his life working with his hands. He looked at me with a quizzical expression and waited for an answer. I assured him that I would be happy to meet with him and then asked whether he had a Bible. He had a New Testament, but he had never read it. I gave him his first assignment: Before meeting with him the next week, I asked him to start reading the Gospel of John, beginning with chapter three.

He showed up the following week carrying his New Testament with him. I asked him how his reading had gone the past week. He replied, "I'm sorry, but I didn't do what you asked me to do."

Hiding my disappointment, I asked whether he had read anything. His face brightened. "Yes," he said. "I didn't begin with John 3. I started with the book of Matthew."

Again, I had to bite my lip. Reading through the first chapter of Matthew was just like reading a phone directory and hardly inspiring reading.

"How was it?" I asked. Chuck's reply staggered me.

"I loved it. This showed me that God loves people, remembers them by name, and I know that He must therefore also know me personally."

I breathed an inward sigh of relief. Chuck went on: "I just couldn't put this book down. I kept reading and reading. I went through the whole book of Matthew, and then I went through Mark and Luke and John. Then I read through the book of Acts and I'm now reading the book of Romans."

This man was oozing a hunger and enthusiasm for the Scriptures I had never encountered before. There was no question in my mind that here was one of the key evidences of the new birth in him: a deep love and hunger for the Word of God. I am not sure how much I was able to help him, but Chuck sure blessed me.

Then there was Jim, who worked at the phone company in San Jose. He had been to my Sunday school class and had invited me to come to his home one evening. At his kitchen table, I gave Jim a clear presentation of the gospel and he then opened his heart to receive the Savior. Although I have experienced this joy many times, I never cease to be thrilled and marvel at the miracle of the new birth taking place.

But Frieda was another story. She had been a pastor's wife with a family. Her marriage failed in part due to the fact that she suffered from a severe eating disorder, anorexia nervosa. She had then become a schoolteacher in a Christian school. She continued to struggle with anorexia, often collecting leftover food in restaurants and stuffing it in her purse. On Sunday mornings at the church coffee hour she would do the same with donuts.

One day Frieda approached me and asked me to pray for her because she felt restless and disturbed in her spirit. I did. Soon she was back, and again asked me to pray. When I asked what the problem was, she said it was "demons."

I discounted this at first, but eventually agreed that I would test for demonic activity in her life. Alice, along with an elder from the church, a young minister, and I all met Frieda at her home. We started our time together with a brief study in the Word dealing with deception. We acknowledged that Satan is the great deceiver, that sin deceives us, that others can deceive us, and that we can even deceive ourselves.

This was followed by a time of prayer. I pointed out that James 4:7 clearly states that before we can resist the devil we need to submit ourselves to God and give Him total authority over our lives. I told Frieda that it was essential for her to *first* submit to God and *then* resist the devil. In her prayer she spoke only about resisting Satan and had difficulty expressing her commitment to submit to God. Even after urging her to do so, she was unable to verbalize this. This gave me an immediate clue.

I asked Frieda for permission to test whether there were demons present in her life. She said yes, this was the reason she had wanted me to come. I said I would speak to her, but in effect address any demons in her life and command them to make themselves known.

When I asked any demons present to identify themselves, the response was immediate and convincing. From Frieda's mouth, but in a gruff, masculine voice, the demons responded:

"We do not have to listen to you."

I responded: "Yes, you do. I come to you with the authority of the Lord Jesus Christ, and I command you to tell me who you are!"

After some further urging, the demons, and there were a number of them, grudgingly admitted who they were, but insisted that they had total rights over Frieda.

I challenged that. "Frieda belongs to the Lord Jesus Christ," I said, "because He has bought her with His own blood on the cross. You have no rights on her, and in the name of the Lord Jesus Christ, I command you to leave."

A lengthy back-and-forth argument followed, in which the demons became more and more belligerent. Through their spokesman, they said, "We will not leave."

While all of this was going on, Frieda was slumped on her sofa. She did not speak in her usual voice, and seemed oblivious to what was happening. My wife and the two church leaders sat and prayed quietly, sometimes out loud, especially when the demons spoke.

Finally, I asked the demons to tell me when they had first invaded Frieda's life. The answer was precise: "When she was thirteen." Again I told them that they had no right to stay and had to leave. Again they refused. "We don't have to leave," the voice said, "because Frieda likes us to stay."

It was then that I broke off further contact with them and spoke directly to Frieda. When I addressed her, she immediately sat up and paid attention. I asked whether she understood what had been going on since I made contact with the demons. She replied that she wasn't aware of anything that had happened.

I related what the demons had said, including the fact that they had moved into her life when she was thirteen.

"Frieda," I said, "what happened when you were thirteen?"

With her head bowed, Frieda quietly told us that she had been sexually abused as a thirteen-year-old and that this abuse had continued for several years. I then asked her about the demons' claim that "Frieda likes us to stay." Frieda avoided my eyes, but nodded her head. "That is true too."

I was deeply saddened when I had to tell her that unless she was totally willing to submit to God and renounce Satan in her life, there could not be any help forthcoming. Here was the reason she found it so difficult in her opening prayer to verbalize her submission to God.

This was the last time we saw Frieda. We later heard that she had been in a car accident and was hospitalized. After that, her parents moved her back east to live with them. She died not long after.

I wish Frieda's life had turned out differently. It was a sad experience for all of us. It also taught us a tremendous lesson: even true believers can come under the control of demonic powers when they refuse to submit to the authority and lordship of Jesus Christ. Frieda failed to do this, and it allowed the enemy to move in. Rejection and rebellion against Christ's authority make any believer vulnerable. I committed myself afresh to obey Him fully, no matter what it cost.

The rest of my ministry at the church during this time was deeply satisfying. Still, something gnawed at me. I guess that once you have been exposed to this vast world, it is hard to limit to yourself to one small area of geography. Yet I was sure that God wanted me to stay at Los Gatos Christian Church—that is, until something happened which again showed me God's creative ways of bringing about change.

It is always a great feeling when people appreciate your ministry, and it was a special joy when this translated into changed lives. I had been teaching a class on financial principles from a biblical perspective. After one class, a young high school coach shared the blessing this class had been to him and how it had led him to make major financial changes in his life. He had been enamored by his new little sports car, but this had plunged him into a financial tailspin. He had decided to sell his car and buy a secondhand vehicle.

The young coach came to the next class beaming. "I am free!" he said. A little thing, true. But what a change it produced in his life.

I had been asked to teach the small adult Sunday school class at Los Gatos. When it began to grow, we shifted into larger rooms and finally divided into two classes. Emphasis on real-life issues, learning how to internalize Scripture through regular reading of the Word, and memorization revealed a refreshing hunger on the part of many. About seventy in the class read through the Bible from cover to cover for the first time in their lives. I still hear from some of these people today.

It was soon after this that I began to receive phone calls early on Sunday mornings. People wanted to know in which service of the three morning services I would be preaching. Then other questions surfaced, including, "When will you start a church for us to attend?"

This scared me! I had followed the invitation of Marvin

Rickard to assist him in his ministry, not to provide competition. Even though we had differing gifts and abilities, I did not want to have anything to do with a church split. As Alice and I prayed, we came to the strong conclusion that our time at LGCC was coming to a close and that I should hand in my resignation. This I did, to take effect the end of December 1980.

I had no idea what God had in mind for us at that moment. But one thing was clear: It was my responsibility to listen to His direction, and as the Great Shepherd, He knew where to lead me. Along with Job in the Old Testament, I could pray: "I know that you can do all things; no plan of yours can be thwarted" (Job 42:2).

I was committed to pursuing the purposes of God for my life, and I knew beyond the shadow of a doubt that He would lead in the days ahead.

As a teenager growing up in Shanghai, I had made it a habit to memorize favorite hymns as well as Scripture. One of these came to mind, one I had often sung. These verses once again brought me comfort and confidence:

> How good is the God we adore,
> Our faithful unchangeable Friend;
> His love is as great as His power,
> And knows neither measure nor end.
>
> 'Tis Jesus the first and the last,
> Whose Spirit shall guide us safe home;
> We'll praise Him for all that is past,
> We'll trust Him for all that's to come.[9]

44

THERE WERE GIANTS IN THE LAND

February 1981

Stuttgart, Germany

As soon as word got out that I had resigned from my position at Los Gatos Christian Church, phone calls from good friends started to come in. Everyone graciously offered to help me discover the next step for our lives. Seldom had I experienced such genuine kindness and friendship. They offered to introduce me to other organizations and make phone calls on my behalf, and made all sorts of helpful suggestions. Many of the potential ministries sounded attractive and challenging.

Then one lunch in a Chinese restaurant in San Jose in early December 1980 decided it all. My good friend and Brazil team member Bill Keyes, now OC's personnel director, set it up. "Would you be willing to meet with me and Clyde Cook for lunch?" he asked.

Dr. Cook was now president of One Challenge International. As we ate, he presented me with a challenge. "God is calling us into Europe," he said. "But we lack leadership. You're the obvious man for the job. Unless you come back, we will not move forward."

Could this be real? I asked myself. I had always harbored a dream of working in Europe, in my native Germany. How my heart had responded when Daws Trotman first approached me about going there and ministering to my own people. Yet the door had never opened—I had gone to Taiwan instead.

That was twenty-eight years earlier!

Ten years in Taiwan, two terms in Brazil, and seven years at OC headquarters…a long journey to Germany! But I had come to realize that God's ways are infinitely higher than our ways. Now it seemed that my dream of nearly three decades was finally coming true.

An old proverb says: You may take the boy out of the country, but you can't take the country out of the boy. This was certainly true in my case. Even though I had not lived in Germany, there remained a strong German root within me. It felt that this new assignment was a reconnecting with my past—a going home.

I requested and was granted permission to visit Germany and "test the soil." I left San Francisco on February 4, 1981, taking with me Bill Rapier, a young missionary with OC whom I had recruited to join our potential team for Germany.

Flying across the Atlantic that night, I began to wonder how all of this was going to work out. Yes, there was the thrill of going to my home country. But how would we go about researching the feasibility of locating a team there, let alone beginning a ministry?

We were on TWA Flight 740, originating in New York and headed for Frankfurt, Germany. About 4 A.M., when we were somewhere over the Atlantic, I turned to Bill and asked him to join me at the back of the 747 for a time of prayer. It was something I desperately needed. I recognized that I did not have it within me to accomplish this task. We simply turned to our Lord and asked Him to go before us and guide us on a clear path.

When we arrived in Germany, an old classmate and friend dating back to my days in Shanghai met us. Werner Bürklin had returned to Germany while I had moved to America. He had also experienced God's call on his life and had become a key leader with Youth for Christ in Germany, as well as in Europe. Billy Graham had asked him to also be the director of his organization in Germany—a good contact for me to begin with. However, Werner made it clear from the start that the one man I needed to see was Peter Schneider. As executive director of the German Evangelical Alliance, he was without doubt one of the most influential evangelicals in the country. The alliance was an umbrella organization for all evangelical elements in Germany, including the state church.

I had known for some time that the most strategic way of evangelizing a nation was to link your ministry to an existing internal structure that had the potential for reaching the nation. In Germany, that structure was the Lutheran Church. It seemed that every mission organization working there had avoided the Lutherans because of their unresponsiveness or liberal theology. But I was convinced that they were the door to Germany—and now I learned that Peter Schneider represented the key to that door.

He was a busy man and hard to get a hold of. We finally established contact, even though it meant crashing a special luncheon he had with the Billy Graham board in Germany. I hopped a train to Stuttgart, and once there, grabbed a taxi to the hotel where we had decided to rendezvous. I walked into the hotel lobby just as Peter and his committee were breaking for lunch.

We sat in the hotel restaurant. After a brief introduction, he cut to the chase. "Herr Wilhelm, we have an abundance of American religious groups in Germany," he said. "What do you think OC can do in Germany that no one else is doing? What are you trying to sell?"

His questions—firm, direct, and to the point—were just

what I expected from a German. I knew that my answers could open or close the doors for OC in Germany.

As I began describing OC's ministry and objectives, his probing questions continued: "Why do you want to work in Germany? Do you have a specialized program you want to offer? What makes you different from others already working here?"

Peter was sincere and polite. There was no question that he too realized Germany was a spiritually needy country and that workers were needed. But when I hesitated to provide him with a plan and schematic for our ministry, he was not sure what role OC would play in his country. Something inside blocked me from laying out the full-orbed modus operandi the mission would follow once it came to Germany. Instead, I talked in generalities—and got nowhere.

As the luncheon drew to a close, I recognized that we had made no progress, especially when I heard these ominous words: "We need to give this a lot of prayer and thought over the next few months. We need to move very slowly."

Was this just a polite way of saying, "Thanks, but no thanks"? The questions Peter asked were tough and legitimate. I did not think he could close the door for us to enter Germany as a mission, but was God sending me a message? Was He closing the door to what had seemed such a challenging idea? Was this really His plan for OC, for our lives?

You can imagine the questions and emotions surging through my mind and heart after this encounter. To top it off, I had just covered in my daily Bible reading the passage in Numbers 13 where a group of twelve men sent by Moses are on a fact-finding trip. The majority report is overwhelming: "The land we have seen is a beautiful land, a rich land, a fertile land. But it has very strong cities in it and there are giants in the land. They would crush us, and we felt like grasshoppers" (my paraphrase).

I identified with this story, and with the ten spies. We too were here to spy out the land. We had seen its big cities, its castles along the Rhine river, the meadows and forests. In fact, it seemed that today I had lunch with one of those giants. Ten of Moses' spies decided it was too tough: "We can't take possession of it, we can't do it." That's how I felt during my lunch meeting with Peter Schneider. I had a hard time choking down my food. I wanted to be a Caleb and a Joshua, yet I felt more like a grasshopper.

Writing home to Alice that evening, I said, "I want to respond like Caleb did—but tonight I don't really feel like it. I really wish you were here—but I am thankful that you are praying for me."

What had started out as such a promising day had ended on such a discouraging note. *Lord,* I prayed, *is this the end of my dream?*

Thank God, it wasn't. Without praying friends, the story would have ended right here. But there was more.

45

So, You Are That Hans Wilhelm

February 19, 1981

Frankfurt, Germany

Just before saying goodbye to Peter Schneider in Stuttgart, he turned to me and said, "It really hasn't been fair for you to have just this brief time with me. We really need more time."

Pulling out his pocket calendar, he said, "This really is a bad week, but Thursday night I am free. I will be in Frankfurt. Would you be able to join me there for the evening so we can talk?"

I quickly agreed. I booked a room at the hotel where Peter was staying and cancelled other appointments I'd already made. *I better not blow this one*, I thought. *Otherwise, I might as well pack up and go home.*

In honor of German punctuality, Bill Rapier and I walked into the hotel lobby at the stroke of 8 P.M. Peter Schneider was already seated there waiting for us. "Let's get a room," he said in a businesslike tone. He spoke to a manager who opened up a conference room for us. The three of us marched in and sat down at one end of a long conference table.

"I really don't know where to begin," I said. It occurred to me that since Peter had treated me like a German, I might as well respond in kind. I said, "Herr Schneider, the question you asked me the other day is a good question. I have given it a lot of thought. Here is what I am going to do."

As these words crossed my lips, I honestly did not have the slightest idea what I was going to say. But another thought came to me: *Why don't you share a bit of your background with him, so that he can get to know you before you plunge into the heavy stuff?*

That is exactly what I did. I talked about my early childhood growing up in China as son of missionary parents serving with the Liebenzell Mission. Of course, Peter knew about this mission, and it began to establish a link. I told him about the war years, my time in Shanghai, and my infatuation with the Hitler Youth movement. At that point, Peter interrupted. "Your story sounds a lot like mine," he said. "I was in the Hitler Youth too."

I shared how the trauma at the end of World War II allowed me to recognize my need of a Savior and how God brought people into my life that encouraged me in my Christian growth. When I mentioned Dawson Trotman and the Navigators, a strange look appeared on his face. He said, "So you are *that* Hans Wilhelm?"

I replied, "Yes, I am."

Peter began to recount a strange and unbelievable story. He too had met Daws Trotman when he visited Germany, and had been invited to come to the States to visit the Navigators.

"Twenty-five years ago, I first heard this name Hans Wilhelm," he said. "People in the States kept asking me, 'Do you know this Hans Wilhelm from Germany? Surely you must know him?' Now I finally meet you."

The ice had been broken. From that point forward, Peter's whole demeanor was different. He listened enthusiastically as I reviewed OC's history, beginning with Dick Hillis in Taiwan and its spread throughout Asia and then into Latin America. Each country required a different approach, and I illustrated this from the different things we had experienced.

All of a sudden, Peter stopped me and said, "That is exactly what we need in Germany!"

I was taken aback because I had been so involved in telling our story.

"I haven't told you anything about what we hope to do in Germany," I said. "I have just been telling you what and how we are operating in other fields."

"No, that is exactly what we need in Germany," Peter said.

"Herr Schneider, I still find it difficult to answer your previous question as to what specifically we are going to do here in Germany and how it differs from what others here are not doing. The reason I find it hard to answer this question is because it seems to me very presumptuous as an outsider to come in and tell you what the German church really needs. We cannot give you a prepackaged program. This is where you and other people here are so important to us. We need to learn what the real needs are and then only can we work together to develop something."

Peter looked at me. "That is exactly what I wanted to hear you say. You would be amazed—and this is the reason why I asked you this question—how many people come, especially from America, and have their programs all mapped out: Here is what you need. And they don't have the slightest idea. There is such a thing as German pride. We don't need that. But you understand this, because you are German."

Then without dropping a beat, he asked, "When can you come?"

This sudden shift in Peter was nothing less than dramatic. Three days earlier he had voiced serious questions about the presence of another "American" mission organization. Now he was extending a warm invitation to come to Germany.

As we continued to talk, Peter began to share some of his own ministry concerns, brother to brother. The ties between us grew tighter by the minute. His mind started to let the creative juices flow; he had all sorts of ideas for us.

"You know, this is really God's way of putting things together here," he said. "The timing of your coming is really God's timing."

He used the German word *Gottesfügung*—something ordained by God.

When I told him that twenty-eight years earlier the Navigators had considered sending me to Germany, he quickly interjected, "Twenty-eight years ago we weren't ready for you. This time we are. We really are. You know it is important that you come.

"By the way, I never asked you, are you an American citizen? Do you have an American passport? Listen, don't tell anybody that you are an American. Your father was a German, your mother was a German, you are a German and don't tell anybody differently. You just work here on the basis of being a German. That is very important. Because when you come, they know that you are a German and anybody you bring with you can come in under that and there is no cloud of suspicion that here is some foreign element.

"I know all the evangelical leaders and pastors in Germany and I will open my files to you and introduce you to anyone. How soon can you come? I hope it will be very soon!"

I had to pinch myself—could all this be for real? Was I dreaming?

In my next letter to Alice, I wrote:

> This past week, especially the past few days, have been the most important of the trip. Our meeting with Peter Schneider was the breakthrough I really needed to know whether God really wanted us to come and minister here."

Once again I had experienced in a powerful way that when God opens doors, no man can shut them. He had truly directed our steps, given us the right words to speak, and answered the prayers of many.

A few days later, back in California, I reported to the mission leadership God's gracious dealings with us and the confirmation

He had given regarding future ministry in Germany. We concluded together that this was from Him and preparations got underway for a new chapter in our lives.

46

AKTION GEMEINDEAUFBAU

1982

Germany

There were three specific prayer requests concerning Germany which I had shared with my friends at OC. We needed open doors for ministry. Then God needed to provide us with a team of coworkers. Finally, we had to have financial resources.

Each of these prayers was answered in an abundant way. I have already mentioned how God opened the door for us through Peter Schneider. Then there was the assembling of a team. Among the people who answered God's call to join us were Ralphe and Lanett Forster.

I'd been introduced to Ralphe and Lanett just before I went on my survey trip to Germany. Ralphe was chief engineer at the Stanford Court Hotel in San Francisco. Both he and his wife had immigrated to the States from Germany twenty years earlier. As I shared with them our burden and concern to return to our "Fatherland," they both responded with great enthusiasm. They began to pray for us earnestly, they took on a good part of our support, they stayed in touch.

A few months later, as I chatted with Ralphe on the phone, I sensed God wanting me to challenge Ralphe to join our team in Germany.

"Ralphe, we have appreciated your prayers and we have valued your financial help," I said. "But there is something more than that I am going to ask you to give. Will you and Lanett pray about joining our team?"

There was a long silence on the phone. Finally, Ralphe responded.

"Hans, you will never believe this," he said. "For quite a long time, I have been burdened to return to Germany as a missionary. I went to my pastor and asked his advice concerning this and whom I should contact. His reply was, 'Ralphe, don't do anything. When the right time comes, someone will come to you and ask you.' And now you are doing just that."

However, Ralphe had one main concern—he had not been to seminary.

"But that is exactly why I want you to come, Ralphe," I said. "We need strong Christian laymen who can demonstrate to other laymen that you don't have to be a theologian to be a witness for Christ and lead home Bible studies. We have enough seminary-trained men on our team. I want you!"

Needless to say, it was a wonderful day when we welcomed Ralphe and Lanett Forster to our team in Germany. For ten years they served Him with great fruitfulness.

Following Peter Schneider's counsel and seeking to minimize our American image, we soon incorporated under the name *Aktion Gemeindeaufbau,* the German phrase for church growth. This became the catchphrase for the German *Landeskirche*, often referred to as the state church. Much disillusionment had taken place, with a massive exodus from its membership. This forced its leadership to seek a new approach to help its church retain members and build them up. It seemed that God had allowed us to step on the scene at precisely the right time.

Things developed faster than we could have imagined. We were able to establish contacts with key leaders whom God brought into our lives. These German leaders embraced us wholeheartedly, and soon we became founding members of the German Church Growth Association. In the meantime, our staff continued to grow. Within a few years we were ten families.

Language study was the primary focus for our team in those first years. Alice faced this challenge as well. During our time in Taiwan and later in Brazil, she had already acquired two foreign languages, Chinese and Portuguese. Now she was looking at another daunting challenge in learning German. She rose to the occasion and tackled it bravely, though it did not come easy. She even took an intensive course at the well-known Defense Language Institute in Monterey, California, though this involved several weeks of separation from me. Later on, she spent several weeks with a family in East Germany where all she heard was German. It was total immersion.

I, however, was able to plunge into ministry opportunities from day one. In one meeting I was asked where in Germany I had come from. I admitted that I had never lived in Germany after the age of four. No one believed me! They told me my accent and dialect gave it away. I must have come from Saxony, my dad's home state.

In a letter to friends in early 1984, I shared the following experience:

> He was a young Roman Catholic priest from Poland and had moved to West Germany a couple of years ago. Now I was seated next to him in his little parish church. The fellowship room in which we were meeting was crowded; some were standing. I guess we had nearly a hundred

there. For a village church in Germany that was a considerable number.

What made this particular group so interesting was that there were not only Catholics, but also Protestants meeting together for a weeklong series of Bible messages which I had been asked to give. The two little village churches, one Protestant and the other Catholic, had an agreement: each year they would alternate in having this Bible week in their churches and both congregations would participate.

So, night after night, I was able to open the Word and speak to this hungry group for at least one hour. For many, it was the first time they had someone teach them directly from the Bible and encourage them to bring their Bibles to church with them. Oh, yes—they fumbled through the pages and found the passages by thumbing through the index, but they were right with me! I have seldom encountered such an attentive audience. How grateful I was for this opportunity to share the good news of life in Christ.

Life in Germany was not always as easy or enjoyable as this. There were other challenges that caused me to rely heavily on the Lord.

One day, I had just finished eating lunch at home when the telephone rang. A familiar voice greeted me. It was a leading elder of a fast-growing church in Bavaria. As we chatted, my heart sank. He reported major difficulties that had arisen in their church. Would I be willing to intervene with the pastor?

Five minutes later, the phone rang again. This time it was the pastor of the church on the line. Without knowing anything about the previous phone call, he shared with me that the enemy was attacking on all fronts. Would I be willing to pray and fast with him for their church?

You can imagine the turmoil in my soul as I pondered what I should do. Both sides were my friends and both had sought me out independently of each other. I could not refuse this assignment, no matter how difficult.

As I drove the two hundred miles the next morning, it seemed the longest two-hour drive (there is no speed limit on the German autobahns) I'd ever made. I cried out to the Lord for wisdom and for Him to give me counsel that would bring peace to this troubled church.

Seated around the dining room table in the pastor's home were his three leading elders. One after the other voiced his concerns and expressed lack of confidence in his leadership, in his personal integrity, and in his ministry. As the afternoon progressed, the discussion grew in intensity until one of the men stated that he could no longer remain in the church. The other two followed suit. And the pastor, too, was forced to agree that under these circumstances he could no longer remain. Bitterness of heart and deep sorrow was etched on all their faces when they turned to me and said, "What should we do?"

It is at moments like these that you become totally aware of your own insufficiency and cry out to God. It is also at moments like these that you experience the blessing of faithful friends at home who pray for you.

God gave me the right words for these leaders. Part of the message God gave me was from Hebrews.

> Make every effort to live in peace with all men
> and to be holy; without holiness no one will see
> the Lord. See to it that no one misses the grace
> of God and that no bitter root grows up to cause
> trouble and defile many. (Hebrews 12:14–15)

We went on our knees together and the Spirit of God did His gracious work in each heart. There was the right response to His grace. What a joy to see these men embrace each other and find restoration of fellowship. Praise God for His faithfulness!

The trip home that evening was even faster—my heart was singing. But I also drove with the distinct impression that the battle was not over. We had a strong enemy who was set on destroying the church Christ was building.

I was reminded of the apostle John's message in 1 John 3:8: "The reason the Son of God appeared was to destroy the devil's work."

This put in proper focus the purpose for our being in Germany. He had called us to be co-laborers with Him in building His church. What a privilege!

47

TWO SOVIET WOMEN

December 1984

East Germany

My father's ancestral home in East Germany was very close to the Czech border. More than fifty years had passed since I had been there as a small child. Now that we lived in West Germany, we looked forward to the day when we could once again visit the old homestead and get to know family we only knew from pictures and hearsay.

Crossing from the West to the East required a special visitors visa issued by the Democratic German Republic (Communist Germany), also known as the DDR. By the time we finished filling in all the application forms, the authorities had a pretty clear picture of our family history and background.

We packed the trunk of our car with food items which we knew were not available to our relatives in the "other" Germany. We had heard that coffee, loved by all Germans, sold there for fourteen dollars a pound, while bread and potatoes were relatively inexpensive. Buying meat meant a long wait in line. People stood in line for hours to pick up a couple of oranges. Dessert on a special occasion consisted of each person receiving one slice!

We set out in our car packed with fruit, produce, canned food, used clothing, toys, and, of course, coffee and chocolate. At the border we handed over our passports and guards inspected our car. Specifically, they asked if we were bringing in any newspapers, magazines, or books. These items were strictly *verboten*. East Germans were permitted to read only what the government approved. Once the guards were assured that we carried no contraband, the border crossing beam rose and we were allowed to go through.

What a welcome awaited us!

Up to this point, I had never met any relatives apart from my immediate family. Now, for the first time, we greeted aunts, uncles, and cousins I'd known by name only. They rolled out the welcome mat for us. Though they could not find or afford much of what we took for granted, they had saved up for our coming. Only the best was good enough for their "American" family. I felt the warmth of family bonds in a new way, and blessed beyond words. We spent hours sitting in living rooms of various family members, getting acquainted and sharing about our lives.

Zschorlau, the little village in the province of Saxony where my dad was born, was in the Erzgebirge, a mineral-rich area where coal, and later uranium, was mined. In 1903, a Methodist evangelist held a series of evangelistic meetings here. Among others, my grandfather was converted. A miner, he eventually became an itinerant lay preacher. My dad was the first missionary who left that area to go to China.

Since this was just a couple of weeks before Christmas, the warmth and joy of the season seemed to flow into our lives. Each home had been decorated with lights, crèches, ornaments, and other carvings which originated in that area and have now become world famous. Even though they lived in an atheistic society, there seemed to be no problem with celebrating Christmas. As we walked through the village square and saw the festive decorations and marketable goods for sale, Christmas carols rang out over the loudspeakers, including Bing Crosby crooning "I'm Dreaming of a White Christmas."

On Sunday, we worshiped together in the same little church where my father had preached years before. It was packed, but the pastor was extremely cautious in what he said. All sermons were taped and came under government scrutiny.

Our sixteen-year-old cousin, Connie, had chosen to identify with the church. She was "watched" as she left her confirmation, and later was denied entrance into the school to become a gym teacher. There was a price that had to be paid. While we were there, she placed an order to be eligible to buy a car. The normal waiting period for everyone was ten to fourteen years. She hoped to get her car by the time she was in her late twenties.

The fence, or wall in Berlin, ran the entire length of the country, separating East and West Germany. We thought that it was to keep the East Germans from escaping to the West until we heard that the reason given over there was to keep the West Germans from entering East Germany! I guess this was all a matter of perspective. No one was allowed to leave the country except women over sixty and men over sixty-five under certain conditions, as well as those physically disabled or otherwise undesirable.

Our twenty-two-year-old nephew, who had just started teaching school, sighed as he told us, "I would love to just see the Alps in Switzerland for myself someday. But I will have to wait forty-three more years." I swallowed hard when I heard this. Another world? Yes, and we just lived a few hours away.

Meeting my dad's best friend and brother-in-law, Uncle Max, was unforgettable. He was ninety-three and in poor health, but he had wanted to see me before he died. He loved the Lord with all his heart and maintained a steadfast Christian testimony throughout the difficult war and postwar years.

Three days after our return to the west, Uncle Max peacefully passed away.

Crossing the border to leave East Germany and return to the West was another story. We handed our customs slip to the East German border guard. He read it, read it again, and then kept looking at it. Then he politely ordered us out of the car and told us to put our suitcases on a nearby table. Another guard passed a mirror underneath the car, while a third carefully searched under the spare tire. Obviously, they were looking for someone.

With a mischievous smile, Alice admitted declaring on her customs slip that she was bringing out two Soviet women. Then the guard checked the backseat and saw two magazines, each titled *Soviet Women*. The dimples on his cheeks betrayed his sense of humor for a quick flash. Then he politely thanked us and allowed us to leave East Germany. Needless to say, Alice and I both chuckled the rest of the way home.

48

CAN ANYTHING GOOD
COME OUT OF AMERICA?

April 1985

Germany

We were a group of about fourteen men, mostly pastors and leaders of Christian organizations in Germany. The one thing we all had in common was a strong commitment to see the Body of Christ built up, renewed, and growing.

As we sat around a large table, one of the pastors opened his New Testament and turned to Mark 2. We read what Jesus said about pouring "new wine into new wineskins" (v. 22).

"Our job, as I see it," the pastor said, "is to pour new wine into new wineskins in old wine cellars."

This aptly described the challenge we faced in ministering to the established church in Germany. There was no question that we were dealing with some old wine cellars when it came to the institution of the church in this country, and in fact all over Europe. Centuries of encrusted patterns had left their mark.

The temptation was great to get involved in a "fight against the barnacles."

Yet I was more than ever convinced that God had not called us to change and correct the institution of the church. Rather, He had sent us to proclaim the availability of new life through a personal relationship with the Lord Jesus Christ.

As a team, we experienced exciting days as we met church leaders and laypeople from different parts of the country whose hearts beat with ours in wanting to see spiritual renewal sweep through this land. However, we were convinced that only as individual lives underwent spiritual transformation would church renewal come.

In so many ways, pastors held the key to what happened in the church. We began to actively seek them out, share our vision, and extend hands of partnership to help them. We discovered in this process that many of these leaders did not understand what it meant to know Christ in a personal way. Unbelievable as it sounds, one of the top church leaders in the state where we lived told me when I visited his office, "I can't say that I have experienced personal conversion."

Instead of being discouraged by this remark, I walked out sensing that this was an opportunity for God to demonstrate His ability and power to change lives.

For that reason, we set as one of our key objectives to expose pastors to healthy, growing churches in order to stimulate their vision. We did this by conducting church growth study tours to the United States. The German pastors visited key churches, which provided for interaction with American pastors who had a vision for growth.

Our German guests were exposed to such pastors as the late D. James Kennedy, John MacArthur, Jack Hyles, and Robert Schuller. They also had the opportunity to interact with renowned missiologists and church growth thinkers such as Donald McGavran, Arthur Glasser, Ralph Winter, Eddie Gibbs, and Peter Wagner, under whose tutelage I was studying for my doctorate in church growth at Fuller Theological Seminary.

In a letter following the trip, I tried to summarize what happened after one of these tours.

> Have you ever been at a total loss for words? Then you know how I feel! My heart is bursting with gratitude and praise to the Lord for all He is doing in a next-to-impossible situation.
>
> Imagine yourself boarding a plane with over twenty German pastors and leaders headed towards New York. You know they wonder if "anything good can come out of America?"…
>
> Our first encounter was at a lively, black church in New York where the pastor asked his congregation to give them a hearty welcome. As our reserved German pastors extended their hands, our black brothers and sisters brushed them aside and gave each one a bear hug, one they will never forget the rest of their lives! But what impressed them even more was the group who met a half hour before the service to pray.
>
> We saw and studied growing churches in action in Indiana, Illinois, New York, California, and Florida. All had different approaches, but all had the same priorities: a strong commitment to the Scriptures, personal conversion, strong visionary leadership, and training of laypeople for Christian living and ministry.
>
> These German pastors went with skepticism, but returned with a new vision for their own churches.

Specifically, these were comments from several of these men who went:

"For the first time in years I can see that there is a real future for our church. We can and must find new ways of service, worship, and outreach. If we will put Jesus Christ, the Living Lord, at the center of our proclamation, then we indeed have a great future ahead of us."

"Everywhere we went, we saw churches working upon the Ephesians 4:11–12 principle. Namely, that the pastor's function is not to be a 'solo actor' but a trainer, to equip the saints for the work of the ministry. From now on, that's how we want to operate here in our church"…

"I am the pastor of an historic eight-hundred-year-old church and I have the opportunity every Sunday to greet visitors from all over Germany. Up to this time, I have talked to them only about the history of the church, its magnificent stain-glass windows, the hand-carved altar, etc. From now on, after seeing what Dr. James Kennedy did, I am going to take this opportunity to personally challenge each visitor to consider these two questions: 1. If you were to die tonight, would you be sure that you would go to heaven? And 2. On what basis would God let you into heaven?"

Later, another church leader told us: "These trips are the single most important thing being done currently to raise the vision of German pastors and laymen for church growth." We were beginning to see "new wine poured into new wineskins." The old wine cellars were slowly giving way to new ones.

One person who never questioned our coming to Germany or that anything good could come out of America was Fritz

Schwarz. He was a pastor and district superintendent in northern Germany and father of the church growth movement in the nation.

I once sat in a meeting where he addressed fifty pastors and asked them for a definition of the gospel. Goethe, the German Shakespeare, once said, "The Germans make everything difficult, both for themselves and for everyone else." Perhaps that is why there has always been a German problem. Fritz realized that, and he fearlessly called for a return to a biblical foundation of what he termed "the simple gospel."

To Fritz, the gospel message was basically simple and could be described in a few minutes. After his challenge to the pastors, however, there was an awkward silence in the room. None of the pastors volunteered to answer. In their minds, volumes could be written to give an introduction to the definition of the gospel.

Later, after Fritz described his "simple gospel," one of the pastors made the skeptical remark: "We would like to hear what this kind of gospel sounds like."

Fritz Schwarz felt that if German theology could link arms with the pragmatic American approach it would make up for the lack of the training received by German pastors. He took our young American team under his wing. He was not only a brilliant theologian and author of many books, but also a dear brother with a strong personal commitment to Jesus Christ. Together, along with other like-minded leaders, we laid the foundation for a national organization which brought key leaders together.

A few months after Fritz joined us on one of our church growth study tours, he invited me to participate with him in a series of pastor conferences in Switzerland. I looked forward to this special time with him. At the last minute, however, I received a call that Fritz had to back out due to a physical problem. Disappointed, I went on without him.

Shortly after my return, I received another call. Fritz Schwarz, only fifty-five, had died of a massive heart attack. I was shocked. "Why now, Lord, just when we needed his help?" I asked. But here again we experienced His amazing grace. I knew we must give thanks even for this and focus our confidence and expectation on Him alone: "The Lord gave and the Lord has taken away; May the name of the Lord be praised" (Job 1:21).

God still had greater things in mind for us. About a year and a half earlier, I'd come across a letter from a church growth leader in Great Britain. What, the writer asked, were the chances of bringing together representatives from all over Europe to discuss how our traditional churches could be moved to effective evangelism and discipleship training? I responded that we were not only interested in this, but that we also wanted to have an active part in seeing this realized. After all, that's why we were in Germany.

Little did I realize that before long the leadership of this effort would be turned over to me. In January 1987, the first European Church Growth Conference was held. Delegates from Belgium, England, Finland, France, The Netherlands, Norway, Sweden, Switzerland, Scotland, and West Germany committed themselves to the formation of a European Church Growth Association. It was an historic event born out of a critical concern for the continent. Europe was increasingly becoming an irreligious land. Church attendance had declined dramatically; approximately 1.8 million people were giving up their church membership.

At our final meeting, an executive committee was elected, and I was asked to serve as its founding chairman. This was a special privilege and honor for me, and a token of God's blessing and comfort after the death of Fritz Schwarz.

Back in 1953, prior to my leaving for Taiwan as a missionary, I had spoken at a Navigators men's conference in California. At the conclusion of my messages, I was given a small book along with a word of thanks. The book, *Your God Is Too Small* by J. B. Phillips, was not meant to be a critique of my messages, but rather a reminder that in our limited understanding, God does not seem to be big enough to handle all our needs in this confused world.

I felt that once again He had to remind me of this truth. After seeing Him at work in Germany, I rested in this thought and assurance.

Then something brought back memories of Brazil and elsewhere. Thoughts about being too comfortable once again hit me. I must confess that I was totally blindsided when this happened. I knew that I couldn't "put God in a box," yet I struggled mightily when something unexpected loomed before me.

I was about to find out just what that "something unexpected" was.

49

INSIDE AFRICA

April 1987

Southern Africa

One of our special activities while living in Germany was getting out on Saturdays and joining the *volksmarches* throughout the neighboring countryside. These so-called marches were really hikes. Hundreds of people walked together through forest paths, meadows, smaller villages, and out-of-the-way places. This way we got to learn about sights hidden from the general public.

Instead of making these 10-kilometer, 20-kilometer, or 42-kilometer (marathon) walks, Alice and I ran them. We enjoyed these immensely; besides, they were good for keeping up physical fitness. While in Germany, I ran ten marathons and Alice did four. For all of these, we were in our fifties. I have the medals to prove it!

Gradually, my responsibilities increased in Germany. Since we as a mission also had ministry teams in France and Greece, regular trips to touch base with our staff became part of my schedule as Europe area director. In this capacity, I made frequent trips to our headquarters in California for consultations and leadership conferences.

During the five preceding years, OC grew at a rapid rate. Our missionary force had more than doubled; this meant that leaders needed to be trained to meet the demands for future expansion into more countries. In 1986, I was privileged to be part of a six-man teaching team that traveled to three locations in Asia, Europe, and Latin America, where we met with present and potential future leaders or our missionary teams for an intensive training period.

"Around the world in eighty days"—so went that familiar tune from years ago. We did it in less than half that time. This trip and others required me to be away from home for lengthy periods. Whenever possible, on shorter distances, I took Alice along with me, and was always glad for her input and read on situations, especially as they dealt with personnel issues. These seemed to dominate the agenda. Since half of our personnel were women, Alice's role in assisting me was highly valuable and appreciated.

When the mission sent its first team to Africa, Kenya was the target country. The team was large, and apart from the leader, a native Kenyan, most were first-term missionaries. This meant we provided a lot of pastoral oversight, as well as help in the formation of basic field ministry and strategy.

The mission then asked me, in addition to my European responsibilities, to assume the role of giving oversight to the new ministry in Africa. This, of course, meant adding more trips and reports to my already loaded schedule. I did not make it any easier on myself when I enrolled at Fuller Theological Seminary for doctoral studies in the area of church growth. This required occasional trips to the States for intensive courses, as well as tons of reading and the usual term papers.

I finally submitted my doctoral thesis, *Church Renewal in Germany, Is It Possible? A Study of the Established Protestant Church.* I can assure you that I was glad when this was all over and I received my doctor of ministry degree at graduation ceremonies at Fuller. I was happy to have our daughter, Lita, with me for that occasion, representing the rest of the family unable to come.

Despite the demands on my time, I thrived on all of these opportunities and felt that I was just where I should be. When OC's president paid a visit to Germany, one of the key pastors with whom we were working turned to him and thanked him warmly for sending us. He added, "I hope they won't have to leave. We need them here."

In April 1987, I was invited to participate in the Discipling Zimbabwe Congress in Harare (Salisbury) hosted by OC. When the decision was made to deploy a team to the southern Africa region, the mission asked me to assume its leadership, which would require a move from Germany to Africa.

I wrestled with this decision. I was excited about the open doors in Africa and the overwhelming response on the part of church leadership in welcoming us. On the other hand, I also knew that my job in Germany was not done. Although I had turned over the field leadership to capable men on our team, I had an uneasy feeling about leaving, especially when I felt that our commitment to the German church had not been fulfilled. Was it right to cut and run?

When I sought the counsel of godly men, there seemed to be no question that I should stay on in Germany and oversee the work in Africa from a distance. Finally, however, the mission prevailed and urged me to make the change, with the appeal that my presence was more needed in Africa than in Germany.

I have always believed that God is bigger than any human authority, but now I had to practice what I preached.

We packed our bags and off we went—to Swaziland, a little land-locked country bordering South Africa and Mozambique. Before long we were four families, the advance team for reaching out into the southern cone of Africa. The shift from Germany to a largely underdeveloped continent brought certain challenges with it. But our experiences on other mission fields helped with our adjustment. Alice was particularly glad that this change did not involve learning another language, since English was the common language in these former English colonies.

We quickly learned that life inside Africa was going to be different. During a conference in Zimbabwe, Alice and I were eating breakfast with our pastor friends. Fried liver and beans wasn't exactly our standard breakfast fare, but that's exactly what we had. If that did not get us, something else did. As we ate, a pastor from neighboring Malawi told us a heartbreaking and stomach-wrenching story.

"A Mozambican pastor was regularly crossing the border from his country into Malawi to bring back Bibles and Christian literature," the pastor said. "One day, while he was gone, Communist soldiers came to his home asking where he was. They suspected him of spying and ordered his wife to report to them as soon as he returned.

"When he came back, she dutifully informed the authorities. The soldiers returned, and with his wife and six children looking on, shot him point blank. Then, tearing out his intestines, they roasted them over a fire, burned the Bibles, and forced his wife to eat her husband's intestines. For several months she suffered from terrible nausea while seeking to care for her family."

It was hard for us to eat another bite after a story like this. We were exposed to the terrible struggle for survival some of our African believer-friends faced. Yet their courage to maintain their faith in light of all this inspired us.

We had shifted from a nominally Christian continent in Europe to Africa, where the gospel had made huge inroads into what used to be called the "dark continent." The seed of the gospel had fallen on good ground and the response to it had been immense. Different from the rational Western approach, which questioned and sought to dissect all spiritual matters, the African had a built-in sense and appreciation for the supernatural and therefore a keen sensitivity to the transcendent world. God's role and rule in our lives was never disputed. It was taken for granted.

This came like a breath of fresh air to us and we jumped into it with both feet. We knew that God's ways were above our ways. Since He had brought us to Africa, we also knew that He had a purpose to accomplish in and through our lives.

50

THIS IS EXACTLY WHAT WE NEED

1989

Swaziland

Our team of four families gradually started to grow as several more families joined us in Swaziland. One of the primary reasons for selecting this little country was to provide us with access to other African nations. If we had established residence in South Africa, many countries would not have allowed us entry due to their hostile relationships with its apartheid regime. Even though we also had ministry in South Africa, we were able to get around this complication by possessing two passports. We used one exclusively in South Africa, and the other for all other countries. We just had to be careful to pull out the right passport at the airport when going through immigration and customs!

A special thrill for us was to welcome our son Marty, his wife, Karen, and their two children, Karl and Heidi, to Swaziland in 1989. Just as Papa and Mutti never tried to influence the direction of my life's calling, so Alice and I felt that it was not our place to push him into a missionary career. In fact, in his preteen years,

Marty was a handful. His mother often prayed in exasperation, "Lord take him home, before he becomes a juvenile delinquent." Alice really meant it. But when he was nine, Marty invited Christ into his life and a huge change took place. Not that he turned into a saint overnight, but there was a new spiritual sensitivity to right and wrong, and becoming more teachable.

I took Marty with me on a ministry trip to Europe in 1977, when we traveled with evangelist Luis Palau to meetings in Wales, England, and Germany. It was during that time that God impressed upon Marty the purpose He had for his life: serving Him. College work at Multnomah University and seminary studies at Fuller Theological Seminary wove a thread into his life, and all pointed toward Africa. After marrying his college sweetheart, Karen Johnson, Marty eventually joined OC. The mission agreed to send him to Swaziland.

What a privilege it was to have family with us and to start working together in ministry. As we began to minister as a father-son team, it not only blessed us but also became an example and inspiration to many of the pastors we taught during our large conferences and seminars in different countries.

Marty provided immeasurable help in helping us refine materials and resources for our ministry. Beyond that, he established contact with the Mozambican community in Swaziland and initiated a teaching ministry among them. Ever since our arrival in Africa, we had prayed that God would give us an opening to effectively influence the spiritual leadership of that nation.

The opening came at a general assembly of the Conference of Churches in Swaziland, made up of the key pastoral leaders of all the churches in the country. Our team was invited to provide the speakers, and we invited one of our fellow-missionaries in Kenya to lead the morning Bible studies and deliver the evening messages. I was asked to present the basic church growth lectures for four hours each day.

From the start, I felt a special sense of freedom and authority with my teaching. Hour after hour, they sat and responded with real enthusiasm to the challenge of church growth and world missions. I seldom had a more receptive audience.

On the second day, the prime minister of Swaziland attended and presented his greetings. He ended his remarks with this exhortation: "When you selected the theme of church growth for this conference, you could not have chosen a better topic. May I exhort you to follow Christ's command to make disciples of all nations."

It must have been unique in modern history that a prime minister of a country had given church leaders such a mandate!

At the conference closing, Pastor Isaac, president of the Swaziland Conference of Churches, stood up. "This is exactly what we need," he said. "I want every pastor in Swaziland to receive training in church growth by OC. Let's turn Swaziland upside down!"

Needless to say, this was a huge encouragement to all of us.

Later, our team was invited to have tea at the prime minister's office. It was my privilege to pray for him in his responsibilities of leadership for this nation.

Soon invitations came to hold training seminars for pastors in South Africa, Zimbabwe, Malawi, Zambia, Botswana, and Tanzania. Requests even came from Nigeria for similar ministries.

Again we were witnessing God's gracious hand of blessing as opportunities increased. But as Paul wrote to the Corinthians, there were not only doors for effective work that were opened, but there was also opposition that came along with them. There were struggles within the team, conflicts with mission leadership, and health issues. All of these were used by the enemy to distract us from the work to which God had called us. Yet with His help we marched on, confident that He who had begun a good work in and through us would carry it on to completion.

51

A BROKEN WRISTWATCH

October 1989

Malawi, Africa

It was the last day of our church growth conference in Malawi. I had been challenging nearly two hundred pastors all week with God's plan of desiring to use the African church to reach the world with the gospel. Throughout the week, a powerful sense of God's presence prevailed.

The meetings especially moved one pastor. Augustino was a simple man, equipped with only a grade-school education. Several months earlier, he had fled with his wife and baby from the atrocities of civil war in Mozambique.

Once across the border, they found shelter in a refugee camp. They arrived with nothing. Even the clothes on their backs were from the Red Cross. Yet, full of God's love, they began ministering to their fellow countrymen in the refugee camp. Many responded to the gospel, and soon a new church was born.

On this final day of the conference, Augustino approached me. He did not speak English, unlike most of the pastors in southern Africa. But he had heard that I had lived in Brazil. He talked to me in Portuguese, the *lingua franca* of Mozambique.

"What you shared has deeply touched my heart," he said. "I know that we need to have a part in reaching not only Africa, but the world for Christ. I have no money to offer. All I can give is this."

He reached into his pocket and pulled out an old wristwatch. It was obvious it had seen years of use. The band was broken, though Augustino had tried to fix it with discarded dental floss. The crystal was clouded and scratched. Yet it still ticked.

Immediately, I realized that this gift was a sacrifice beyond measure. The young pastor had literally nothing of material value. His wife didn't even have a blanket to protect their baby from the chilling cold of African nights. How could I accept this family's most valuable possession? I quickly handed it back to him and said, "No, dear brother, I cannot accept this."

But the Mozambican insisted.

"*Senhor,* this watch is not for you," he said. "Please, sell it for me and use the money to help spread the gospel in Africa and to others who have never heard, since I cannot go."

I was stunned. What commitment, what a vision this man had! Out of their poverty, this family was giving what was most precious to them so that others around the world might come to know Christ.

There was no question in my mind who the true missionary was in this case. He stood right in front of me.

A year later, I saw Augustino again. We were back again in Malawi for another pastoral training conference. He was overjoyed when he saw us, and with excitement told us all that God had done for him that past year. His ministry had grown from pastoring one church to five churches among his fellow refugees, under primitive circumstances. He urged us to come back and help. He desperately needed New Testaments and Bibles for his people. We were able to provide him with a little money to buy some of them.

What about the wristwatch? I still have it in my possession. By looking at it, you would think it has little value. Yet over the years, I have related the story of Augustino's watch many times, to many people. After each telling, either my listeners or myself, or both, are moved to reach into our pockets and give again for the sake of spreading the gospel in Africa and beyond. That little timepiece has inspired the flow of countless dollars toward the cause of Christ. For this reason, Augustino's watch is not for sale. It is priceless.

In Mark 14 we read the account of Mary anointing Jesus at Bethany. Jesus called her act of sacrifice something beautiful, saying, "She did what she could" (v. 8). Then He added these significant words: "...wherever the gospel is preached throughout the world, what she has done will also be told, in memory of her" (v. 9).

Augustino was a true disciple of the Savior. I am glad and honored to have met him. His story too continues to be told.

52

MAKING THE SECOND HALF THE BEST HALF

Summer 1991

Cupertino, California

Both Alice and I turned sixty in 1991. As we faced this new milestone in our lives, we looked ahead to the future. We were excited about the prospects of the next decade or more, as God would give us health and strength. Both of us felt physically in top condition and were eager to make the coming years count for His glory. We read a stimulating book by Edmund Janss entitled *Making the Second Half the Best Half.* It challenged us to take a personal inventory and make a fresh commitment to see this happen in our lives. This in turn led us to make some radical changes.

The most profound one was our decision to resign (again) from OC after nearly forty years of ministry. OC had been our life during these past decades as we ministered on five continents—in Asia, Africa, Europe, North and South America. Deep personal relationships and friendships had been forged over the years. It was not an easy decision. We both wrestled before the Lord to know His will for our lives.

In a real sense, it meant leaving the security of a mission family and stepping out in faith and trusting Him in a new way for everything. It was easy to think that this kind of faith was more for the younger generation just beginning their ministry. But just as Jesus commanded Peter to step out of the boat and walk on unknown waters, we too heard that voice deep within. Earnest appeals by the mission leadership for us to stay were part of the struggle and did not make it any easier.

I had no idea what the next step would be, but finally concluded that I needed to follow in the footsteps of Abraham, who by faith "obeyed and went, even though he did not know where he was going" (Hebrews 11:8).

If we took the first step of obedience, we were sure that He would be faithful and show us the next step at the right time.

I once read a quote by Hudson Taylor, that great apostle to China in the nineteenth century, saying that "God is ready to give us all that we need, when we need it." This is especially true when it comes to finding clear direction for our lives.

Once the decision was made, there was a deep peace within that we were proceeding in His will and that the best was still ahead of us. We visited with Dick Hillis shortly after returning to the States. "Hans," he said, "these first forty years have just been years of preparation. Now you are ready for the real task God has for you."

I must admit that I did not feel a bit like Moses, who had a similar experience when God called him from the backside of the Midian desert at age eighty. But if he could do it with God's help at eighty, who was I to shrink back at age sixty?

My first thought was that after a brief furlough, we might return to Africa. I sensed that much work still needed to be done there. We could go back on short-term projects and assignments. What our organizational support structure would be was not clear, but we always knew that God would provide for our financial needs and the ministry He had for us to do.

Once again, an old hymn came to mind, one I had memorized and sung as a teenager in China. Here is the final verse:

> If we could see, if we could know
> We often say,
> But God in love a veil doth throw
> Across our way.
> We cannot see what lies before,
> And so we cling to Him the more,
> He leads us till this life is o'er,
> Trust and Obey.

Trust and obey were the key words that were to be our compass as we eagerly anticipated His purpose for our lives.

After resigning from OC, a number of invitations came knocking at our doors. These were challenging opportunities and responsibilities. One organization offered me a position to head up ministry encompassing the whole continent of Africa. Another asked me to pray about leading their ministries in South America.

We prayed, but did not sense the Spirit's confirmation.

Then something extraordinary happened. It came totally unexpected and unsought, yet with such force and conviction that there remained no doubt it was from His leading.

So often, we tend to limit God when we envision what He will do and how He will handle a situation. But then God, again and again, delights to surprise us and reveal Himself as the One who knows the end from the beginning. It was Paul who wrote to the church in Rome, "Oh, the depth of the riches of the wisdom and knowledge of God! How unsearchable his judgments, and his paths beyond tracing out!" (Romans 11:33).

A visitor rang the doorbell of our home in Cupertino, California. We'd purchased this home when we first returned from Brazil in 1972 and had lived in it while we were in the

States for ten years working at OC headquarters. When we went to Germany, our kids lived in it, and while in Africa we rented it out. When we returned, we had a home to come back to.

I opened the door and welcomed Joseph Wong into our home. He was the lead elder of a large Chinese congregation in San Jose, CCiC (Chinese Church in Christ). In fact, before going to Germany in 1982, this church assumed a substantial part of our missionary support and faithfully maintained it. They'd told me that since my parents came from Germany to China to bring the gospel to their people, they wanted to play a part as we returned to Germany and ministered to the German people.

Joseph had a message from the Lord for us. He did not say this in so many words, but to me it came through crystal clear.

"God brought you back from Africa to come and work among us Chinese people," he said. "After all, you are Chinese and you belong to us. There are many Chinese people in Brazil—they need you."

Over the next couple of weeks, we were avalanched from every direction by people we knew, as well as some who were total strangers. All had one theme: You need to go back and minister to the Chinese. We couldn't believe what was happening.

China had always had a special place in my heart. But after all these years, this was totally out of the blue. The calls kept coming, and we began to pay attention. My heart began to burn within me. Before long, there was that sweet confirmation of His Spirit to our spirit that this was His will for us. There seemed to be a new call on our lives for a new task.

Along with this call, God gave us a fresh vision for China and what He wanted us to do. As I prayed, a number of things began to crystallize in my mind. I wrote them down.

> Although the church there has grown faster than in any other country, despite persecution, we are still faced with the fact that one billion are unevangelized.

Just as God miraculously opened doors for the gospel into Eastern Europe by demolishing "walls and Iron Curtains," I believe that in the not-too-distant future the doors to China will also swing open.

Specifically, I am praying for ten thousand harvesters to go to China when the doors open and reap the harvest He has been preparing during these past few decades.

It is my firm conviction that the Chinese people, principally those living in North America (over two million), hold the greatest potential for providing a major missionary thrust to see this accomplished.

I further believe that the time has come for Chinese believers to be gripped in a new way by this missionary challenge and to shoulder this responsibility.

Several immediate ministries ensued.

I agreed to link forces with a growing Chinese church in the San Jose area for the next couple of years. Besides teaching and preaching every week, I endeavored to stimulate their vision and challenge, motivate, and equip them.

Soon other Chinese churches asked for the same kind of help. Then an invitation came to go to Brazil and acquaint myself with what was taking place among the one hundred thousand–plus Chinese in São Paulo. I had not been back to Brazil for more than ten years and was looking forward to it. Some Chinese friends provided the funds to make the trip.

I particularly looked forward to seeing Clarence Pi. This visit would provide new direction for me.

53

CHINESE INTERNATIONAL MISSIONS

December 1991

São Paulo, Brazil

Chinese International Missions was born in the heart of Clarence Pi.

I met Clarence in 1981 during my first contact with CCiC in San Jose. As a young engineer in Silicon Valley, he was already vitally interested in seeing God's kingdom built in Chinese communities of the Bay Area. I sensed in him a restless spirit that sought something more than earning a living. When I challenged him to seek God's will by pursuing biblical and theological training, he promptly enrolled at Multnomah University. We continued our relationship, though by this time I was ministering in Germany.

Whenever my visits brought me back to the States, I looked forward to informal times over a cup of coffee with Clarence. We each shared what God was doing in our lives.

While I was in Africa, Clarence, along with his wife, Christine, and their children, moved to Brazil to serve as missionaries. They began to see fruit in the lives of the Chinese community there. Clarence had a special burden to unite the various Chinese churches, and God began to use him as a catalyst to bring the churches together around a project close to Clarence's heart: the formation of a Chinese theological seminary.

It was in December 1991, on my visit to Brazil, that Clarence opened his heart to me and shared his vision of a Chinese missionary organization which would reach around the world, mobilizing Chinese believers to be obedient to the Great Commission.

This immediately clicked with me, because I too had started to pray since my return from Africa that God would raise up a mighty army of Chinese missionaries. I boldly started—and still continue today—to pray for ten thousand missionaries.

With excitement, Clarence and I began to dream, talk, pray, and plan for the Lord to bring this together. And He did.

During subsequent times together, Clarence and I met with key Chinese and missionary leaders here in the States to explore the possibilities of forming this new missionary agency, which would be directed by Chinese and would work closely with over a thousand Chinese churches across America. Everywhere, we were met with an overwhelmingly positive response.

As we began to assemble a potential board of directors, God led us to the Lord and wise counselors. Much work needed to be done in formulating a constitution and bylaws to provide documentation for incorporation.

Clarence wanted me to lead this organization, citing my experience and age, but I firmly resisted his persistent urging. I countered that this was to be a Chinese mission and had to be led by a Chinese. I was willing, however, to help get it going. In my mind, I thought of a commitment of five years.

I had just read a statement by Arnold Toynbee, the great historian-philosopher. He said that the twenty-first century would be largely under the control of the Chinese. China's economy was beginning to boom as it emerged from its Communist shadows, and I believed that spiritually it also was ready to make a move forward. These were all the more reasons that Chinese needed to take a lead in Christian missions.

And so in June 1992—barely six months from that first meeting in Brazil—Chinese International Missions (CIM) was born. Part of its purpose statement read, "It is our goal not only to reach our fellow Chinese scattered over all the world including those on the mainland of China, but also to reach out cross-culturally."

Clarence Pi was unanimously chosen to serve as executive director, and I, privileged to be the only "foreigner" in this group, was appointed as associate director.

Uruguay and Chile were the first two countries in which CIM found opportunities to minister. Missionary staff recruited in Hong Kong joined the fledgling organization as things began to move forward. Chinese communities in other countries expressed their need for help, and we began to pray earnestly for laborers. Before long, Clarence and his family moved to South Africa to lay the groundwork for ministry among a growing Chinese population.

I had one unforgettable experience on a CIM trip to South America. While visiting one of our missionary couples in Santiago, Chile, my past intersected with my present. Here is the story as I wrote it to friends:

> Joseph and Maria Hsu, our missionary couple in Santiago, picked me up at the airport, along with Mr. Chu from their church. On the way to their home we stopped off at a Chinese restaurant to get a bite to eat. Our conversation soon centered on the bowl of red-hot Chinese chili peppers I was eating. When Mr. Chu asked me where I had developed a taste for these, I told him that I had grown up in Hunan province in Chinawhere this was very customary. He asked me further, what

town I had lived in. To my utter amazement, Mr. Chu replied that he had grown up in the same place. Then I couldn't believe my ears when he told me that as a boy he had heard about a German missionary who had a bicycle and he had seen him walk with his son along the city wall. "That was my dad and me!" I shouted excitedly.

Mr. Chu had immigrated to Chile and just four years ago turned to Christ. Now he was serving as a lay elder in reaching out to the Chinese community of fifteen hundred in Santiago.

It truly was a long way from Shaoyang, China, to Santiago, Chile. But God had allowed me once again to witness His infinite power to reach across the oceans and the years and establish that link which holds us together in Christ.

While all this was going on, I continued an active ministry at home with CCiC, as well as with other churches when opportunities presented themselves. On one of these occasions, I had just finished speaking to a group of postgraduate Chinese scholars from Stanford University in California when one of them asked me a question which stunned me: "Why doesn't God love the Chinese?"

That evening, I'd shared with them the beautiful story of the lost son from Luke 15, and the father who was waiting for him to return home. For many of these students, it was the first time they had ever heard the gospel, since most came from mainland China.

Quickly, I assured the student that God loved the whole world, and because there were so many Chinese, He had a vey special love for them.

I was totally unprepared for the next question.

"But if He loves us, why hasn't He allowed us to hear this Good News before?"

I struggled to answer. It certainly was not because God did

not love the Chinese. Had He not commanded His followers to go to the ends of the earth and tell them? Now, nearly two thousand years later, there were still billions of people who had never heard. About one billion of these were Chinese.

But here sitting in front of me were some of China's finest scholars, asking whether God really loved them. What an indictment to us who call ourselves His faithful followers!

Yet God in His grace let the light of the gospel shine into their hearts that night. A number of them invited Christ into their lives.

That evening, I was challenged afresh to pray that God might send laborers into China where so many men and women had never heard the Good News of Jesus Christ.

54

CHINA REVISITED

May 1997

Nanchang, Jiangxi, China

My old friend Werner Bürklin was on the line, the same Werner who first welcomed us to Germany fifteen years earlier. It was an amazing circle of events going way back to my teenage years in Shanghai. Werner and I were classmates there and had also been members of the Hitler Youth Movement. Now World War II was over and Hitler long dead. Yet God wonderfully used these events to help bring me to Christ. Several of my schoolmates also found the Savior and heard God's call.

Werner was one of these. He returned to Germany and I went to the States. Before long, he directed Youth for Christ in all of Europe, later served with Billy Graham, and twice directed his International Conferences for Itinerant Evangelists (Amsterdam '83 and '86).

During one of these congresses, God renewed Werner's vision for China. He began to visit China several times each year. There he developed deep relationships with church leaders that eventually led to invitations to come with international teams of western Christian leaders to conduct training seminars in China's Bible schools and theological seminaries. Eventually, Werner founded China Partner, Inc.

Now our paths were crossing again. On the phone, Werner asked me to be part of this teaching team. Would I pray about it?

There are some things which you immediately recognize as God's leading, and this was one of them. I accepted, and traveled to China in May 1997. I wrote the following letter to friends about my visit.

> I returned a few days ago from a three-week trip to China and Korea. What an experience! You can't imagine the emotions I felt being back in the country of my birth. It was exactly in May 1950 that our family took the long train ride from Shanghai to Tianjing (close to Beijing) to board an old American troop transporter which was to bring us to the U.S.A.
>
> In these forty-seven years a lot has changed, and yet, a lot remained the same.
>
> There have always been a lot of people in China, but now there are a lot more. When I grew up we learned that China had a population of 400 million. Now there are three times that many— 1.3 billion! But what was even more exciting was the growth of the church of Christ in that country.
>
> When we left China in 1950, there were about 700,000 believers. Then Communism took over with its atheistic totalitarianism. During the Cultural Revolution (1966–1976), all churches were closed and all religions banned. Hundreds

of thousands, perhaps millions (including many Christians) were persecuted and died. After the death of the Communist leaders Mao Zedong and Zhou En lai in 1976, things gradually began to change. And under China's new leader, Deng Xiaoping, in 1979 the first churches were reopened.

During our time in China we were able to preach and teach with total freedom. I will never forget the first Sunday there—May 4. I had been invited to speak in a church in Nanchang at an 8 A.M. service. When I arrived there fifteen minutes early, the church courtyard was already filled with several hundred people who had been unable to get into the building where 1,000 or more sat tightly squeezed together. You should have seen their faces lighting up when I greeted them in Chinese and told them that it was so good to come "home." There seemed no shortage of Bibles; in fact, they were selling them in the church's bookstore! And how hungry they were for spiritual food. What a privilege to preach with total freedom!

I thought a lot about my dear dad and mom who had given nearly thirty years of their lives to minister in China. How they would have rejoiced if they had seen this—maybe they did.

Most moving, however, was a visit we made to Shenyang, in northern China close to the Korean border. Before the sermon, a beautifully robed choir stood and sang, "All to Jesus I surrender, all to Him I freely give." My thoughts went back to the dark days these believers had gone through.

Many of them, no doubt, had lost loved ones to the sword, others had suffered and survived violence we know little about. Yet here they were, singing "All to Jesus I surrender." What a lesson and challenge to us believers in the Western world who know so little about suffering and following the Savior's footsteps.

At the close of the service, I turned to the pastor and said, "You had about two thousand people in the service this morning. You have a very large church."

The pastor smiled and replied, "Oh, I forgot to tell you, we have five services like this every Sunday."

"Do you have about eight thousand members, then?" I asked incredulously, thinking that I might have misunderstood him.

Again, there was that wistful smile. "Actually, we have twenty-two thousand members and to accommodate this large number we have to rotate them every other week so that all will have an opportunity to attend also." I learned that when they were not able to attend the main service, members would attend meetings in one of a hundred local house churches.

I was blown away, and more so when I learned that when the church was reopened in 1979, there were only 220 in attendance. This church had averaged over one thousand baptisms each year since then.

What was behind this phenomenal growth?

Again, I pulled one of the Chinese church leaders aside and asked him this question. I have never forgotten the precise and clear answer he gave me.

"There are three reasons," he said. "This is not due to any man's work. It is clearly the work of the Holy Spirit. It is the result of persecution we have suffered, and when we suffer, God manifests His grace. We have not had foreigners come and tell us of their religion these past forty years. This is not a foreign import; it is our religion, our faith."

We taught two consecutive weeks in two Bible schools/seminaries. There is no question that the biggest need in the church in China is the need for more pastors, preachers, evangelists, and teachers. With thousands coming to know Christ, there is only one ordained pastor for every ten thousand believers in the registered church.

As we taught in these schools, we sensed their eagerness to listen and learn from us, scribbling down notes as fast as they could. I was overwhelmed with their genuine warmth and the reception they gave us. Even Communist party members and representatives of the Religious Affairs Bureau sat with us at the reception dinners and thanked us for coming "home" to China and helping the church.

Needless to say, my heart was deeply moved. I was so grateful that God allowed me to see with my own eyes what He is doing in China.

55

A Cab Driver's Blessing

1997

Shanghai, China

The open doors to teach in Bible schools and seminaries in China continued to provide wonderful opportunities to give biblical instruction to young students preparing for the ministry. Many of my Chinese friends in the States looked at this skeptically at first because it was done within the framework of the registered church in China. In time they did acknowledge that these were unusual opportunities. My personal conviction was that I was willing to go wherever God opened the door to minister the Word without interference.

One of the members of our team was Ed Lyman, an evangelist, teacher, and most of all, a man with a powerful singing voice. The ministry of this gifted tenor (while in the service, he had been called the "Singing Marine") blessed all who heard him. We developed a close personal friendship on trips to China. When in the States, I valued him as a good friend, a man with a kindred spirit.

There were about twenty seminaries spread all over China and during the next few years we were able to teach in most of them. That this was even possible in a Communist country was a miracle.

Along with teaching in the schools, we also had the privilege of preaching in churches each Sunday we were there. I was awed that I was able to stand in front of one or two thousand people in a couple of the largest churches in two cities and preach the message of salvation. I thought again of my father, who in all his years of pioneer missionary work had probably never spoken to more than two hundred people at one time. These early pioneers sowed the seed. We were able to view the harvest they never saw.

I was so grateful for other unforgettable experiences. For example, there was the prayer meeting in a seminary where the director voiced the deep conviction of everyone, saying, "We Chinese are praying that one day Beijing's Tiananmen Square will be filled with thousands of Christians praising God, not under the flag of Communism, but under the flag of Jesus Christ." My heart tingled with excitement as I heard these words not just once, but again and again.

Since open evangelism was not permitted, the seminary students of this same school found creative ways to share their faith publicly. Each wore a colorful jacket with the words "Jesus loves me" emblazoned on the back in bold letters in both English and Chinese. On weekends, they carried red backpacks marked with the Chinese characters for "Jesus is Lord" as they moved through the streets or through the countryside. Even pastors openly identified with Christ by wearing ties with "God is love" embroidered on them. This often led to questions from interested parties. If asked, of course, the students and pastors had to respond!

Another memory: one day, a young man passing by one of the Bible schools heard singing from inside. He walked up the stairs and asked, "Can someone here tell me how I can get to know God?"

Two church leaders who suffered greatly during the Cultural Revolution in the sixties will also always be etched in my memory. One had lost a father and four family members; all were killed by Communists. Another was falsely accused and had to suffer severe punishment. When I asked them how they were able to work in this kind of setting, they simply replied, "We have chosen to forgive them."

Something which impressed me deeply was the dynamic role women were playing in building of the kingdom of God in China. We visited several new churches, including a house gathering of ten, which grew in nine years to six hundred members. The sparkplug was Mrs. Sun, who had been a devout Buddhist. When she found the Lord, she immediately began sharing the Good News with her family. Then neighbors started coming to her home. Since she was a new believer, she attended a church service in another village and then shared what she had learned. Now they had a building seating about five hundred—all paid for at the dedication.

I spoke briefly one morning to a weekly Bible study attended by 1,000 women. Even the enrollment in Bible schools had a majority of female students, many of whom would pastor churches upon completion of their studies. It was no surprise, therefore, to see some of the largest churches in China pastored by women.

During many visits, I had the occasion of meeting with the top leadership of the China Christian Council, which embodied the official church of China. Some were without doubt true followers of Christ, and I could embrace them as such. At all times, they were polite and cordial in their interactions with us. Werner Bürklin had spent years cultivating their friendship and this provided us with strategic opportunities for ministry.

A very special remembrance was a visit to the former Shanghai Free Christian Church with my son and grandson. This is the church where in 1945 I had my personal encounter with Christ. I showed them the pillar behind which I hid when I entered the crowded hall. It was there that God's Word spoke so powerfully to me about the need of my own soul. My life had gone through a fundamental change, from darkness to light!

One morning, as I headed for the train station in Shanghai, I got into a lively conversation with my taxi driver. I soon discovered that he also knew the Lord and faithfully attended one of the large churches in the city. He reminded me of something I had observed earlier, that if you wanted to get a seat at a Sunday morning service, you had to show up at least an hour early.

When the cab driver let me off at the train station, he grabbed my hand and said, "Will you promise me that you will come back to China again? We need you!"

When I assured him that I would, he had one more message for me: "God bless you."

This was the first time and only time I was blessed by a cab driver. And it happened in Shanghai.

56

FROM AMSTERDAM TO ZAMBIA

1998

Arnold, California

In 1998, Alice and I moved to a little mountain town, Arnold, in the California Sierra mountains. This was quite a change from city life, but we enjoyed it immensely. The tranquil pace, the majestic scenery of the mountains surrounded by Redwood trees—it all seemed the perfect fit for us at this stage of life.

Two years later, an official-looking manila envelope arrived in the mail at our post office box. It was an invitation from the Billy Graham organization to present two seminars in German on evangelism and follow-up at its Amsterdam 2000 Conference of Preaching Evangelists.

I felt greatly honored, since I knew many German leaders could have better handled this subject. But since they insisted, I gladly accepted and was off to Amsterdam, The Netherlands, to join ten thousand other participants from 190 countries. This was certainly one of the most representative Christian gatherings ever held. Dr. Billy Graham, due to health factors, could not attend in person but sent greetings via satellite.

It was an opportunity to catch up with many old friends in ministry over the past decades and to refresh our friendships. As I presented my seminar one morning, an elderly gentleman entered the room and sat at the back. During the break, he came up to me. I recognized my dear friend and mentor, Roy Robertson, whom I had met in China more than fifty years before as a teenager. He had discipled me and built major principles into my life which provided me with a solid foundation. He had seen my name on the program and had come to see what his "Timothy" had to say. Unfortunately, he did not understand a word I uttered, since it was all in German!

The year 2000 proved to be a busy one for me. Here is a brief glimpse at my schedule:

February	China Symposium with a delegation of leaders from China in California
March	International student conference at Yosemite Park, California
April	Washington, D.C. annual missions conference for Chinese church
May	Training seminars in three cities in China
June	China conference in Germany

July/August	Amsterdam 2000 congress
September	Pastors conferences in Tanzania and Zambia
October	China ministry board meetings in Hong Kong

While China occupied much of my time and attention, I stayed involved in Africa through annual pastor conferences in Zambia. Our son, Marty, who had lived and ministered in Africa for more than twelve years, invited me to join him in conferences for pastors in Tanzania and Zambia.

That September, our team of eight set out on a 4,400-mile trip in two Land Rovers, traversing northern South Africa through Zimbabwe and Zambia into Tanzania. As we followed the footsteps of David Livingstone, the Scottish pioneer missionary to Africa, through rough terrain, we gained new appreciation for this missionary/explorer who gave his life in the heart of Africa. We stopped briefly at the site where his heart was buried. While his body was shipped back to England, Africans felt that his heart belonged to Africa. What a tribute to the man!

For a number of years, Marty's burden had been to minister to rural pastors in out-of-the-way places. That we did. Many came and hungrily received what we taught in morning-to-night sessions that covered topics such as pastoral leadership, spiritual gifts, discipleship, growth in maturity, church planting, and stewardship and finances. Marty and I carried the bulk of the instruction, sometimes teaching five or six hours a day, but we loved every minute of it. Accommodations were whatever the bush offered. Marty and some of our team contracted malaria and had to be flown back to Johannesburg, South Africa. But all of that was just par for the course.

In 2003, Marty and his family returned to the States. Two more children had joined his family: Kari, born in Swaziland in

1990; and Mark, born in South Africa in 1992. The decision to return was not easy, but he wanted to be home when he guided his children through the transition period from high school to college. The family decided to establish roots in Arnold to be close to Alice and me. Of course, we welcomed having them and our grandchildren close by, just a two-minute walk through the trees from our home.

Marty began teaching as an adjunct professor at William Jessup University near Sacramento, having earned his doctorate in theology at the University of South Africa. He soon became a popular teacher with his students. He also started a ministry among men in our area and established many new relationships.

But Marty's heart was still in missions. He continued regular teaching in different parts of the world.

I was also glad to have our daughter Lita live in close proximity. After many years as a successful marketing executive with FedEx and Apple Computers, she felt compelled to do something for her country, especially in light of the 9/11 terrorist attacks. She reactivated her reserve status with the U.S. Army and after training in psychological operations was deployed in Afghanistan for 2003, a few weeks after she was married to William Lott. This was a very positive experience for her, and thanks to the Internet we were able to stay in regular contact. She is continuing her service for our country as a warrant officer in military intelligence.

As parents, we are proud of our children, and thank God for the way they have responded to His direction in their lives. What a blessing it was to celebrate our fiftieth wedding anniversary with them in 2006—a special time just with our own family!

I am also grateful for regular contact with my sisters, Eva in Germany and Anita and Peggy in Scottsbluff, Nebraska. After several decades in the Washington, D.C., area and Florida, Peg decided to return to Nebraska and live close to Anita. E-mail, Internet, and phone contacts keep us up to date on each other.

We have also had several opportunities to host extended family from Germany to maintain the bonds established long ago.

Whenever home, I maintain a weekend ministry in Chinese churches in the San Jose area. I learned to play golf, since our home was just a mile from the beautiful Sequoia Woods golf course. And I developed a close camaraderie with other seniors, a privilege I had never experienced before. When winter came, I enjoyed hitting the ski slopes at nearby Bear Valley, since as a "super senior" the season tickets amounted to less than forty dollars. Alice linked up with a group of ladies calling themselves WIB's (women in boots) and hiked all over the mountains in summer and snow-shoed in winter.

Living in Arnold meant a weekly roundtrip of approximately 350 miles to San Jose for Sunday preaching assignments. By the end of 2008, I had made over 330 of these roundtrips. Preaching at least twice each Sunday, I felt personally and spiritually invigorated, and grateful for the privilege of opening the Word week after week and seeing the fruit of changed lives. We connected with many couples on a deep and intimate level. Marriage counseling, weddings, and funerals also kept us busy.

As opportunities for teaching ministries in China declined, God opened up new avenues to serve Him there through my association as a board member of ChinaSource, which provides resources, information, and networking facilities to many organizations.

In September 2004, I was invited by a Chinese missionary organization to conduct a pastors and evangelists conference for 135 leaders of the Karen people in Burma, now known as Myanmar. The theme was "born to reproduce," an old Navigator concept. I taught for seventeen hours and was amazed at their attentiveness and eagerness to learn. My prayer was that the seed sown in that difficult land would indeed be reproduced in the lives of many Burmese.

Following those meetings, several of us had an opportunity to visit a world-famous pagoda. Shwedagon pagoda is the most sacred place of Rangoon, the capital city of Burma. Built about 2,500 years ago, the pagoda itself has a spire one hundred meters high, covered with eight thousand plates of gold.

Burma is one of the poorest countries of Southeast Asia, yet amazing opulence rubs shoulders with extreme poverty. What moved me, however, was watching worshipers kneeling and kowtowing in front of the Buddha statues. Desperation and hopelessness marked the faces of these people. They were seeking, but not finding.

As I watched, I knew they were not alone. It is a picture multiplied many times over in our world today. Millions of people on every continent are in the same situation. Looking, seeking, but not finding. They are lost.

I moved about that huge temple in Rangoon, snapped pictures to help me remember the sights, and thought of a passage in Matthew. I asked the Lord to give me much more compassion than I felt. When Jesus was around crowds of people, He saw them as helpless. He said to His disciples:

> "The harvest is plentiful but the workers are few.
> Ask the Lord of the harvest, therefore, to send out
> workers into his harvest field." (Matthew 9:38)

During the many trips I made to China over the years, I was able to see much of this land of my birth. From Harbin in the distant north to Guangzhou in the south, from cities like Shanghai on the eastern seaboard to Urumxi in the Gobi desert on the western border near Kazakhstan, and many other places in between, I got a new glimpse of this vast country and the many people whom God loved so much. Again and again, I was stirred by the thought of 25,000 of them going daily into a Christless eternity. They need to hear, but someone has to go and tell them!

David Morken, evangelist, friend, and mentor, first introduced me to the following song by Mrs. A. Head when I was a teen in

Shanghai. I memorized it then. It has come to mind many times since.

> Stir me, oh stir me, Lord, I care not how,
> But stir my heart in passion for the world,
> Stir me to give, to go, but most to pray;
> Stir, till the blood-red banner be unfurled
> O'er lands that still in heathen darkness lie,
> O'er deserts where no cross is lifted high.
>
> Stir me, oh, stir me, Lord, Thy heart was stirred
> By love's intensest fire, till Thou didst give
> Thine only Son, Thy best beloved One,
> E'en to the dreadful cross, that I might live.
> Stir me to give myself so back to Thee,
> That Thou canst give Thyself again through
> me.[10]

The theme of Bob Pierce, founder of World Vision, was "Let my heart be broken by the things that break the heart of God." How much I have needed to learn this important truth. The Lord has allowed me literally to travel from "A to Z"—to live in five continents of the world and set foot in about a hundred different countries. How blessed I have been. I have seen so much. But with that comes the awesome responsibility to pass on to others what I have seen and heard. I will always be deeply conscious of that.

THE LAST WORD

Now you have read my story. It has been a long one, but then, I have lived a long and full life. Yet there is one more thing I want to say before you lay this book down.

Over the years, I discovered again and again that God indeed had a purpose for my life. Sometimes these purposes were not readily visible or understandable to me. But as I chose to submit to His direction, in the end they resonated in my heart as the "good and acceptable and perfect will of God."

A quote from Oswald Chambers puts this eloquently:

> If we are in communion with God and recognize that He is taking us into His purposes, we shall no longer try to find out what His purposes are. As we go on in the Christian life it gets simpler, because we are less inclined to say—Now why did God allow this and that? Behind the whole thing lies the compelling of God. "There's a divinity that shapes our ends." A Christian is one who trusts the wits and the wisdom of God, and not his own wits. If we have a purpose of our own, it destroys the simplicity and the leisureliness which ought to characterize the children of God.[11]

If there is one thing I have learned during these past seventy-eight years, it is this: Life is a very precious gift from God. You have just one go at it, then it is gone. That is why you must make the most of it. You must make it count.

My friend and fellow classmate at Fuller Seminary, Rick Warren, put it this way: "People ask me, 'What is the purpose of life?' And I respond: 'In a nutshell, life is preparation for eternity. We were made to last forever, and God wants us to be with Him in Heaven.'"[12]

My final word is this:

> "Live life, then, with a due sense of responsibility, not as men who do not know the meaning and purpose of life but as those who do. Make the best use of your time, despite all the difficulties of these days. Don't be vague, but firmly grasp what you know to be the will of the Lord." (Ephesians 4:15–17 PHILLIPS)

If you haven't already, stop right now and make this commitment. You will never regret it!

June 2009
Arnold, California

MY MENTORS

I am very conscious that God has been gracious to me in a special way by bringing people into my life that immensely blessed me. It began with my godly parents, who laid the foundation by their example of what it means to follow God in good times as well as bad. Never once did I hear them complain when things were tough, even during the war years.

When it came time to leave China, they both would have preferred to return home to Germany. Instead, they felt that for the sake of their children, they needed to make a new start in America, hard as it was for them. I admire them for that. Though they never urged me to enter the ministry, I know that at my birth they dedicated me to the Lord for His service. They rejoiced when God directed me to follow in their footsteps. I am deeply indebted to them for their support, their prayers, and their unflagging encouragement of my work.

However, it is my wife Alice - the love of my life - who had the greatest impact on my life. She is a woman who deeply loves Scripture and steadfastly keeps on memorizing it. For more than fifty years she has faithfully stood by my side and fulfilled her God-given role as a true "helpmate." She knows when to encourage and when to rebuke. There were times when I didn't like the latter, but I always came back and thanked her for being true to her convictions. Even when my travels and responsibilities took me away from home a good share of the time, she understood and encouraged me to do what God had laid on my heart. I am eternally grateful to her for helping shape and mold my life to fulfill God's purposes in me.

I want to mention some of the other men and women who also left a deep mark on my life. There are many more, but here is a list of some of them. I am deeply grateful to each one:

David Adeney—China missionary and neighbor who taught me to love Chinese students

Bill Bright—Founder of Campus Crusade, provided opportunity for evangelism at UCLA

Stuart Briscoe—Bible teacher extraordinaire, fellow jogger, who often refreshed my soul

Werner Bürklin—China classmate and friend, opened the door for ministry in China

Phineas Chauke—South African pastor/evangelist/church planter who knew how to pray

Norm & Muriel Cook—Fellow OC missionaries, best man at wedding, and faithful friends

Larry Coy—A special friend who gave me handles to real issues in life

Norman Cummings—OC executive director and friend, who linked administration with ministry

Timothy Dzao—One of China's great evangelists, friend of my father, and mine too

Brent Fulton—A gifted, humble visionary who saw China and communicated it to others

Arthur Glasser—China missionary, a special friend and supporter for sixty-plus years

Bill Gothard—Taught me basic life principles which have followed me all my life

Greg Gripentrog—OC president and friend who always served with excellence

Dick Hillis—Founder of OC, a true mentor and friend who demonstrated servanthood

Bishop Frank Houghton—General director of China Inland Mission, impacted my early life

David Hubbard—Fuller Seminary president, professor, and friend who opened the Word

Jim Kemp—Fellow OC missionary and friend who brought enthusiasm wherever he went

Bill Keyes—Fellow missionary and friend, always positive, steady, and faithful

Eleanor Kingman—A Chinese lady, who encouraged me in following Christ as a teenager

Joerg Knoblauch—German businessman and friend who longed to see churches grow

Paul Landrey—Fellow OC missionary in Brazil, team member, and friend

Bill Lawrence—Former pastor, fellow board member, friend, gifted articulator of truth

Ed Lyman—Comrade-in-arms in China ministry and friend, who sang to the glory of God

John MacArthur—Friend and Bible teacher who ministered to me through his books

Donald McGavran—Father of the church growth movement, visionary, and personal friend

Paul McKaughan—Fellow missionary in Brazil, missions executive, faithful friend

Hubert Mitchell—Missionary leader who had his priorities straight, a true friend

John E. Mitchell—Multnomah founder, one who knew and lived the Scriptures

Jim Montgomery—Fellow OC missionary who had a disciple-whole-nation vision

David Morken—Missionary evangelist, taught me to love the Word and great hymns

Ed Murphy—Fellow OC missionary, coworker in Africa, friend, and gifted Bible teacher

Henry Mumba—Zambian pastor and friend who taught me servanthood and humility

Luis Palau—OC president and world evangelist, with a passion for evangelism

Jim Peterson—Navigator friend in Brazil, taught me to apply discipleship cross-culturally

Bob Pierce—Evangelist and founder of World Vision, with a big and generous heart

Bill Rapier—Fellow OC missionary in Germany and Africa, a man with a servant's heart

Roy Robertson—First Navigator missionary who personally discipled me in China

Lorne & Lucille Sanny—Navigator president, my second parents when I came to the U.S.

Rod Sargent—A true Navigator, always there when I needed him

Peter Schneider—A German giant who opened a big door for OC in Germany

Fritz Schwarz—Father of German church growth movement, guided our German fledgling team

Ken Strachan—Latin America Mission president, taught me to trust Him even in dark hours

Anna Swarr—China missionary, willing to sacrifice time to disciple a young Christian

James Taylor III—Fellow missionary and friend who loved China wholeheartedly

Dawson Trotman—Founder of Navigators, a giant among men, gave me a second chance

Ary Velloso—Fellow OC missionary and pastor in Brazil, friend, and counselor

Bob Vernon—Former Los Angeles assistant police chief, friend, supporter, and example

Peter Wagner—Fuller professor who believed in church growth and taught it well

Rick Warren—Fellow Fuller doctoral student who taught me to have a big vision

Joseph Wong—Humble Chinese church leader who set an example in spirituality

SIGNIFICANT DATES

1896   Karl Max Wilhelm and Anna Elisabetha Giessel born in Germany

1923   Missionary Max Wilhelm sails for China

1925   Fiancée Anna arrives in China, Max captured by bandits

1927   Max and Anna married in Hong jiang, Hunan

1929   Eva-Maria born in Jinping, Guizhou, China

1931   Hans-Martin born in Jinping, Guizhou

1932   Anita Gisela born in Hong jiang, China; family returns to Germany

1933   Esther Elisabeth born in Zwickau, Germany

1934   Karl Friedrich Oskar (Fred) born in Bad Liebenzell, Germany

1935   Return to China, flee from Communists on Long March

1936   Start school in Changsha, Hunan

1937   Edelgard Margarethe (Peggy) born in Changsha, Hunan; start of Sino-Japanese war, Changsha in flames

1939   Outbreak of World War II, missionary school moves to interior

1941   Japanese bombing raid on our city, Pearl Harbor; house arrest

1942   Lei yang internment camp; expelled from China

1943   Hitler Youth; Kaiser-Wilhelm-Schule in Shanghai, China

1945   End of World War II; found Christ and new life

1946   Shanghai British School; Shanghai Free Christian Church

1949   St. John's University, Shanghai; Communist rule in China

1950   Exit China, enter U.S.A.; begin work with the Navigators in California; Anita's escape from East Germany

1951   Graduate from Pasadena City College, enroll at UCLA

1952   Ministry with Campus Crusade and Bill Bright at UCLA

1953   B.A. in history from UCLA; full-time ministry with Navigators; Eva and Anita arrive in U.S.A.

1954   Commissioned to Formosa as missionary with the Navigators

1956   Engagement to Alice Bell, March wedding, Hong Kong honeymoon

1957   Furlough and deputation in U.S.A.

1958 Naturalized as U.S. citizens; return to Taiwan; Marty born in Taiwan

1960 Lita born in Taipei, Taiwan

1963 Lita healed from leukemia; furlough and enrollment at Fuller Seminary

1965 Call to Brazil; studies with Donald McGavran; family reunion

1966 Ordination, M.Div. from Fuller; arrival in Brazil

1967 Appointed field director, Brazil; Esther and Papa pass away

1970 Building a new team, Brazil para Cristo ministry

1971 First OC leadership conference (team paper), Larry Coy seminar

1972 Call to return to serve at OC headquarters; Bill Gothard seminars

1973 Appointed associate executive director for OC administration

1974 Mutti dies in Schooley's Mountain, New Jersey

1976 Appointed executive vice-president of OC

1977 Dick Hillis resigns OC leadership, Luis Palau becomes president

1979 Clyde Cook, OC president; left OC; pastor, discipleship at LGCC

1981 Return to OC, survey trip to Germany

1982 Departure for Germany, building of German team

1983   Marty and Karen Johnson wedding; Larry Keyes becomes OC president

1987   Move to Swaziland, Africa; appointed Europe/Africa area director

1989   D.Min. from Fuller; Lausanne II in Manila; Marty and family in Africa

1990   First international Wilhelm clan reunion in Germany (East & West Germany, Africa, USA)

1991   Return to U.S.; resign from OC; join World Outreach Ministries

1992   Ministry with CCiC church, Chinese International Missions

1997   Ministry in China with Werner Bürklin, China Partner

1998   Move to Arnold, California

2000   Amsterdam 2000 Congress; elected to ChinaSource board

2003   Marty and family move from Africa to Arnold; Lita marries Will Lott and is deployed with U.S. Army to Afghanistan

2004   Brother Fred dies; Burma pastors conference in Rangoon, Burma

2006   Celebrate our golden wedding with family in Arnold

NOTES

1. Glimpses of Christian History No. 160, "Betty and John Stam: Young Missionaries Martyred," http://www.chinstitute.org/GLIMPSEF/Glimpses/glmps160.html.

2. *The Best of Max Lucado on Jesus,* CD-ROM (Nashville, Tenn.: Thomas Nelson Publishers).

3. "Life Is Not to Do But to Become," http://www.naga.gov.ph/forum/index.php?topic=1188.0;wap2.

4. Anita (Wilhelm) Osborn, *Echoes of the Past* (Victoria, B.C., Canada: Trafford Publishing, 2003). To order, e-mail wd.osborn@charter.net or write to 17 Regency Court, Scottsbluff, Neb., 69361.

5. "Famous Preacher Quotes," Forgotten Word Ministries, http://forgottenword.org/quotes.html.

6. "Only One Life," According to the Scriptures, http://www.accordingtothescriptures.org/doctrine/onlyonelife.html.

7. Dietrich Bonhoeffer, *Letters and Papers from Prison* (New York: Touchstone, 1997).

8.   Geraldine Taylor, *Behind the Ranges* (Chicago: Moody Press, 1975).

9.   Joseph Hart, "This God Is the God We Adore," http://www.stempublishing.com/hymns/biographies/hart.html.

10.   A. Head, *Keswick Hymn-book* (London: Marshall, Morgan & Scott, 1936), 350.

11.   Oswald Chambers, August 5, *My Utmost for His Highest* (New York: Dodd, Mead, 1935).

12.   Rick Warren, interview with Paul Bradshaw, as reported on "Living With Purpose," http://www.ccnews.org/index.php?mod=Story&action=show&id=2449&countryid=207&stateid=0.

For additional copies of this book or inquiries from the author
you may contact

chinahansbook@gmail.com